A

YANKEE IN CANADA,

WITH

ANTI–SLAVERY AND REFORM
PAPERS.

BY

HENRY D. THOREAU,

GREENWOOD PRESS, PUBLISHERS
NEW YORK

81922

Originally published in 1892: Boston

First Greenwood Reprinting 1969

SBN 8371-2044-6

PRINTED IN UNITED STATES OF AMERICA

CONTENTS.

A YANKEE IN CANADA.

———◆———

"New England is by some affirmed to be an island, bounded on the north with the River Canada (so called from Monsieur Cane)."—Josselyn's Rarities.

And still older, in Thomas Morton's "New English Canaan," published in 1632, it is said, on page 97, "From this Lake [Erocoise] Northwards is derived the famous River of Canada, so named, of Monsier de Cane, a French Lord, who first planted a Colony of French in America."

CHAPTER I.

CONCORD TO MONTREAL.

I FEAR that I have not got much to say about Canada, not having seen much; what I got by going to Canada was a cold. I left Concord, Massachusetts, Wednesday morning, September 25th, 1850, for Quebec. Fare, seven dollars there and back; distance from Boston, five hundred and ten miles; being obliged to leave Montreal on the return as soon as Friday, October 4th, or within ten days. I will not stop to tell the reader the names of my fellow-travellers; there were said to be fifteen hundred of them. I wished only to be set down in Canada, and take one honest walk there as I might in Concord woods of an afternoon.

The country was new to me beyond Fitchburg. In Ashburnham and afterward, as we were whirled rapidly along, I noticed the woodbine (*Ampelopsis quinquefolia*), its leaves now changed, for the most part on dead trees, draping them like a red scarf. It was a little exciting, suggesting bloodshed, or at least a military life, like an epaulet or sash, as if it were dyed with the blood of the trees whose wounds it was inadequate to stanch. For now the bloody autumn was come, and an Indian warfare was waged through the forest. These military trees appeared very numerous, for our rapid progress connected those that were even some miles apart. Does the woodbine prefer the elm? The first view of Monadnoc was obtained five or six miles this side of Fitzwilliam, but nearest and best at Troy and beyond. Then there were the Troy cuts and embankments. Keene Street strikes the traveller favorably, it is so wide, level, straight, and long. I have heard one of my relatives, who was born and bred there, say that you could see a chicken run across it a mile off. I have also been told that when this town was settled they laid out a street four rods wide, but at a subsequent meeting of the proprietors one rose and remarked, "We have plenty of land, why not make the street eight rods wide?" and so they voted that it should be eight rods wide, and the town is known far and near for its handsome street. It was a cheap way of securing comfort, as well as fame, and I wish that all new towns would take pattern from this. It is best to lay our plans widely in youth, for then land is cheap, and it is but too easy to contract our views afterward. Youths so laid out, with broad avenues and parks, that they may make handsome and liberal old men! Show me a youth whose mind is like some Washington city of magnificent distances, prepared for the most remotely successful and glorious life after all, when those spaces shall be built over and the idea of the founder be realized. I trust that every New England boy will begin by laying out a Keene Street through his head, eight rods wide. I know one such Washington city of a man, whose lots as yet are only surveyed and staked out, and except a cluster of shanties here and there, only the Capitol stands there for all structures, and any day you may see from afar his princely idea borne coachwise along the spacious but yet empty avenues. Keene is built on a remarkably large and level interval, like the bed of a lake, and the surrounding hills, which are remote from its street, must afford some good walks.

The scenery of mountain towns is commonly too much crowded. A town which is built on a plain of some extent, with an open horizon, and surrounded by hills at a distance, affords the best walks and views.

As we travel northwest up the country, sugar-maples, beeches, birches, hemlocks, spruce, butternuts, and ash trees prevail more and more. To the rapid traveller the number of elms in a town is the measure of its civility. One man in the cars has a bottle full of some liquor. The whole company smile whenever it is exhibited. I find no difficulty in containing myself. The Westmoreland country looked attractive. I heard a passenger giving the very obvious derivation of this name, West-more-land, as if it were purely American, and he had made a discovery; but I thought of "my cousin Westmoreland" in England. Every one will remember the approach to Bellows Falls, under a high cliff which rises from the Connecticut. I was disappointed in the size of the river here; it appeared shrunk to a mere mountain stream. The water was evidently very low. The rivers which we had crossed this forenoon possessed more of the character of mountain streams than those in the vicinity of Concord, and I was surprised to see everywhere traces of recent freshets, which had carried away bridges and injured the railroad, though I had heard nothing of it. In Ludlow, Mount Holly, and beyond, there is interesting mountain scenery, not rugged and stupendous, but such as you could easily ramble over, — long narrow mountain vales through which to see the horizon. You are in the midst of the Green Mountains. A few more elevated blue peaks are seen from the neighborhood of Mount Holly, perhaps Killington Peak is one. Some times, as on the Western Railroad, you are whirled over mountainous embankments, from which the scared horses in the valleys appear diminished to hounds. All the hills blush; I think that autumn must be the best season to journey over even the *Green* Mountains. You frequently exclaim to yourself, what *red* maples! The sugar-maple is not so red. You see some of the latter with rosy spots or cheeks only, blushing on one side like fruit, while all the rest of the tree is green, proving either some partiality in the light or frosts, or some prematurity in particular branches. Tall and slender ash-trees, whose foliage is turned to a dark mulberry color, are frequent. The butternut, which is a remarkably spreading tree, is turned completely yellow, thus proving its relation to the hickories. I was also struck by the bright yellow tints of the yellow-birch. The sugar-maple is remarkable for its clean ankle. The groves of these trees looked like vast forest sheds, their branches stopping short at a uniform height, four or five feet from the ground, like eaves, as if they had been trimmed by art, so that you could look under and through the whole grove with its leafy canopy, as under a tent whose curtain is raised.

As you approach Lake Champlain you begin to see the New York mountains. The first view of the Lake at Vergennes is impressive, but rather from association than from any peculiarity in the scenery. It lies there so small (not appearing in that proportion to the width of the State that it does on the map), but beautifully quiet, like a picture of the Lake of Lucerne on a music-box, where you trace the name of Lucerne among the foliage; far more ideal than ever it looked on the map. It does not say, "Here I am, Lake Champlain," as the conductor might for it, but having studied the geography thirty years, you crossed over a hill one afternoon and beheld it. But it is only a glimpse that you get here. At Burlington you rush to a wharf and go on board a steamboat, two hundred and thirty-two miles from Boston. We left Concord at twenty minutes before eight in the morning, and were in Burlington about six at night, but too late to see the lake. We got our first fair view of the lake at dawn, just before reaching Plattsburg, and saw blue ranges of mountains on either hand, in New York and in Vermont, the former especially grand. A few white schooners, like gulls, were seen in the distance, for it is not waste and solitary like a lake in Tartary; but it was such a view as leaves not much to be said; indeed, I have postponed Lake Champlain to another day.

The oldest reference to these waters that I have yet seen is in the account of Cartier's discovery and exploration of the St. Lawrence in 1535. Samuel Champlain actually discovered and paddled up the Lake in July, 1609, eleven years before the settlement of Plymouth, accompanying a war-party of the Canadian Indians against the Iroquois. He describes the islands in it as not inhabited, although they are pleasant, — on account of the continual wars of the Indians, in consequence of which they withdraw from the rivers and lakes into the depths of the land, that they may not be surprised. " Continuing our course," says he, " in this lake, on the western side, viewing the country, I saw on the eastern side very high mountains, where there was snow on the summit. I inquired of the savages if those places were inhabited. They replied that they were, and that they were Iroquois, and that in those places there were beautiful valleys and plains fertile in corn, such as I have eaten in this country, with an infinity of other fruits." This is the earliest account of what is now Vermont.

The number of French Canadian gentlemen and ladies among the passengers, and the sound of the French language, advertised us by this time that we were being whirled towards some foreign vortex. And now we have left Rouse's Point, and entered the Sorel River, and passed the invisible barrier between the States and Canada. The shores of the Sorel, Richelieu, or St. John's River, are flat and reedy, where I had expected something more rough and mountainous for a natural boundary between two nations. Yet I saw a difference at once, in the few huts, in the pirogues on the shore, and as it were, in the shore itself. This was an interesting scenery to me, and the very reeds or rushes in the shallow water, and the tree-tops in the swamps, have left a pleasing impression. We had still a distant view behind us of two or three blue mountains in Vermont and New York. About nine o'clock in the forenoon we reached St. John's, an old frontier post three hundred and six miles from Boston and twenty-four from Montreal. We now discovered that we were in a foreign country, in a station-house of another nation. This building was a barn-like structure, looking as if it were the work of the villagers combined, like a log-house in a new settlement. My attention was caught by the double advertisements in French and English fastened to its posts, by the formality of the English, and the covert or open reference to their queen and the British lion. No gentlemanly conductor appeared, none whom you would know to be the conduc-

tor by his dress and demeanor; but erelong we began
to see here and there a solid, red-faced, burly-looking
Englishman, a little pursy perhaps, who made us
ashamed of ourselves and our thin and nervous countrymen,— a grandfatherly personage, at home in his
great-coat, who looked as if he might be a stage proprietor, certainly a railroad director, and knew, or had
a right to know, when the cars did start. Then there
were two or three pale-faced, black-eyed, loquacious
Canadian French gentlemen there, shrugging their
shoulders; pitted as if they had all had the small-pox.
In the mean while some soldiers, red-coats, belonging
to the barracks near by, were turned out to be drilled.
At every important point in our route the soldiers
showed themselves ready for us; though they were
evidently rather raw recruits here, they manœuvred
far better than our soldiers; yet, as usual, I heard some
Yankees talk as if they were no great shakes, and
they had seen the Acton Blues manœuvre as well.
The officers spoke sharply to them, and appeared to
be doing their part thoroughly. I heard one suddenly
coming to the rear, exclaim, "Michael Donouy, take his
name!" though I could not see what the latter did or
omitted to do. It was whispered that Michael Donouy
would have to suffer for that. I heard some of our
party discussing the possibility of their driving these
troops off the field with their umbrellas. I thought
that the Yankee, though undisciplined, had this advantage at least, that he especially is a man who, everywhere
and under all circumstances, is fully resolved to better
his condition essentially, and therefore he could afford
to be beaten at first; while the virtue of the Irishman,
and to a great extent the Englishman, consists in merely

maintaining his ground or condition. The Canadians here, a rather poor-looking race, clad in gray homespun, which gave them the appearance of being covered with dust. were riding about in caleches and small one-horse carts called charettes. The Yankees assumed that all the riders were racing, or at least exhibiting the paces of their horses, and saluted them accordingly. We saw but little of the village here, for nobody could tell us when the cars would start; that was kept a profound secret, perhaps for political reasons; and therefore we were tied to our seats. The inhabitants of St. John's and vicinity are described by an English traveller as "singularly unprepossessing," and before completing his period he adds, "besides, they are generally very much disaffected to the British crown." I suspect that that "besides" should have been a because.

At length, about noon, the cars began to roll towards La Prairie. The whole distance of fifteen miles was over a remarkably level country, resembling a Western prairie, with the mountains about Chambly visible in the northeast. This novel, but monotonous scenery, was exciting. At La Prairie we first took notice of the tinned roofs, but above all of the St. Lawrence, which looked like a lake; in fact it is considerably expanded here; it was nine miles across diagonally to Montreal. Mount Royal in the rear of the city, and the island of St. Helen's opposite to it, were now conspicuous. We could also see the Sault St. Louis about five miles up the river, and the Sault Norman still farther eastward. The former are described as the most considerable rapids in the St. Lawrence; but we could see merely a gleam of light there as from a cobweb in the sun. Soon the city of Montreal was discovered with its tin

roofs shining afar. Their reflections fell on the eye like
a clash of cymbals on the ear. Above all the church of
Notre Dame was conspicuous, and anon the Bonsecours
market-house, occupying a commanding position on the
quay, in the rear of the shipping. This city makes the
more favorable impression from being approached by
water, and also being built of stone, a gray limestone
found on the island. Here, after travelling directly
inland the whole breadth of New England, we had
struck upon a city's harbor, — it made on me the
impression of a seaport, — to which ships of six hundred
tons can ascend, and where vessels drawing fifteen feet
lie close to the wharf, five hundred and forty miles from
the Gulf; the St. Lawrence being here two miles wide.
There was a great crowd assembled on the ferry-boat
wharf and on the quay to receive the Yankees, and
flags of all colors were streaming from the vessels to
celebrate their arrival. When the gun was fired, the
gentry hurrahed again and again, and then the Canadian caleche-drivers, who were most interested in the
matter, and who, I perceived, were separated from the
former by a fence, hurrahed their welcome; first the
broadcloth, then the homespun.

It was early in the afternoon when we stepped ashore.
With a single companion, I soon found my way to the
church of Notre Dame. I saw that it was of great size
and signified something. It is said to be the largest
ecclesiastical structure in North America, and can seat
ten thousand. It is two hundred and fifty-five and a
half feet long, and the groined ceiling is eighty feet
above your head. The Catholic are the only churches
which I have seen worth remembering, which are not
almost wholly profane. I do not speak only of the rich

and splendid like this, but of the humblest of them as
well.   Coming from the hurrahing mob and the rattling
carriages, we pushed aside the listed door of this church,
and found ourselves instantly in an atmosphere which
might be sacred to thought and religion, if one had any.
There sat one or two women who had stolen a moment
from the concerns of the day, as they were passing ; but,
if there had been fifty people there, it would still have
been the most solitary place imaginable.   They did not
look up at us, nor did one regard another.   We walked
softly down the broad-aisle with our hats in our hands.
Presently came in a troop of Canadians, in their homespun, who had come to the city in the boat with us, and
one and all kneeled down in the aisle before the high
altar to their devotions, somewhat awkwardly, as cattle
prepare to lie down, and there we left them.   As if you
were to catch some farmer's sons from Marlboro, come
to cattle-show, silently kneeling in Concord meeting--
house some Wednesday !   Would there not soon be a
mob peeping in at the windows ?   It is true, these Roman Catholics, priests and all, impress me as a people
who have fallen far behind the significance of their
symbols.   It is as if an ox had strayed into a church
and were trying to bethink himself.   Nevertheless, they
are capable of reverence ; but we Yankees are a people
in whom this sentiment has nearly died out, and in this
respect we cannot bethink ourselves even as oxen.   I
did not mind the pictures nor the candles, whether tallow or tin.   Those of the former which I looked at
appeared tawdry.   It matters little to me whether the
pictures are by a neophyte of the Algonquin or the
Italian tribe.   But I was impressed by the quiet religious atmosphere of the place.   It was a great cave

in the midst of a city; and what were the altars and
the tinsel but the sparkling stalactics, into which you
entered in a moment, and where the still atmosphere
and the sombre light disposed to serious and profitable
thought? Such a cave at hand, which you can enter
any day, is worth a thousand of our churches which are
open only Sundays, — hardly long enough for an airing,
— and then filled with a bustling congregation, — a
church where the priest is the least part, where you
do your own preaching, where the universe preaches
to you and can be heard. I am not sure but this Catholic religion would be an admirable one if the priest
were quite omitted. I think that I might go to church
myself sometimes some Monday, if I lived in a city
where there was such a one to go to. In Concord,
to be sure, we do not need such. Our forests are such
a church, far grander and more sacred. We dare not
leave *our* meeting-houses open for fear they would be
profaned. Such a cave, such a shrine, in one of our
groves, for instance, how long would it be respected?
for what purposes would it be entered, by such baboons
as we are? I think of its value not only to religion,
but to philosophy and to poetry; besides a reading-
room, to have a thinking-room in every city! Perchance the time will come when every house even will
have not only its sleeping-rooms, and dining-room, and
talking-room or parlor, but its thinking-room also, and
the architects will put it into their plans. Let it be
furnished and ornamented with whatever conduces to
serious and creative thought. I should not object to
the holy water, or any other simple symbol, if it were
consecrated by the imagination of the worshippers.

I heard that some Yankees bet that the candles were

not wax, but tin. A European assured them that they were wax; but, inquiring of the sexton, he was surprised to learn that they were tin filled with oil. The church was too poor to afford wax. As for the Protestant churches, here or elsewhere, they did not interest me, for it is only as caves that churches interest me at all, and in that respect they were inferior.

Montreal makes the impression of a larger city than you had expected to find, though you may have heard that it contains nearly sixty thousand inhabitants. In the newer parts it appeared to be growing fast like a small New York, and to be considerably Americanized. The names of the squares reminded you of Paris, — the Champ de Mars, the Place d'Armes, and others, and you felt as if a French revolution might break out any moment. Glimpses of Mount Royal rising behind the town, and the names of some streets in that direction, make one think of Edinburgh. That hill sets off this city wonderfully. I inquired at a principal bookstore for books published in Montreal. They said that there were none but school-books and the like; they got their books from the States. From time to time we met a priest in the streets, for they are distinguished by their dress, like the *civil* police. Like clergymen generally, with or without the gown, they made on us the impression of effeminacy. We also met some Sisters of Charity, dressed in black, with Shaker-shaped black bonnets and crosses, and cadaverous faces, who looked as if they had almost cried their eyes out, their complexions parboiled with scalding tears; insulting the daylight by their presence, having taken an oath not to smile. By cadaverous I mean that their faces were like the faces of those who have been dead and buried for a year, and then untombed, with the life's grief upon them, and yet, for some unaccountable reason, the process of decay arrested.

> " Truth never fails her servant, sir, nor leaves him
> With the day's shame upon him."

They waited demurely on the sidewalk while a truck laden with raisins was driven in at the seminary of St. Sulpice, never once lifting their eyes from the ground.

The soldier here, as everywhere in Canada, appeared to be put forward, and by his best foot. They were in the proportion of the soldiers to the laborers in an African ant-hill. The inhabitants evidently rely on them in a great measure for music and entertainment. You would meet with them pacing back and forth before some guard-house or passage-way, guarding, regarding, and disregarding all kinds of law by turns, apparently for the sake of the discipline to themselves, and not because it was important to exclude anybody from entering that way. They reminded me of the men who are paid for piling up bricks and then throwing them down again. On every prominent ledge you could see England's hands holding the Canadas, and I judged by the redness of her knuckles that she would soon have to let go. In the rear of such a guard-house, in a large gravelled square or parade-ground, called the Champ de Mars, we saw a large body of soldiers being drilled, we being as yet the only spectators. But they did not appear to notice us any more than the devotees in the church, but were seemingly as indifferent to fewness of spectators as the phenomena of nature are, whatever they might have been thinking under their helmets of the Yankees that were to come. Each man wore white kid gloves. It was one of the most interesting

sights which I saw in Canada. The problem appeared
to be how to smooth down all individual protuberances
or idiosyncrasies, and make a thousand men move as
one man, animated by one central will; and there was
some approach to success. They obeyed the signals of
a commander who stood at a great distance, wand in
hand; and the precision, and promptness, and harmony
of their movements could not easily have been matched.
The harmony was far more remarkable than that of any
choir or band, and obtained, no doubt, at a greater cost.
They made on me the impression, not of many individuals, but of one vast centipede of a man, good for all
sorts of pulling down; and why not then for some kinds
of building up? If men could combine thus earnestly,
and patiently, and harmoniously to some really worthy
end, what might they not accomplish? They now put
their hands, and partially perchance their heads, together, and the result is that they are the imperfect
tools of an imperfect and tyrannical government. But
if they could put their hands and heads and hearts and
all together, such a co-operation and harmony would be
the very end and success for which government now exists in vain, — a government, as it were, not only with
tools, but stock to trade with.

I was obliged to frame some sentences that sounded
like French in order to deal with the market-women,
who, for the most part, cannot speak English. According to the guide-book the relative population of
this city stands nearly thus: two fifths are French Canadian; nearly one fifth British Canadian; one and a
half fifth English, Irish, and Scotch; somewhat less
than one half fifth Germans, United States people, and
others. I saw nothing like pie for sale, and no good

cake to put in my bundle, such as you can easily find in our towns, but plenty of fair-looking apples, for which Montreal Island is celebrated, and also pears, cheaper, and I thought better than ours, and peaches, which, though they were probably brought from the South, were as cheap as they commonly are with us. So imperative is the law of demand and supply that, as I have been told, the market of Montreal is sometimes supplied with green apples from the State of New York some weeks even before they are ripe in the latter place. I saw here the spruce wax which the Canadians chew, done up in little silvered papers, a penny a roll; also a small and shrivelled fruit which they called *cerises* mixed with many little stems somewhat like raisins, but I soon returned what I had bought, finding them rather insipid, only putting a sample in my pocket. Since my return, I find on comparison that it is the fruit of the sweet viburnum (*Viburnum Lentago*), which with us rarely holds on till it is ripe.

I stood on the deck of the steamer John Munn, late in the afternoon, when the second and third ferry-boats arrived from La Prairie, bringing the remainder of the Yankees. I never saw so many caleches, cabs, charettes, and similar vehicles collected before, and doubt if New York could easily furnish more. The handsome and substantial stone quay, which stretches a mile along the river-side, and protects the street from the ice, was thronged with the citizens who had turned out on foot and in carriages to welcome or to behold the Yankees. It was interesting to see the caleche drivers dash up and down the slope of the quay with their active little horses. They drive much faster than in our cities. I have been told that some of them come nine miles into

the city every morning and return every night, without
changing their horses during the day. In the midst of
the crowd of carts, I observed one deep one loaded with
sheep with their legs tied together, and their bodies
piled one upon another, as if the driver had forgotten
that they were sheep and not yet mutton. A sight, I
trust, peculiar to Canada, though I fear that it is not.

CHAPTER II.

QUEBEC AND MONTMORENCI.

ABOUT six o'clock we started for Quebec, one hundred and eighty miles distant by the river; gliding past
Longueil and Boucherville on the right, and *Pointe aux
Trembles,* "so called from having been originally covered
with aspens," and *Bout de l'Isle,* or the end of the island,
on the left. I repeat these names not merely for want
of more substantial facts to record, but because they
sounded singularly poetic to my ears. There certainly
was no lie in them. They suggested that some simple,
and, perchance, heroic human life might have transpired
there. There is all the poetry in the world in a name.
It is a poem which the mass of men hear and read.
What is poetry in the common sense, but a string of
such jingling names? I want nothing better than a
good word. The name of a thing may easily be more
than the thing itself to me. Inexpressibly beautiful
appears the recognition by man of the least natural fact,
and the allying his life to it. All the world reiterating

this slender truth, that aspens once grew there; and the swift inference is, that men were there to see them. And so it would be with the names of our native and neighboring villages, if we had not profaned them.

The daylight now failed us, and we went below; but I endeavored to console myself for being obliged to make this voyage by night, by thinking that I did not lose a great deal, the shores being low and rather unattractive, and that the river itself was much the more interesting object. I heard something in the night about the boat being at William Henry, Three Rivers, and in the Richelieu Rapids, but I was still where I had been when I lost sight of *Pointe aux Trembles*. To hear a man who has been waked up at midnight in the cabin of a steamboat, inquiring, " Waiter, where are we now?" is, as if at any moment of the earth's revolution round the sun, or of the system round its centre, one were to raise himself up and inquire of one of the deck hands, "Where are we now?"

I went on deck at daybreak, when we were thirty or forty miles above Quebec. The banks were now higher and more interesting. There was an "uninterrupted succession of white-washed cottages" on each side of the river. This is what every traveller tells. But it is not to be taken as an evidence of the populousness of the country in general, hardly even of the river banks. They have presented a similar appearance for a hundred years. The Swedish traveller and naturalist, Kalm, who descended this river in 1749, says: "It could really be called a village, beginning at Montreal and ending at Quebec, which is a distance of more than one hundred and eighty miles; for the farm-houses are never above five arpens, and sometimes but three asunder, a few

places excepted." Even in 1684 Hontan said that the
houses were not more than a gunshot apart at most.
Erelong we passed Cape Rouge, eight miles above Quebec, the mouth of the Chaudière on the opposite or
south side, New Liverpool Cove with its lumber rafts
and some shipping; then Sillery and Wolfe's Cove and
the Heights of Abraham on the north, with now a view
of Cape Diamond, and the citadel in front. The approach to Quebec was very imposing. It was about six
o'clock in the morning when we arrived. There is but
a single street under the cliff on the south side of the
cape, which was made by blasting the rocks and filling
up the river. Three-story houses did not rise more than
one fifth or one sixth the way up the nearly perpendicular rock, whose summit is three hundred and forty-
five feet above the water. We saw, as we glided past,
the sign on the side of the precipice, part way up, pointing to the spot where Montgomery was killed in 1775.
Formerly it was the custom for those who went to
Quebec for the first time to be ducked, or else pay a
fine. Not even the Governor General escaped. But
we were too many to be ducked, even if the custom had
not been abolished.*

Here we were, in the harbor of Quebec, still three
hundred and sixty miles from the mouth of the St.
Lawrence, in a basin two miles across, where the greatest depth is twenty-eight fathoms, and though the water

* Hierosme Lalemant says in 1648, in his relation, he being Superior: "All those who come to New France know well enough the
mountain of Notre Dame, because the pilots and sailors, being ar
rived at that part of the Great River which is opposite to those high
mountains, baptize ordinarily for sport the new passengers, if they
do not turn aside by some present the inundation of this baptism
which one makes flow plentifully on their heads."

is fresh, the tide rises seventeen to twenty-four feet, — a harbor "large and deep enough," says a British traveller, "to hold the English navy." I may as well state that, in 1844, the county of Quebec contained about forty-five thousand inhabitants (the city and suburbs having about forty-three thousand); about twenty-eight thousand being Canadians of French origin; eight thousand British; over seven thousand natives of Ireland; one thousand five hundred natives of England; the rest Scotch and others. Thirty-six thousand belong to the Church of Rome.

Separating ourselves from the crowd, we walked up a narrow street, thence ascended by some wooden steps, called the Break-neck Stairs, into another steep, narrow, and zigzag street, blasted through the rock, which last led through a low massive stone portal, called Prescott Gate, the principal thoroughfare into the Upper Town. This passage was defended by cannon, with a guard-house over it, a sentinel at his post, and other soldiers at hand ready to relieve him. I rubbed my eyes to be sure that I was in the nineteenth century, and was not entering one of those portals which sometimes adorn the frontispieces of new editions of old black-letter volumes. I thought it would be a good place to read Froissart's Chronicles. It was such a reminiscence of the Middle Ages as Scott's novels. Men apparently dwelt there for security. Peace be unto them! As if the inhabitants of New York were to go over to Castle William to live! What a place it must be to bring up children! Being safe through the gate we naturally took the street which was steepest, and after a few turns found ourselves on the Durham Terrace, a wooden platform on the site of the old castle of St. Louis, still one hundred and fifteen feet below the summit of the citadel, overlooking the Lower Town, the wharf where we had landed, the harbor, the Isle of Orleans, and the river and surrounding country to a great distance. It was literally a *splendid* view. We could see six or seven miles distant, in the northeast, an indentation in the lofty shore of the northern channel, apparently on one side of the harbor, which marked the mouth of the Montmorenci, whose celebrated fall was only a few rods in the rear.

At a shoe-shop, whither we were directed for this purpose, we got some of our American money changed into English. I found that American hard money would have answered as well, excepting cents, which fell very fast before their pennies, it taking two of the former to make one of the latter, and often the penny, which had cost us two cents, did us the service of one cent only. Moreover, our robust cents were compelled to meet on even terms a crew of vile half-penny tokens, and bung-town coppers, which had more brass in their composition, and so perchance made their way in the world. Wishing to get into the citadel, we were directed to the Jesuits' Barracks, — a good part of the public buildings here are barracks, — to get a pass of the Town Major. We did not heed the sentries at the gate, nor did they us, and what under the sun they were placed there for, unless to hinder a free circulation of the air, was not apparent. There we saw soldiers eating their breakfasts in their mess-room, from bare wooden tables in camp fashion. We were continually meeting with soldiers in the streets, carrying funny little tin pails of all shapes, even semicircular, as if made to pack conveniently. I supposed that they contained their dinners, — so many slices of bread and butter to each, perchance. Some-

times they were carrying some kind of military chest
on a sort of bier or hand-barrow, with a springy, un
dulating, military step, all passengers giving way to
them, even the charette-drivers stopping for them to
pass, — as if the battle were being lost from an inadequate supply of powder. There was a regiment of
Highlanders, and, as I understood, of Royal Irish, in
the city; and by this time there was a regiment of
Yankees also. I had already observed, looking up even
from the water, the head and shoulders of some General
Poniatowsky, with an. enormous cocked hat and gun,
peering over the roof of a house, away up where the
chimney caps commonly are with us, as it were a cari-
cature of war and military awfulness; but I had not
gone far up St. Louis Street before my riddle was
solved, by the apparition of a real live Highlander
under a cocked hat, and with his knees out, standing
and marching sentinel on the ramparts, between St.
Louis and St. John's Gate. (It must be a holy war
that is waged there.) We stood close by without fear
and looked at him. His legs were somewhat tanned,
and the hair had begun to grow on them, as some of our
wise men predict that it will in such cases, but I did not
think they were remarkable in any respect. Notwithstanding all his warlike gear, when I inquired of him
the way to the Plains of Abraham, he could not answer
me without betraying some bashfulness through his
broad Scotch. Soon after, we passed another of these
creatures standing sentry at the St. Louis Gate, who let
us go by without shooting us, or even demanding the
countersign. We then began to go through the gate,
which was so thick and tunnel-like, as to remind me of
those lines in Claudian's Old Man of Verona, about the

getting out of the gate being the greater part of a journey; — as you might imagine yourself crawling through an architectural vignette *at the end* of a black-letter volume. We were then reminded that we had been in a fortress, from which we emerged by numerous zigzags in a ditch-like road, going a considerable distance to advance a few rods, where they could have shot us two or three times over, if their minds had been disposed as their guns were. The greatest, or rather the most prominent, part of this city was constructed with the design to offer the deadest resistance to leaden and iron missiles that might be cast against it. But it is a remarkable meteorological and psychological fact, that it is rarely known to rain lead with much violence, except on places so constructed. Keeping on about a mile we came to the Plains of Abraham, — for having got through with the Saints, we come next to the Patriarchs. Here the Highland regiment was being reviewed, while the band stood on one side and played, — methinks it was *La Claire Fontaine*, the national air of the Canadian French. This is the site where a real battle once took place, to commemorate which they have had a sham fight here almost every day since. The Highlanders manœuvred very well, and if the precision of their movements was less remarkable, they did not appear so stiffly erect as the English or Royal Irish, but had a more elastic and graceful gait, like a herd of their own red deer, or as if accustomed to stepping down the sides of mountains. But they made a sad impression on the whole, for it was obvious that all true manhood was in the process of being drilled out of them. I have no doubt that soldiers well drilled are, as a class, peculiarly destitute of originality and independence. The officers appeared like men dressed above their condition. It is impossible to give the soldier a good education, without making him a deserter. His natural foe is the government that drills him. What would any philanthropist, who felt an interest in these men's welfare, naturally do, but first of all teach them so to respect themselves, that they could not be hired for this work, whatever might be the consequences to this government or that; — not drill a few, but educate all. I observed one older man among them, gray as a wharf-rat, and supple as the Devil, marching lock-step with the rest who would have to pay for that elastic gait.

We returned to the citadel along the heights, plucking such flowers as grew there. There was an abun‧dance of succory still in blossom, broad-leaved golden rod, buttercups, thorn-bushes, Canada thistles, and ivy, on the very summit of Cape Diamond. I also found the bladder-campion in the neighborhood. We there enjoyed an extensive view, which I will describe in another place. Our pass, which stated that all the rules were "to be strictly enforced," as if they were determined to keep up the semblance of reality to the last gasp, opened to us the Dalhousie Gate, and we were conducted over the citadel by a bare-legged Highlander in cocked hat and full regimentals. He told us that he had been here about three years, and had formerly been stationed at Gibraltar. As if his regiment, having per chance been nestled amid the rocks of Edinburgh Castle, must flit from rock to rock thenceforth over the earth's surface, like a bald eagle, or other bird of prey, from eyrie to eyrie. As we were going out, we met the Yankees coming in, in a body, headed by a red-coated officer called the commandant, and escorted by many

citizens, both English and French Canadian. I therefore immediately fell into the procession, and went round
the citadel again with more intelligent guides, carrying,
as before, all my effects with me. Seeing that nobody
walked with the red-coated commandant, I attached myself to him, and though I was not what is called well-
dressed, he did not know whether to repel me or not,
for I talked like one who was not aware of any de-
ficiency in that respect. Probably there was not one
among all the Yankees who went to Canada this time,
who was not more splendidly dressed than I was. It
would have been a poor story if I had not enjoyed some
distinction. I had on my "bad-weather clothes," like
Olaf Trygesson the Northman, when he went to the
Thing in England, where, by the way, he won his bride.
As we stood by the thirty-two-pounder on the summit
of Cape Diamond, which is fired three times a day, the
commandant told me that it would carry to the Isle of
Orleans, four miles distant, and that no hostile vessel
could come round the island. I now saw the subter-
ranean or, rather, "casemated barracks" of the soldiers,
which I had not noticed before, though I might have
walked over them. They had very narrow windows,
serving as loop-holes for musketry, and small iron chim-
neys rising above the ground. There we saw the soldiers
at home and in an undress, splitting wood, — I looked to
see whether with swords or axes, — and in various ways
endeavoring to realize that their nation was now at peace
with this part of the world. A part of each regiment,
chiefly officers, are allowed to marry. A grandfatherly,
would-be witty Englishman could give a Yankee whom
he was patronizing no reason for the bare knees of the
Highlanders, other than oddity. The rock within the

citadel is a little convex, so that shells falling on it would roll toward the circumference, where the barracks of the soldiers and officers are; it has been proposed, therefore, to make it slightly concave, so that they may roll into the centre, where they would be comparatively harmless; and it is estimated that to do this would cost twenty thousand pounds sterling. It may be well to remember this when I build my next house, and have the roof "all correct" for bombshells.

At mid-afternoon we made haste down *Sault-au-Matelot* street, towards the Falls of Montmorenci, about eight miles down the St. Lawrence, on the north side, leaving the further examination of Quebec till our return. On our way, we saw men in the streets sawing logs pit-fashion, and afterward, with a common wood-saw and horse, cutting the planks into squares for paving the streets. This looked very shiftless, especially in a country abounding in water-power, and reminded me that I was no longer in Yankee land. I found, on inquiry, that the excuse for this was, that labor was so cheap; and I thought, with some pain, how cheap men are here! I have since learned that the English traveller, Warburton, remarked, soon after landing at Quebec, that everything was cheap there but men. That must be the difference between going thither from New and from Old England. I had already observed the dogs harnessed to their little milk-carts, which contain a single large can, lying asleep in the gutters regardless of the horses, while they rested from their labors, at different stages of the ascent in the Upper Town. I was surprised at the regular and extensive use made of these animals for drawing, not only milk, but groceries, wood, &c. It reminded me that the dog commonly is not put

to any use. Cats catch mice ; but dogs only worry the
cats. Kalm, a hundred years ago, saw sledges here for
ladies to ride in, drawn by a pair of dogs. He says
"A middle-sized dog is sufficient to draw a single per
son, when the roads are good "; and he was told by old
people, that horses were very scarce in their youth, and
almost all the land-carriage was then effected by dogs.
They made me think of the Esquimaux, who, in fact,
are the next people on the north. Charlevoix says, that
the first horses were introduced in 1665.

We crossed Dorchester Bridge, over the St. Charles,
the little river in which Cartier, the discoverer of the
St. Lawrence, put his ships, and spent the winter of
1535, and found ourselves on an excellent macadamized
road, called *Le Chemin de Beauport*. We had left Concord Wednesday morning, and we endeavored to realize
that now, Friday morning, we were taking a walk in
Canada, in the Seigniory of Beauport, a foreign country,
which a few days before had seemed almost as far off as
England and France. Instead of rambling to Flint's
Pond or the Sudbury Meadows, we found ourselves, after
being a little detained in cars and steamboats, — after
spending half a night at Burlington, and half a day at
Montreal, — taking a walk down the bank of the St.
Lawrence to the Falls of Montmorenci and elsewhere.
Well, I thought to myself, here I am in a foreign country ; let me have my eyes about me, and take it all in.
It already looked and felt a good deal colder than it had
in New England, as we might have expected it would.
I realized fully that I was four degrees nearer the pole,
and shuddered at the thought ; and I wondered if it
were possible that the peaches might not be all gone
when I returned. It was an atmosphere that made me

think of the fur-trade, which is so interesting a department in Canada, for I had for all head-covering a thin
palm-leaf hat without lining, that cost twenty-five cents,
and over my coat one of those unspeakably cheap, as
well as thin, brown linen sacks of the Oak Hall pattern,
which every summer appear all over New England, thick
as the leaves upon the trees. It was a thoroughly Yankee costume, which some of my fellow-travellers wore
in the cars to save their coats a dusting. I wore mine,
at first, because it looked better than the coat it covered,
and last, because two coats were warmer than one,
though one was thin and dirty. I never wear my best
coat on a journey, though perchance I could show a
certificate to prove that I have a more costly one, at
least, at home, if that were all that a gentleman required. It is not wise for a traveller to go dressed. I
should no more think of it than of putting on a clean
dicky and blacking my shoes to go a-fishing; as if you
were going out to dine, when, in fact, the genuine travel
ler is going out to work hard, and fare harder, — to eat
a crust by the wayside whenever he can get it. Honest
travelling is about as dirty work as you can do, and a
man needs a pair of overalls for it. As for blacking my
shoes in such a case, I should as soon think of blacking
my face. I carry a piece of tallow to preserve the
leather, and keep out the water; that's all; and many
an officious shoe-black, who carried off my shoes when
I was slumbering, mistaking me for a gentleman, has
had occasion to repent it before he produced a gloss on
them.

My pack, in fact, was soon made, for I keep a short
list of those articles which, from frequent experience, I
have found indispensable to the foot-traveller; and, when

I am about to start, I have only to consult that, to be
sure that nothing is omitted, and, what is more important, nothing superfluous inserted. Most of my fellow-
travellers carried carpet-bags, or valises. Sometimes
one had two or three ponderous yellow valises in his
clutch, at each hitch of the cars, as if we were going to
have another rush for seats; and when there was a rush
in earnest, and there were not a few, I would see my
man in the crowd, with two or three affectionate lusty
fellows along each side of his arm, between his shoulder
and his valises, which last held them tight to his back,
like the nut on the end of a screw. I could not help
asking in my mind, What so great cause for showing
Canada to those valises, when perhaps your very nieces
had to stay at home for want of an escort? I should
have liked to be present when the custom-house officer
came aboard of him, and asked him to declare upon his
honor if he had anything but wearing apparel in them.
Even the elephant carries but a small trunk on his journeys. The perfection of travelling is to travel without
baggage. After considerable reflection and experience,
I have concluded that the best bag for the foot-traveller
is made with a handkerchief, or, if he study appearances,
a piece of stiff brown paper, well tied up, with a fresh
piece within to put outside when the first is torn. That
is good for both town and country, and none will know
but you are carrying home the silk for a new gown for
your wife, when it may be a dirty shirt. A bundle which
you can carry literally under your arm, and which will
shrink and swell with its contents. I never found the
carpet-bag of equal capacity, which was not a bundle of
itself. We styled ourselves the Knights of the Umbrella
and the Bundle; for wherever we went, whether to Notre

Dame or Mount Royal, or the Champ-de-Mars, to the
Town Major's or the Bishop's Palace, to the Citadel,
with a bare-legged Highlander for our escort, or to the
Plains of Abraham, to dinner or to bed, the umbrella
and the bundle went with us ; for we wished to be ready
to digress at any moment. We made it our home nowhere in particular, but everywhere where our umbrella
and bundle were. It would have been an amusing cir-
cumstance, if the Mayor of one of those cities had po-
litely asked us where we were staying. We could only
have answered, that we were staying with his Honor for
the time being. I was amused when, after our return,
some green ones inquired if we found it easy to get ac-
commodated ; as if we went abroad to get accommo-
dated, when we can get that at home.

We met with many charettes, bringing wood and stone
to the city. The most ordinary looking horses travelled
faster than ours, or, perhaps they were ordinary looking,
because, as I am told, the Canadians do not use the
curry-comb. Moreover, it is said, that on the approach
of winter their horses acquire an increased quantity of
hair, to protect them from the cold. If this be true,
some of our horses would make you think winter were
approaching, even in midsummer. We soon began to
see women and girls at work in the fields, digging potatoes alone, or bundling up the grain which the men cut.
They appeared in rude health, with a great deal of color
in their cheeks, and, if their occupation had made them
coarse, it impressed me as better in its effects than making shirts at fourpence apiece, or doing nothing at all ;
unless it be chewing slate pencils, with still smaller results. They were much more agreeable objects, with
their great broad-brimmed hats and flowing dresses,

than the men and boys. We afterwards saw them doing
various other kinds of work; indeed, I thought that we
saw more women at work out of doors than men. On
our return, we observed in this town a girl with Indian
boots, nearly two feet high, taking the harness off a dog.
The purity and transparency of the atmosphere were
wonderful. When we had been walking an hour, we
were surprised, on turning round, to see how near the
city, with its glittering tin roofs, still looked. A village
ten miles off did not appear to be more than three or
four. I was convinced that you could see objects distinctly there much farther than here. It is true the
villages are of a dazzling white, but the dazzle is to be
referred, perhaps, to the transparency of the atmosphere
as much as to the whitewash.

We were now fairly in the village of Beauport, though
there was still but one road. The houses stood close upon
this, without any front-yards, and at any angle with it,
as if they had dropped down, being set with more reference to the road which the sun travels. It being about
sundown, and the Falls not far off, we began to look
round for a lodging, for we preferred to put up at a private house, that we might see more of the inhabitants.
We inquired first at the most promising looking houses,
if, indeed, any were promising. When we knocked, they
shouted some French word for come in, perhaps *entrez*,
and we asked for a lodging in English; but we found,
unexpectedly, that they spoke French only. Then we
went along and tried another house, being generally
saluted by a rush of two or three little curs, which
readily distinguished a foreigner, and which we were
prepared now to hear bark in French. Our first question
would be, *Parlez-vous Anglais?* but the invariable an

swer was, *Non, monsieur;* and we soon found that the
inhabitants were exclusively French Canadians, and nobody spoke English at all, any more than in France;
that, in fact, we were in a foreign country, where the
inhabitants uttered not one familiar sound to us.   Then
we tried by turns to talk French with them, in which we
succeeded sometimes pretty well, but for the most part,
pretty ill.   *Pouvez-vous nous donner un lit cette nuit?*
we would ask, and then they would answer with French
volubility, so that we could catch only a word here and
there.   We could understand the women and children
generally better than the men, and they us; and thus,
after a while, we would learn that they had no more
beds than they used.

So we were compelled to inquire: *Y a-t-il une maison
publique ici?* (*auberge* we should have said, perhaps, for
they seemed never to have heard of the other), and they
answered at length that there was no tavern, unless we
could get lodgings at the mill, *le moulin*, which we had
passed; or they would direct us to a grocery, and almost
every house had a small grocery at one end of it.   We
called on the public notary or village lawyer, but he had
no more beds nor English than the rest.   At one house
there was so good a misunderstanding at once established
through the politeness of all parties, that we were encouraged to walk in and sit down, and ask for a glass of
water; and having drank their water, we thought it was
as good as to have tasted their salt.   When our host and
his wife spoke of their poor accommodations, meaning
for themselves, we assured them that they were good
enough, for we thought that they were only apologizing
for the poorness of the accommodations they were about
to offer us, and we did not discover our mistake till they

took us up a ladder into a loft, and showed to our eyes
what they had been laboring in vain to communicate to our
brains through our ears, that they had but that one apartment with its few beds for the whole family. We made
our *a-dieus* forthwith, and with gravity, perceiving the
literal signification of that word. We were finally taken
in at a sort of public-house, whose master worked for
Patterson, the proprietor of the extensive saw-mills
driven by a portion of the Montmorenci stolen from the
fall, whose roar we now heard. We here talked, or mur-
dered French all the evening, with the master of the
house and his family, and probably had a more amusing
time than if we had completely understood one another.
At length they showed us to a bed in their best chamber, very high to get into, with a low wooden rail to it.
It had no cotton sheets, but coarse, home-made, dark
colored, linen ones. Afterward, we had to do with sheets
still coarser than these, and nearly the color of our blankets.   There was a large open buffet loaded with crock-
ery, in one corner of the room, as if to display their
wealth to travellers, and pictures of Scripture scenes,
French, Italian, and Spanish, hung around. Our hostess
came back directly to inquire if we would have brandy
for breakfast. The next morning, when I asked their
names, she took down the temperance pledges of herself
and husband, and children, which were hanging against
the wall. They were Jean Baptiste Binet, and his wife,
Geneviève Binet. Jean Baptiste is the sobriquet of
the French Canadians.

After breakfast we proceeded to the fall, which was
within half a mile, and at this distance its rustling sound,
like the wind among the leaves, filled all the air. We
were disappointed to find that we were in some measure

shut out from the west side of the fall by the private
grounds and fences of Patterson, who appropriates not
only a part of the water for his mill, but a still larger
part of the prospect, so that we were obliged to trespass.
This gentleman's mansion-house and grounds were formerly occupied by the Duke of Kent, father to Queen
Victoria. It appeared to me in bad taste for an individual, though he were the father of Queen Victoria, to
obtrude himself with his land titles, or at least his fences,
on so remarkable a natural phenomenon, which should,
in every sense, belong to mankind.   Some falls should
even be kept sacred from the intrusion of mills and
factories, as water privileges in another than the mill-
wright's sense.   This small river falls perpendicularly
nearly two hundred and fifty feet at one pitch.   The St.
Lawrence falls only one hundred and sixty-four feet at
Niagara.   It is a very simple and noble fall, and leaves
nothing to be desired; but the most that I could say of
it would only have the force of one other testimony to
assure the reader that it is there.   We looked directly
down on it from the point of a projecting rock, and saw
far below us, on a low promontory, the grass kept fresh
and green by the perpetual drizzle, looking like moss.
The rock is a kind of slate, in the crevices of which
grew ferns and golden-rods.   The prevailing trees on
the shores were spruce and arbor-vitæ, — the latter very
large and now full of fruit, — also aspens, alders, and the
mountain-ash with its berries.   Every emigrant who arrives in this country by way of the St. Lawrence, as he
opens a point of the Isle of Orleans, sees the Montmo
renci tumbling into the Great River thus magnificently
in a vast white sheet, making its contribution with emphasis.   Roberval's pilot, Jean Alphonse, saw this fall

thus, and described it, in 1542. It is a splendid intro-
duction to the scenery of Quebec. Instead of an arti
ficial fountain in its square, Quebec has this magnificent
natural waterfall to adorn one side of its harbor. Within
the mouth of the chasm below, which can be entered
only at ebb tide, we had a grand view at once of Quebec and of the fall. Kalm says that the noise of the
fall is sometimes heard at Quebec, about eight miles
distant, and is a sign of a northeast wind. The side of
this chasm, of soft and crumbling slate too steep to climb,
was among the memorable features of the scene. In the
winter of 1829 the frozen spray of the fall, descending
on the ice of the St. Lawrence, made a hill one hundred
and twenty-six feet high. It is an annual phenomenon
which some think may help explain the formation of
glaciers.

In the vicinity of the fall we began to notice what
looked like our red-fruited thorn bushes, grown to the
size of ordinary apple-trees, very common, and full of
large red or yellow fruit, which the inhabitants called
pommettes, but I did not learn that they were put to any
use.

CHAPTER III.

ST. ANNE.

By the middle of the forenoon, though it was a rainy day, we were once more on our way down the north bank of the St. Lawrence, in a northeasterly direction, toward the Falls of St. Anne, which are about thirty miles from Quebec. The settled, more level, and fertile portion of Canada East may be described rudely as a triangle, with its apex slanting toward the northeast, about one hundred miles wide at its base, and from two to three, or even four hundred miles long, if you reckon its narrow northeastern extremity; it being the immediate valley of the St. Lawrence and its tributaries, rising by a single or by successive terraces toward the mountains on either hand. Though the words Canada East on the map stretch over many rivers and lakes and unexplored wildernesses, the actual Canada, which might be the colored portion of the map, is but a little clearing on the banks of the river, which one of those syllables would more than cover. The banks of the St. Lawrence are rather low from Montreal to the Richelieu Rapids, about forty miles above Quebec. Thence they rise gradually to Cape Diamond, or Quebec. Where we now were, eight miles northeast of Quebec, the mountains which form the northern side of this triangle were only five or six miles distant from the river, gradually departing farther and farther from it, on the west, till they reach the Ottawa, and making haste to meet it on the east, at Cape Tourmente, now in plain sight about twenty miles distant. So that we were travelling in a

very narrow and sharp triangle between the mountains
and the river, tilted up toward the mountains on the
north, never losing sight of our great fellow-traveller on
our right. According to Bouchette's Topographical Description of the Canadas, we were in the Seigniory of
the Côte de Beaupré, in the county of Montmorenci, and
the district of Quebec; in that part of Canada which
was the first to be settled, and where the face of the
country and the population have undergone the least
change from the beginning, where the influence of the
States and of Europe is least felt, and the inhabitants
see little or nothing of the world over the walls of Quebec. This Seigniory was granted in 1636, and is now
the property of the Seminary of Quebec. It is the
most mountainous one in the province. There are
some half a dozen parishes in it, each containing a
church, parsonage-house, grist-mill, and several saw-
mills. We were now in the most westerly parish called
Ange Gardien, or the Guardian Angel, which is bounded
on the west by the Montmorenci. The north bank of
the St. Lawrence here is formed on a grand scale. It
slopes gently, either directly from the shore, or from the
edge of an interval, till, at the distance of about a mile,
it attains the height of four or five hundred feet. The
single road runs along the side of the slope two or three
hundred feet above the river at first, and from a quarter
of a mile to a mile distant from it, and affords fine views
of the north channel, which is about a mile wide, and of
the beautiful Isle of Orleans, about twenty miles long by
five wide, where grow the best apples and plums in the
Quebec District.

Though there was but this single road, it was a con-
tinuous village for as far as we walked this day and the

next, or about thirty miles down the river, the houses being as near together all the way as in the middle of one of our smallest straggling country villages, and we could never tell by their number when we were on the skirts of a parish, for the road never ran through the fields or woods. We were told that it was just six miles from one parish church to another. I thought that we saw every house in Ange Gardien. Therefore, as it was a muddy day, we never got out of the mud, nor out of the village, unless we got over the fence; then indeed, if it was on the north side, we were out of the civilized world. There were sometimes a few more houses near the church, it is true, but we had only to go a quarter of a mile from the road to the top of the bank to find ourselves on the verge of the uninhabited, and, for the most part, unexplored wilderness stretching toward Hudson's Bay. The farms accordingly were extremely long and narrow, each having a frontage on the river. Bouchette accounts for this peculiar manner of laying out a village by referring to "the social character of the Canadian peasant, who is singularly fond of neighborhood," also to the advantage arising from a concentration of strength in Indian times. Each farm, called *terre*, he says, is, in nine cases out of ten, three arpents wide by thirty deep, that is, very nearly thirty-five by three hundred and forty-nine of our rods; sometimes one half arpent by thirty, or one to sixty; sometimes, in fact, a few yards by half a mile. Of course it costs more for fences. A remarkable difference between the Canadian and the New England character appears from the fact that in 1745, the French government were obliged to pass a law forbidding the farmers or *censitaires* building on land less than one and a half arpents

front by thirty or forty deep, under a certain penalty, in
order to compel emigration, and bring the seigneur's
estates all under cultivation ; and it is thought that they
have now less reluctance to leave the paternal roof than
formerly, " removing beyond the sight of the parish
spire, or the sound of the parish bell." But I find that
in the previous or seventeenth century, the complaint,
often renewed, was of a totally opposite character,
namely, that the inhabitants dispersed and exposed
themselves to the Iroquois. Accordingly, about 1664,
the king was obliged to order that " they should make
no more clearings except one next to another, and that
they should reduce their parishes to the form of the
parishes in France as much as possible." The Canadians
of those days, at least, possessed a roving spirit of adventure which carried them further, in exposure to
hardship and danger, than ever the New England colo-
nist went, and led them, though not to clear and colo-
nize the wilderness, yet to range over it as *coureurs de
bois,* or runners of the woods, or as Hontan prefers to
call them *coureurs de risques,* runners of risks ; to say
nothing of their enterprising priesthood ; and Charlevoix
thinks that if the authorities had taken the right steps
to prevent the youth from ranging the woods (*de courir
les bois*) they would have had an excellent militia to
fight the Indians and English.

The road, in this clayey looking soil, was exceedingly
muddy in consequence of the night's rain. We met an
old woman directing her dog, which was harnessed to a
little cart, to the least muddy part of it. It was a beg-
garly sight. But harnessed to the cart as he was, we
heard him barking after we had passed, though we
looked anywhere but to the cart to see where the dog

was that barked. The houses commonly fronted the south, whatever angle they might make with the road; and frequently they had no door nor cheerful window on the roadside. Half the time they stood fifteen to forty rods from the road, and there was no very obvious passage to them, so that you would suppose that there must be another road running by them. They were of stone, rather coarsely mortared, but neatly whitewashed, almost invariably one story high and long in proportion to their height, with a shingled roof, the shingles being pointed, for ornament, at the eaves, like the pickets of a fence, and also one row half-way up the roof. The gables sometimes projected a foot or two at the ridge-pole only. Yet they were very humble and unpretending dwellings. They commonly had the date of their erection on them. The windows opened in the middle, like blinds, and were frequently provided with solid shutters. Sometimes, when we walked along the back side of a house which stood near the road, we observed stout stakes leaning against it, by which the shutters, now pushed half open, were fastened at night; within, the houses were neatly ceiled with wood not painted. The oven was commonly out of doors, built of stone and mortar, frequently on a raised platform of planks. The cellar was often on the opposite side of the road, in front of or behind the houses, looking like an ice-house with us with a lattice door for summer. The very few mechanics whom we met had an old-Bettyish look, in their aprons and *bonnets rouges*, like fools' caps. The men wore commonly the same *bonnet rouge*, or red woollen or worsted cap, or sometimes blue or gray, looking to us as if they had got up with their night-caps on, and, in fact, I afterwards found that they had. Their clothes were of the cloth of the country, *étoffe du pays*, gray or some other plain color: The women looked stout, with gowns that stood out stiffly, also, for the most part, apparently of some home-made stuff. We also saw some specimens of the more characteristic winter dress of the Canadian, and I have since frequently detected him in New England by his coarse gray homespun capote and picturesque red sash, and his well-furred cap, made to protect his ears against the severity of his climate.

It drizzled all day, so that the roads did not improve. We began now to meet with wooden crosses frequently, by the roadside, about a dozen feet high, often old and toppling down, sometimes standing in a square wooden platform, sometimes in a pile of stones, with a little niche containing a picture of the Virgin and Child, or of Christ alone, sometimes with a string of beads, and covered with a piece of glass to keep out the rain, with the words, *pour la vierge*, or *Iniri*, on them. Frequently, on the cross-bar, there would be quite a collection of symbolical knickknacks, looking like an Italian's board; the representation in wood of a hand, a hammer, spikes, pincers, a flask of vinegar, a ladder, &c., the whole, perchance, surmounted by a weathercock; but I could not look at an honest weathercock in this walk without mistrusting that there was some covert reference in it to St. Peter. From time to time we passed a little one-story chapel-like building, with a tin-roofed spire, a shrine, perhaps it would be called, close to the pathside, with a lattice door, through which we could see an altar, and pictures about the walls; equally open, through rain and shine, though there was no getting into it. At these places the inhabitants kneeled and perhaps breathed a short prayer. We saw one school-house in our walk.

and listened to the sounds which issued from it; but it appeared like a place where the process, not of enlightening, but of obfuscating the mind was going on, and the pupils received only so much light as could penetrate the shadow of the Catholic Church. The churches were very picturesque, and their interior much more showy than the dwelling-houses promised. They were of stone, for it was ordered, in 1699, that that should be their material. They had tinned spires, and quaint ornaments. That of l'Ange Gardien had a dial on it, with the Middle Age Roman numerals on its face, and some images in niches on the outside. Probably its counterpart has existed in Normandy for a thousand years. At the church of Chateau Richer, which is the next parish to l'Ange Gardien, we read, looking over the wall, the inscriptions in the adjacent churchyard, which began with, "*Ici gît*" or "*Repose,*" and one over a boy contained, "*Priez pour lui.*" This answered as well as Père la Chaise. We knocked at the door of the curé's house here, when a sleek friar-like personage, in his sacerdotal robe, appeared. To our *Parlez-vous Anglais?* even he answered, "*Non, Monsieur*"; but at last we made him understand what we wanted. It was to find the ruins of the old *chateau.* "*Ah! oui! oui!*" he exclaimed, and, donning his coat, hastened forth, and conducted us to a small heap of rubbish which we had already examined. He said that fifteen years before, it was *plus considérable.* Seeing at that moment three little red birds fly out of a crevice in the ruins, up into an arbor-vitæ tree, which grew out of them, I asked him their names, in such French as I could muster, but he neither understood me nor ornithology; he only inquired where we had *appris à parler Français ;* we told him, *dans les États-Unis;* and so we bowed him into his house again. I was surprised to find a man wearing a black coat, and with apparently no work to do, even in that part of the world.

The universal salutation from the inhabitants whom we met was *bon jour*, at the same time touching the hat; with *bon jour*, and touching your hat, you may go smoothly through all Canada East. A little boy, meeting us, would remark, " *Bon jour, Monsieur ; le chemin est mauvais*," Good morning, sir; it is bad walking. Sir Francis Head says that the immigrant is forward to " appreciate the happiness of living in a land in which the old country's servile custom of touching the hat does not exist," but he was thinking of Canada West, of course. It would, indeed, be a serious bore to be obliged to touch your hat several times a day. A Yankee has not leisure for it.

We saw peas, and even beans, collected into heaps in the fields. The former are an important crop here, and, I suppose, are not so much infested by the weevil as with us. There were plenty of apples, very fair and sound, by the roadside, but they were so small as to suggest the origin of the apple in the crab. There was also a small red fruit which they called *snells*, and another, also red and very acid, whose name a little boy wrote for me "*pinbéna.*" It is probably the same with, or similar to, the *pembina* of the voyageurs, a species of viburnum, which, according to Richardson, has given its name to many of the rivers of Rupert's Land. The forest trees were spruce, arbor-vitæ, firs, birches, beeches, two or three kinds of maple, bass-wood, wild-cherry, aspens, &c., but no pitch pines (*Pinus rigida*). I saw very few, if any, trees which had been set out for shade or ornament. The water was commonly running streams or springs in the bank by the roadside, and was excellent. The parishes are commonly separated by a stream, and frequently the farms. I noticed that the fields were furrowed or thrown into beds seven or eight feet wide to dry the soil.

At the *Rivière du Sault à la Puce*, which, I suppose, means the River of the Fall of the Flea, was advertised in English, as the sportsmen are English, "The best Snipe-shooting grounds," over the door of a small public-house. These words being English affected me as if I had been absent now ten years from my country, and for so long had not heard the sound of my native language, and every one of them was as interesting to me as if I had been a snipe-shooter, and they had been snipes. The prunella or self-heal, in the grass here, was an old acquaintance. We frequently saw the inhabitants washing, or cooking for their pigs, and in one place hackling flax by the roadside. It was pleasant to see these usually domestic operations carried on out of doors, even in that cold country.

At twilight we reached a bridge over a little river, the boundary between Chateau Richer and St. Anne, *le premier pont de St. Anne*, and at dark the church of *La Bonne St. Anne*. Formerly vessels from France, when they came in sight of this church, gave "a general discharge of their artillery," as a sign of joy that they had escaped all the dangers of the river. Though all the while we had grand views of the adjacent country far up and down the river, and, for the most part, when we turned about, of Quebec in the horizon behind us, and we never beheld it without new surprise and admiration; yet, throughout our walk, the Great River of

Canada on our right hand was the main feature in the landscape, and this expands so rapidly below the Isle of Orleans, and creates such a breadth of level horizon above its waters in that direction, that, looking down the river as we approached the extremity of that island, the St. Lawrence seemed to be opening into the ocean, though we were still about three hundred and twenty-five miles from what can be called its mouth.*

When we inquired here for a *maison publique* we were directed apparently to that private house where we were most likely to find entertainment. There were no guideboards where we walked, because there was but one road; there were no shops or signs, because there were no artisans to speak of, and the people raised their own provisions; and there were no taverns, because there were no travellers. We here bespoke lodging and breakfast. They had, as usual, a large old-fashioned, two-storied box-stove in the middle of the room, out of which, in due time, there was sure to be forthcoming a supper, breakfast, or dinner. The lower half held the fire, the upper the hot air, and as it was a cool Canadian evening, this was a comforting sight to us. Being four or five feet high it warmed the whole person as you stood by it. The stove was plainly a very important article of furniture in Canada, and was not set aside during the summer. Its size, and the respect which was paid to it, told of the severe winters which it had seen and prevailed over. The master of the house, in his

* From McCulloch's Geographical Dictionary we learn that "immediately beyond the Island of Orleans it is a mile broad, where the Saguenay joins it, eighteen miles; at Point Peter upward of thirty at the Bay of Seven Islands, seventy miles; and at the island of Anticosti (about three hundred and fifty miles from Quebec) it rolls a flood into the ocean nearly one hundred miles across."

long-pointed, red woollen cap, had a thoroughly antique
physiognomy of the old Norman stamp. He might
nave come over with Jacques Cartier. His was the
hardest French to understand of any we had heard yet,
for there was a great difference between one speaker
and another, and this man talked with a pipe in hi.
mouth beside, a kind of tobacco French. I asked him
what he called his dog. He shouted *Brock!* (the name
of the breed). We like to hear the cat called *min,* — min !
min ! min ! I inquired if we could cross the river here
to the Isle of Orleans, thinking to return that way when
we had been to the Falls. He answered, " *S'il ne fait pas
un trop grand vent,*" If there is not too much wind. They
use small boats, or pirogues, and the waves are often too
high for them. He wore, as usual, something between a
moccasin and a boot, which he called *bottes Indiennes,* Indian boots, and had made himself. The tops were of calf
or sheep-skin, and the soles of cowhide turned up like a
mocassin. They were yellow or reddish, the leather
never having been tanned nor colored. The women
wore the same. He told us that he had travelled ten
leagues due north into the bush. He had been to the
Falls of St. Anne, and said that they were more beauti
ful, but not greater, than Montmorenci, *plus beau, mais
non plus grand que Montmorenci.* As soon as we had
retired, the family commenced their devotions. A little
boy officiated, and for a long time we heard him muttering over his prayers.

In the morning, after a breakfast of tea, maple-sugar,
bread and butter, and what I suppose is called *potage*
(potatoes and meat boiled with flour), the universal dish
as we found, perhaps the national one, I ran over to the
Church of La Bonne St. Anne, whose matin bell w4

had heard, it being Sunday morning. Our book said that this church had "long been an object of interest, from the miraculous cures said to have been wrought on visitors to the shrine." There was a profusion of gilding, and I counted more than twenty-five crutches suspended on the walls, some for grown persons, some for children, which it was to be inferred so many sick had been able to dispense with; but they looked as if they had been made to order by the carpenter who made the church. There were one or two villagers at their devotions at that early hour, who did not look up, but when they had sat a long time with their little book before the picture of one saint, went to another. Our whole walk was through a thoroughly Catholic country, and there was no trace of any other religion. I doubt if there are any more simple and unsophisticated Catholics anywhere. Emery de Caen, Champlain's contemporary, told the Huguenot sailors that "Monseigneur, the Duke de Ventadour (Viceroy), did not wish that they should sing psalms in the Great River."

On our way to the Falls, we met the habitans coming to the Church of La Bonne St. Anne, walking or riding in charettes by families. I remarked that they were universally of small stature. The toll-man at the bridge over the St. Anne was the first man we had chanced to meet, since we left Quebec, who could speak a word of English. How good French the inhabitants of this part of Canada speak, I am not competent to say; I only know that it is not made impure by being mixed with English. I do not know why it should not be as good as is spoken in Normandy. Charlevoix, who was here a hundred years ago, observes, "The French language is nowhere spoken with greater purity, there being no accent perceptible "; and Potherie said "they had no dialect, which, indeed, is generally lost in a colony."

The falls, which we were in search of, are three miles up the St. Anne. We followed for a short distance a foot-path up the east bank of this river, through handsome sugar-maple and arbor-vitæ groves. Having lost the path which led to a house where we were to get further directions, we dashed at once into the woods, steering by guess and by compass, climbing directly through woods, a steep hill, or mountain, five or six hundred feet high, which was, in fact, only the bank of the St. Lawrence. Beyond this we by good luck fell into another path, and following this or a branch of it, at our discretion, through a forest consisting of large white pines, — the first we had seen in our walk, — we at length heard the roar of falling water, and came out at the head of the Falls of St. Anne. We had descended into a ravine or cleft in the mountain, whose walls rose still a hundred feet above us, though we were near its top, and we now stood on a very rocky shore, where the water had lately flowed a dozen feet higher, as appeared by the stones and drift-wood, and large birches twisted and splintered as a farmer twists a withe. Here the river, one or two hundred feet wide, came flowing rapidly over a rocky bed out of that interesting wilderness which stretches toward Hudson's Bay and Davis's Straits. Ha-ha Bay, on the Saguenay, was about one hundred miles north of where we stood. Looking on the map, I find that the first country on the north which bears a name is that part of Rupert's Land called East Main. This river, called after the holy Anne, flowing from such a direction, here tumbled over a precipice, at present by three channels, how

far down I do not know, but far enough for all our purposes, and to as good a distance as if twice as far. It
matters little whether you call it one, or two, or three
hundred feet; at any rate, it was a sufficient Water-
privilege for us. I crossed the principal channel directly over the verge of the fall, where it was contracted to about fifteen feet in width by a dead tree,
which had been dropped across and secured in a cleft
of the opposite rock, and a smaller one a few feet
higher, which served for a hand-rail. This bridge was
rotten as well as small and slippery, being stripped of
bark, and I was obliged to seize a moment to pass when
the falling water did not surge over it, and mid-way,
though at the expense of wet feet, I looked down probably more than a hundred feet, into the mist and foam
below. This gave me the freedom of an island of precipitous rock, by which I descended as by giant steps,
the rock being composed of large cubical masses, clothed
with delicate close-hugging lichens of various colors, kept
fresh and bright by the moisture, till I viewed the first
fall from the front, and looked down still deeper to
where the second and third channels fell into a remarkably large circular basin worn in the stone. The falling
water seemed to jar the very rocks, and the noise to be
ever increasing. The vista down stream was through a
narrow and deep cleft in the mountain, all white suds at
the bottom; but a sudden angle in this gorge prevented
my seeing through to the bottom of the fall. Returning
to the shore, I made my way down stream through the
forest to see how far the fall extended, and how the
river came out of that adventure. It was to clamber
along the side of a precipitous mountain of loose mossy
rocks, covered with a damp primitive forest, and termi-

nating at the bottom in an abrupt precipice over the
stream. This was the east side of the fall. At length,
after a quarter of a mile, I got down to still water, and,
on looking up through the winding gorge, I could just
see to the foot of the fall which I had before examined;
while from the opposite side of the stream, here much
contracted, rose a perpendicular wall, I will not venture
to say how many hundred feet, but only that it was the
highest perpendicular wall of bare rock that I ever saw.
In front of me tumbled in from the summit of the cliff a
tributary stream, making a beautiful cascade, which was
a remarkable fall in itself, and there was a cleft in this
precipice, apparently four or five feet wide, perfectly
straight up and down from top to bottom, which, from
its cavernous depth and darkness, appeared merely as *a
black streak.* This precipice is not sloped, nor is the
material soft and crumbling slate as at Montmorenci,
but it rises perfectly perpendicular, like the side of a
mountain fortress, and is cracked into vast cubical
masses of gray and black rock shining with moisture,
as if it were the ruin of an ancient wall built by Titans.
Birches, spruces, mountain-ashes with their bright red
berries, arbor-vitæs, white pines, alders, &c., overhung
this chasm on the very verge of the cliff and in the
crevices, and here and there were buttresses of rock
supporting trees part way down, yet so as to enhance,
not injure, the effect of the bare rock. Take it altogether, it was a most wild and rugged and stupendous
chasm, so deep and narrow where a river had worn itself a passage through a mountain of rock, and all
around was the comparatively untrodden wilderness.

This was the limit of our walk down the St. Lawrence. Early in the afternoon we began to retrace our

steps, not being able to cross the north channel and return by the Isle of Orleans, on account of the *trop grand
vent,* or too great wind.   Though the waves did run
pretty high, it was evident that the inhabitants of Montmorenci County were no sailors, and made but little use
of the river.   When we reached the bridge, between
St. Anne and Chateau Richer, I ran back a little way
to ask a man in the field the name of the river which
we were crossing, but for a long time I could not make
out what he said, for he was one of the more unintelligible Jacques Cartier men.   At last it flashed upon me
that it was *La Rivière au Chien,* or the Dog River,
which my eyes beheld, which brought to my mind the
life of the Canadian voyageur and *coureur de bois,* a
more western and wilder Arcadia, methinks, than the
world has ever seen ; for the Greeks, with all their
wood and river gods, were not so qualified to name the
natural features of a country, as the ancestors of these
French Canadians ; and if any people had a right to
substitute their own for the Indian names, it was they.
They have preceded the pioneer on our own frontiers,
and named the *prairie* for us.   *La Rivière au Chien*
cannot, by any license of language, be translated into
Dog River, for that is not such a giving it to the dogs,
and recognizing their place in creation as the French
implies.   One of the tributaries of the St. Anne is named
La Rivière de la Rose ; and farther east are, *La Rivière
de la Blondelle,* and *La Rivière de la Friponne.*   Their
very *rivière* meanders more than our *river.*

Yet the impression which this country made on me
was commonly different from this.   To a traveller from
the Old World, Canada East may appear like a new
country, and its inhabitants like colonists, but to me,

coming from New England, and being a very green
traveller withal, — notwithstanding what I have said
about Hudson's Bay, — it appeared as old as Normandy
itself, and realized much that I had heard of Europe
and the Middle Ages. Even the names of humble
Canadian villages affected me as if they had been those
of the renowned cities of antiquity. To be told by a
habitan, when I asked the name of a village in sight,
that it is *St. Fereole* or *St. Anne*, the *Guardian Angel*
or the *Holy Joseph's;* or of a mountain, that it was
Bélange or *St. Hyacinthe!* As soon as you leave the
States, these saintly names begin. *St. John* is the first
town you stop at (fortunately we did not see it), and
thenceforward, the names of the mountains, and streams,
and villages reel, if I may so speak, with the intoxi-
cation of poetry; — *Chambly, Longueil, Pointe aux
Trembles, Bartholomy,* &c., &c.; as if it needed only a
little foreign accent, a few more liquids and vowels perchance in the language, to make us locate our ideals at
once. I began to dream of Provence and the Trouba-
dours, and of places and things which have no existence
on the earth. They veiled the Indian and the primitive
forest, and the woods toward Hudson's Bay, were only
as the forests of France and Germany. I could not at
once bring myself to believe that the inhabitants who
pronounced daily those beautiful and, to me, significant
names, lead as prosaic lives as we of New England. In
short, the Canada which I saw was not merely a place
for railroads to terminate in and for criminals to run to.

When I asked the man to whom I have referred, if
there were any falls on the Rivière au Chien, — for I saw
that it came over the same high bank with the Montmo
renci and St. Anne, — he answered that there were.

How far? I inquired. *Trois quatres lieue.* How high? *Je pense, quatre-vingt-dix pieds;* that is, ninety feet. We turned aside to look at the falls of the *Rivière du Sault à la Puce,* half a mile from the road, which before we had passed in our haste and ignorance, and we pronounced them as beautiful as any that we saw; yet they seemed to make no account of them there, and, when first we inquired the way to the Falls, directed us to Montmorenci, seven miles distant. It was evident that this was the country for waterfalls; that every stream that empties into the St. Lawrence, for some hundreds of miles, must have a great fall or cascade on it, and in its passage through the mountains was, for a short distance, a small Saguenay, with its upright walls. This fall of La Puce, the least remarkable of the four which we visited in this vicinity, we had never heard of till we came to Canada, and yet, so far as I know, there is nothing of the kind in New England to be compared with it. Most travellers in Canada would not hear of it, though they might go so near as to hear it. Since my return I find that in the topographical description of the country mention is made of " two or three romantic falls " on this stream, though we saw and heard of but this one. Ask the inhabitants respecting any stream, if there is a fall on it, and they will perchance tell you of something as interesting as Bashpish or the Catskill, which no traveller has ever seen, or if they have not found it, you may possibly trace up the stream and discover it yourself. Falls there are a drug; and we became quite dissipated in respect to them. We had drank too much of them. Beside these which I have referred to, there are a thousand other falls on the St. Lawrence and its tributaries which I have not seen nor heard of; and above all there is one which I have heard of, called Niagara, so that I think that this river must be the most remarkable for its falls of any in the world.

At a house near the western boundary of Chateau Richer, whose master was said to speak a very little English, having recently lived at Quebec, we got lodging for the night. As usual, we had to go down a lane to get round to the south side of the house where the door was, away from the road. For these Canadian houses have no front door, properly speaking. Every part is for the use of the occupant exclusively, and no part has reference to the traveller or to travel. Every New England house, on the contrary, has a front and principal door opening to the great world, though it may be on the cold side, for it stands on the highway of nations, and the road which runs by it comes from the Old World and goes to the far West; but the Canadian's door opens into his back-yard and farm alone, and the road which runs behind his house leads only from the church of one saint to that of another. We found a large family, hired men, wife and children, just eating their supper. They prepared some for us afterwards. The hired men were a merry crew of short, black-eyed fellows, and the wife a thin-faced, sharp-featured French Canadian woman. Our host's English staggered us rather more than any French we had heard yet; indeed, we found that even we spoke better French than he did English, and we concluded that a less crime would be committed on the whole if we spoke French with him, and in no respect aided or abetted his attempts to speak English. We had a long and merry chat with the family this Sunday evening in their spacious kitchen. While my companion smoked a pipe and parlez-vous'd with one party, I parleyed and gesticulated to another. The whole family was enlisted, and I kept a little girl writing what was otherwise unintelligible. The geography getting obscure, we called for chalk, and the greasy oiled table-cloth having been wiped, — for it needed no French, but only a sentence from the universal language of looks on my part, to indicate that it needed it, — we drew the St. Lawrence, with its parishes, thereon, and thenceforward went on swimmingly, by turns handling the chalk and committing to the table-cloth what would otherwise have been left in a limbo of unintelligibility. This was greatly to the entertainment of all parties. I was amused to hear how much use they made of the word *oui* in conversation with one another. After repeated single insertions of it, one would suddenly throw back his head at the same time with his chair, and exclaim rapidly, "*oui! oui! oui! oui!*" like a Yankee driving pigs. Our host told us that the farms thereabouts were generally two acres, or three hundred and sixty French feet wide, by one and a half leagues, (?) or a little more than four and a half of our miles deep. This use of the word *acre* as long measure arises from the fact that the French acre or arpent, the arpent of Paris, makes a square of ten perches, of eighteen feet each on a side, a Paris foot being equal to 1.06575 English feet. He said that the wood was cut off about one mile from the river. The rest was "bush," and beyond that the "Queen's bush." Old as the country is, each landholder bounds on the primitive forest, and fuel bears no price. As I had forgotten the French for *sickle*, they went out in the evening to the barn and got one, and so clenched the certainty of our understanding one another. Then, wishing to learn if they used the cradle. and not knowing any French word for this instrument, I set up the knives and forks on the blade of the sickle to represent one; at which they all exclaimed that they knew and had used it. When *snells* were mentioned they went out in the dark and plucked some. They were pretty good. They said they had three kinds of plums growing wild, — blue, white, and red, the two former much alike and the best. Also they asked me if I would have *des pommes*, some apples, and got me some. They were exceedingly fair and glossy, and it was evident that there was no worm in them; but they were as hard almost as a stone, as if the season was too short to mellow them. We had seen no soft and yellow apples by the roadside. I declined eating one, much as I admired it, observing that it would be good *dans le printemps*, in the spring. In the morning when the mistress had set the eggs a-frying she nodded to a thick-set, jolly-looking fellow, who rolled up his sleeves, seized the long-handled griddle, and commenced a series of revolutions and evolutions with it, ever and anon tossing its contents into the air, where they turned completely topsy-turvy and came down t' other side up; and this he repeated till they were done. That appeared to be his duty when eggs were concerned. I did not chance to witness this performance, but my companion did, and he pronounced it a master-piece in its way. This man's farm, with the buildings, cost seven hundred pounds; some smaller ones, two hundred.

In 1827, Montmorenci County, to which the Isle of Orleans has since been added, was nearly as large as Massachusetts, being the eighth county out of forty (in Lower Canada) in extent; but by far the greater part still must continue to be waste land, lying, as it were, under the walls of Quebec.

I quote these old statistics, not merely because of the difficulty of obtaining more recent ones, but also because I saw there so little evidence of any recent growth. There were in this county, at the same date, five Roman Catholic churches, and no others, five curés and five presbyteries, two schools, two corn mills, four saw-mills, one carding-mill, — no medical man, or notary or lawyer, — five shopkeepers, four taverns (we saw no sign of any, though, after a little hesitation, we were sometimes directed to some undistinguished hut as such), thirty artisans, and five river crafts, whose tonnage amounted to sixty-nine tons! This, notwithstanding that it has a frontage of more than thirty miles on the river, and the population is almost wholly confined to its banks. This describes nearly enough what we saw. But double some of these figures, which, however, its growth will not warrant, and you have described a poverty which not even its severity of climate and ruggedness of soil will suffice to account for. The principal productions were wheat, potatoes, oats, hay, peas, flax, maple-sugar, &c., &c.; linen, cloth, or *étoffe du pays*, flannel, and homespun, or *petite étoffe*.

In Lower Canada, according to Bouchette, there are two tenures, — the feudal and the socage. Tenanciers, censitaires, or holders of land *en roture*, pay a small annual rent to the seigneurs, to which " is added some article of provision, such as a couple of fowls, or a goose, or a bushel of wheat." "They are also bound to grind their corn at the *moulin banal*, or the lord's mill, where one fourteenth part of it is taken for his use " as toll. He says that the toll is one twelfth in the United States, wnere competition exists. It is not permitted to exceed one sixteenth in Massachusetts. But worse than this monopolizing of mill rents is what are called *lods et ventes*, or mutation fines. According to which the seigneur has "a right to a twelfth part of the purchase-money of every estate within his seigniory that changes its owner by sale." This is over and above the sum paid to the seller. In such cases, moreover, "the lord possesses the *droit de retrait*, which is the privilege of pre-emption at the highest bidden price within forty days after the sale has taken place," — a right which, however, is said to be seldom exercised. "Lands held by Roman Catholics are further subject to the payment to their curates of one twenty-sixth part of all the grain produced upon them, and to occasional assessments for building and repairing churches," &c., — a tax to which they are not subject if the proprietors change their faith; but they are not the less attached to their church in consequence. There are, however, various modifications of the feudal tenure. Under the socage tenure, which is that of the townships or more recent settlements, English, Irish, Scotch, and others, and generally of Canada West, the landholder is wholly un hackled by such conditions as I have quoted, and "is bound to no other obligations than those of allegiance to the king and obedience to the laws." Throughout Canada "a freehold of forty shillings yearly value, or the payment of ten pounds rent annually, is the qualification for voters." In 1846 more than one sixth of the whole population of Canada East were qualified to vote for members of Parliament, — a greater proportion than enjoy a similar privilege in the United States.

The population which we had seen the last two days,

— I mean the habitans of Montmorenci County, — appeared very inferior, intellectually and even physically, to that of New England. In some respects they were incredibly filthy. It was evident that they had not advanced since the settlement of the country, that they were quite behind the age, and fairly represented their ancestors in Normandy a thousand years ago. Even in respect to the common arts of life, they are not so far advanced as a frontier town in the West three years old. They have no money invested in railroad stock, and probably never will have. If they have got a French phrase for a railroad, it is as much as you can expect of them. They are very far from a revolution; have no quarrel with Church or State, but their vice and their virtue is content. As for annexation, they have never dreamed of it; indeed, they have not a clear idea what or where the States are. The English government has been remarkably liberal to its Catholic subjects in Canada, permitting' them to wear their own fetters, both political and religious, as far as was possible for subjects. Their government is even too good for them. Parliament passed " an act [in 1825] to provide for the extinction of feudal and seigniorial rights and burdens on lands in Lower Canada, and for the gradual conversion of those tenures into the tenure of free and common socage," &c. But as late as 1831, at least, the design of the act was likely to be frustrated, owing to the reluctance of the seigniors and peasants. It has been observed by another that the French Canadians do not extend nor perpetuate their influence. The British, Irish, and other immigrants, who have settled the townships, are found to have imitated the American settlers, and not the French. They reminded me in this of the

Indians, whom they were slow to displace and to whose habits of life they themselves more readily conformed than the Indians to theirs. The Governor-General Denouville remarked, in 1685, that some had long thought that it was necessary to bring the Indians near them in order to Frenchify (*franciser*) them, but that they had every reason to think themselves in an error; for those who had come near them and were even collected in villages in the midst of the colony had not become French, but the French, who had haunted them, had become savages. Kalm said: "Though many nations imitate the French customs, yet I observed, on the contrary, that the French in Canada, in many respects, follow the customs of the Indians, with whom they converse every day. They make use of the tobacco-pipes, shoes, garters, and girdles of the Indians. They follow the Indian way of making war with exactness; they mix the same things with tobacco (he might have said that both French and English learned the use itself of this weed of the Indian); they make use of the Indian bark-boats, and row them in the Indian way; they wrap square pieces of cloth round their feet instead of stockings; and have adopted many other Indian fashions." Thus, while the descendants of the Pilgrims are teaching the English to make pegged boots, the descendants of the French in Canada are wearing the Indian moccasin still. The French, to their credit be it said, to a certain extent respected the Indians as a separate and independent people, and spoke of them and contrasted themselves with them as the English have never done. They not only went to war with them as allies, but they lived at home with them as neighbors. In 1627 the French king declared " that the descendants of the

French, settled in " New France, "and the savages who should be brought to the knowledge of the faith, and should make profession of it, should be counted and reputed French born (*Naturels François*) ; and as such could emigrate to France, when it seemed good to them, and there acquire, will, inherit, &c., &c., without obtaining letters of naturalization." When the English had possession of Quebec, in 1630, the Indians, attempting to practise the same familiarity with them that they had with the French, were driven out of their houses with blows ; which accident taught them a difference between the two races, and attached them yet more to the French. The impression made on me was, that the French Canadians were even sharing the fate of the Indians, or at least gradually disappearing in what is called the Saxon current.

The English did not come to America from a mere love of adventure, nor to truck with or convert the savages, nor to hold offices under the crown, as the French to a great extent did, but to live in earnest and with freedom. The latter overran a great extent of country, selling strong water, and collecting its furs, and converting its inhabitants, — or at least baptizing its dying infants (*enfans moribonds*), — without *improving* it. First, went the *coureur de bois* with the *eau de vie;* then followed, if he did not precede, the heroic missionary with the *eau d'immortalité*. It was freedom to hunt, and fish, and convert, not to work, that they sought. Hontan says that the *coureurs de bois* lived like sailors ashore. In no part of the seventeenth century could the French be said to have had a foothold in Canada; they held only by the fur of the wild animals which they were exterminating. To enable the poor seigneurs

to get their living, it was permitted by a decree passed
in the reign of Louis the Fourteenth, in 1685, " to all
nobles and gentlemen settled in Canada, to engage in
commerce, without being called to account or reputed
to have done anything derogatory." The reader can
infer to what extent they had engaged in agriculture,
and how their farms must have shone by this time.
The New England youth, on the other hand, were never
coureurs de bois nor *voyageurs*, but backwoodsmen and
sailors rather. Of all nations the English undoubtedly
have proved hitherto that they had the most business
here.

Yet I am not sure but I have most sympathy
with that spirit of adventure which distinguished the
French and Spaniards of those days, and made them
especially the explorers of the American Continent, —
which so early carried the former to the Great Lakes
and the Mississippi on the north, and the latter to the
same river on the south. It was long before our fron-
tiers· reached their settlements in the West. So far as
inland discovery was concerned, the adventurous spirit
of the English was that of sailors who land but for a
day, and their enterprise the enterprise of traders.

There was apparently a greater equality of condition
among the habitans of Montmorenci County than in
New England. They are an almost exclusively agri-
cultural, and so far independent, population, each family producing nearly all the necessaries of life for itself.
If the Canadian wants energy, perchance he possesses
those virtues, social and others, which the Yankee lacks,
in which case he cannot be regarded as a poor man.

CHAPTER IV.

THE WALLS OF QUEBEC.

AFTER spending the night at a farm-house in Chateau-
Richer, about a dozen miles northeast of Quebec, we
set out on our return to the city. We stopped at the
next house, a picturesque old stone mill, over the *Chi-
pré*, — for so the name sounded, — such as you will
nowhere see in the States, and asked the millers the age
of the mill. They went up stairs to call the master;
but the crabbed old miser asked why we wanted to
know, and would tell us only for some compensation.
I wanted French to give him a piece of my mind. I
had got enough to talk on a pinch, but not to quarrel;
so I had to come away, looking all I would have said.
This was the utmost incivility we met with in Canada.
In Beauport, within a few miles of Quebec, we turned
aside to look at a church which was just being completed, — a very large and handsome edifice of stone, with
a green bough stuck in its gable, of some significance to
Catholics. The comparative wealth of the Church in
this country was apparent; for in this village we did not
see one good house besides. They were all humble cottages; and yet this appeared to me a more imposing
structure than any church in Boston. But I am no
judge of these things.

Re-entering Quebec through St. John's Gate, we took
a caleche in Market Square for the Falls of the Chaudière, about nine miles southwest of the city, for which
we were to pay so much, beside forty sous for tolls. The
driver, as usual, spoke French only. The number of

these vehicles is very great for so small a town. They are like one of our chaises that has lost its top, only stouter and longer in the body, with a seat for the driver where the dasher is with us, and broad leather ears on each side to protect the riders from the wheel and keep children from falling out. They had an easy jaunting look, which, as our hours were numbered, persuaded us to be riders. We met with them on every road near Quebec these days, each with its complement of two inquisitive-looking foreigners and a Canadian driver, the former evidently enjoying their novel experience, for commonly it is only the horse whose language you do not understand; but they were one remove further from him by the intervention of an equally unintelligible driver. We crossed the St. Lawrence to Point Levi in a French-Canadian ferry-boat, which was inconvenient and dirty, and managed with great noise and bustle. The current was very strong and tumultuous, and the boat tossed enough to make some sick, though it was only a mile across; yet the wind was not to be compared with that of the day before, and we saw that the Canadians had a good excuse for not taking us over to the Isle of Orleans in a pirogue, however shiftless they may be for not having provided any other conveyance. The route which we took to the Chaudière did not afford us those views of Quebec which we had expected, and the country and inhabitants appeared less interesting to a traveller than those we had seen. The Falls of the Chaudiere are three miles from its mouth on the south side of the St. Lawrence. Though they were the largest which I saw in Canada, I was not proportionately interested by them, probably from satiety. I did not see any *peculiar* propriety in the name *Chaudière*, or caldron. I saw here the most brilliant rainbow that I ever imagined. It was just across the stream below the precipice, formed on the mist which this tremendous fall produced; and I stood on a level with the key-stone of its arch. It was not a few faint prismatic colors merely, but a full semi-circle, only four or five rods in diameter, though as wide as usual, so intensely bright as to pain the eye, and apparently as substantial as an arch of stone. It changed its position and colors as we moved, and was the brighter because the sun shone so clearly and the mist was so thick. Evidently a picture painted on mist for the men and animals that came to the falls to look at; but for what special purpose beyond this, I know not. At the farthest point in this ride, and when most inland, unexpectedly at a turn in the road we descried the frowning citadel of Quebec in the horizon, like the beak of a bird of prey. We returned by the river-road under the bank, which is very high, abrupt, and rocky. When we were opposite to Quebec, I was surprised to see that in the Lower Town, under the shadow of the rock, the lamps were lit, twinkling not unlike crystals in a cavern, while the citadel high above, and we, too, on the south shore, were in broad daylight. As we were too late for the ferry-boat that night, we put up at a *maison de pension* at Point Levi. The usual two-story stove was here placed against an opening in the partition shaped like a fireplace, and so warmed several rooms. We could not understand their French here very well, but the *potage* was just like what we had had before. There were many small chambers with doorways but no doors. The walls of our chamber, all around and overhead, were neatly ceiled, and the timbers cased with wood unpainted. The pillows were checkered and tasselled, and the usual long-pointed red woollen or worsted night-cap was placed on each. I pulled mine out to see how it was made. It was in the form of a double cone, one end tucked into the other; just such, it appeared, as I saw men wearing all day in the streets. Probably I should have put it on if the cold had been then, as it is sometimes there, thirty or forty degrees below zero.

When we landed at Quebec the next morning, a man lay on his back on the wharf, apparently dying, in the midst of a crowd and directly in the path of the horses, groaning, " *O ma conscience!* " I thought that he pronounced his French more distinctly than any I heard, as if the dying had already acquired the accents of a universal language. Having secured the only unengaged berths in the Lord Sydenham steamer, which was to leave Quebec before sundown, and being resolved, now that I had seen somewhat of the country, to get an idea of the city, I proceeded to walk round the Upper Town, or fortified portion, which is two miles and three quarters in circuit, alone, as near as I could get to the cliff and the walls, like a rat looking for a hole ; going round by the southwest, where there is but a single street between the cliff and the water, and up the long, wooden stairs, through the suburbs northward to the King's Woodyard, which I thought must have been a long way from his fireplace, and under the cliffs of the St. Charles, where the drains issue under the walls, and the walls are loop-holed for musketry ; so returning by Mountain Street and Prescott Gate to the Upper Town. Having found my way by an obscure passage near the St. Louis Gate to the glacis on the north of the citadel proper, — I believe that I was the only visitor then in the city who got in there, — I enjoyed a prospect nearly as good as from

within the citadel itself, which I had explored some days
before. As I walked on the glacis I heard the sound of
a bagpipe from the soldiers' dwellings in the rock, and
was further soothed and affected by the sight of a soldier's cat walking up a cleeted plank into a high loop-
hole, designed for *mus-catry*, as serene as Wisdom herself, and with a gracefully waving motion of her tail, as
if her ways were ways of pleasantness and all her paths
were peace. Scaling a slat fence, where a small force
might have checked me, I got out of the esplanade into
the Governor's Garden, and read the well-known in-
scription on Wolfe and Montcalm's monument, which
for saying much in little, and that to the purpose, undoubtedly deserved the prize medal which it received:

MORTEM . VIRTUS . COMMUNEM .
FAMAM . HISTORIA .
MONUMENTUM . POSTERITAS .
DEDIT.

Valor gave them one death, history one fame, posterity
one monument. The Government Garden has for nose-
gays, amid kitchen vegetables, beside the common garden flowers, the usual complement of cannon directed
toward some future and possible enemy. I then returned up St. Louis Street to the esplanade and ramparts there, and went round the Upper Town once more,
though I was very tired, this time on the *inside* of the
wall; for I knew that the wall was the main thing in
Quebec, and had cost a great deal of money, and therefore I must make the most of it. In fact, these are
the only remarkable walls we have in North America,
though we have a good deal of Virginia fence, it is true.
Moreover, I cannot say but I yielded in some measure

to the soldier instinct, and, having but a short time to
spare, thought it best to examine the wall thoroughly,
that I might be the better prepared if I should ever be
called that way again in the service of my country. I
committed all the gates to memory in their order, which
did not cost me so much trouble as it would have done
at the hundred-gated city, there being only five; nor
were they so hard to remember as those seven of Bœo-
tian Thebes; and, moreover, I thought that, if seven
champions were enough against the latter, one would be
enough against Quebec, though he bore for all armor
and device only an umbrella and a bundle. I took the
nunneries as I went, for I had learned to distinguish
them by the blinds; and I observed also the foundling
hospitals and the convents, and whatever was attached
to, or in the vicinity of the walls. All the rest I omitted,
as naturally as one would the inside of an inedible shell-
fish. These were the only pearls, and the wall the only
mother-of-pearl for me. Quebec is chiefly famous for
the thickness of its parietal bones. The technical terms
of its conchology may stagger a beginner a little at
first, such as *banlieue, esplanade, glacis, ravelin, cavalier,*
&c., &c., but with the aid of a comprehensive dictionary
you soon learn the nature of your ground. I was surprised at the extent of the artillery barracks, built so
long ago, — *Casernes Nouvelles,* they used to be called,—
nearly six hundred feet in length by forty in depth,
where the sentries, like peripatetic philosophers, were
so absorbed in thought, as not to notice me when I
passed in and out at the gates. Within, are "small arms
of every description, sufficient for the equipment of
twenty thousand men," so arranged as to give a startling
coup d'œil to strangers. I did not enter, not wishing to

get a black eye; for they are said to be "in a state of complete repair and readiness for immediate use." Here, for a short time, I lost sight of the wall, but I recovered it again on emerging from the barrack yard. There I met with a Scotchman who appeared to have business with the wall, like myself; and, being thus mutually drawn together by a similarity of tastes, we had a little conversation *sub mœnibus*, that is, by an angle of the wall which sheltered us. He lived about thirty miles northwest of Quebec; had been nineteen years in the country; said he was disappointed that he was not brought to America after all, but found himself still under British rule and where his own language was not spoken; that many Scotch, Irish, and English were disappointed in like manner, and either went to the States, or pushed up the river to Canada West, nearer to the States, and where their language was spoken. He talked of visiting the States some time; and, as he seemed ignorant of geography, I warned him that it was one thing to visit the State of Massachusetts, and another to visit the State of California. He said it was colder there than usual at that season, and he was lucky to have brought his thick togue, or frock-coat, with him; thought it would snow, and then be pleasant and warm. That is the way we are always thinking. However, his words were music to me in my thin hat and sack.

At the ramparts on the cliff near the old Parliament House I counted twenty-four thirty-two-pounders in a row, pointed over the harbor, with their balls piled pyramid-wise between them, — there are said to be in all about one hundred and eighty guns mounted at Quebec, — all which were faithfully kept dusted by officials, in accordance with the motto, "In time of peace prepare for war"; but I saw no preparations for peace : she was plainly an uninvited guest.

Having thus completed the circuit of this fortress, both within and without, I went no farther by the wall for fear that I should become wall-eyed. However, I think that I deserve to be made a member of the Royal Sappers and Miners.

In short, I observed everywhere the most perfect arrangements for keeping a wall in order, not even permitting the lichens to grow on it, which some think an ornament; but then I saw no cultivation nor pasturing within it to pay for the outlay, and cattle were strictly forbidden to feed on the glacis under the severest penalties. Where the dogs get their milk I don't know, and I fear it is bloody at best.

The citadel of Quebec says, "I *will* live here, and you sha'n't prevent me." To which you return, that you have not the slightest objection; live and let live. The Martello towers looked, for all the world, exactly like abandoned wind-mills which had not had a grist to grind these hundred years. Indeed, the whole castle here was a "folly,"— England's folly, — and, in more senses than one, a castle in the air. The inhabitants and the government are gradually waking up to a sense of this truth; for I heard something said about their abandoning the wall around the Upper Town, and confining the fortifications to the citadel of forty acres. Of course they will finally reduce their intrenchments to the circumference of their own brave hearts.

The most modern fortifications have an air of antiquity about them; they have the aspect of ruins in better or worse repair from the day they are built, because they are not really the work of this age. The very place where the soldier resides has a peculiar tendency to become old and dilapidated, as the word *barrack* implies. I couple all fortifications in my mind with the dismantled Spanish forts to be found in so many parts of the world; and if in any place they are not actually dismantled, it is because that there the intellect of the inhabitants is dismantled. The commanding officer of an old fort near Valdivia in South America, when a traveller remarked to him that, with one discharge, his gun-carriages would certainly fall to pieces, gravely replied, " No, I am sure, sir, they would stand two." Perhaps the guns of Quebec would stand three. Such structures carry us back to the Middle Ages, the siege of Jerusalem, and St. Jean d'Acre, and the days of the Bucaniers. In the armory of the citadel they showed me a clumsy implement, long since useless, which they called a Lombard gun. I thought that their whole citadel was such a Lombard gun, fit object for the museums of the curious. Such works do not consist with the development of the intellect. Huge stone structures of all kinds, both in their erection and by their influence when erected, rather oppress than liberate the mind. They are tombs for the souls of men, as frequently for their bodies also. The sentinel with his musket beside a man with his umbrella is spectral. There is not sufficient reason for his existence. Does my friend there, with a bullet resting on half an ounce of powder, think that he needs that argument in conversing with me? The fort was the first institution that was founded here, and it is amusing to read in Champlain how assiduously they worked at it almost from the first day of the settlement. The founders of the colony thought this an excellent site for a wall, — and no doubt it was a better site, in some

respects, for a wall than for a city, — but it chanced that
a city got behind it. It chanced, too, that a Lower Town
got before it, and clung like an oyster to the outside of
the crags, as you may see at low tide. It is as if you
were to come to a country village surrounded by pali-
sades in the old Indian fashion, — interesting only as a
relic of antiquity and barbarism. A fortified town is
like a man cased in the heavy armor of antiquity, with
a horse-load of broadswords and small arms slung to
him, endeavoring to go about his business. Or is this
an indispensable machinery for the good government of
the country? The inhabitants of California succeed
pretty well, and are doing better and better every day,
without any such institution. What use has this fortress served, to look at it even from the soldiers' point of
view? At first the French took care of it; yet Wolfe
sailed by it with impunity, and took the town of Quebec
without experiencing any hinderance at last from its
fortifications. They were only the bone for which the
parties fought. Then the English began to take care of
it. So of any fort in the world, — that in Boston harbor,
for instance. We shall at length hear that an enemy
sailed by it in the night, for it cannot sail itself, and
both it and its inhabitants are always benighted. How
often we read that the enemy occupied a position which
commanded the old, and so the fort was evacuated.
Have not the school-house and the printing-press occupied a position which commands such a fort as this?

However, this is a ruin kept in remarkably good repair. There are some eight hundred or thousand men
there to exhibit it. One regiment goes bare-legged to
increase the attraction. If you wish to study the muscles of the leg about the knee, repair to Quebec. This

universal exhibition in Canada of the tools and sinews of war reminded me of the keeper of a menagerie showing his animals' claws. It was the English leopard showing his claws. Always the *royal* something or other; as, at the menagerie, the Royal Bengal Tiger. Silliman states that "the cold is so intense in the winter nights, particularly on Cape Diamond, that the sentinels cannot stand it more than one hour, and are relieved at the expiration of that time"; "and even, as it is said, at much shorter intervals, in case of the most extreme cold." What a natural or unnatural fool must that sol dier be, — to say nothing of his government, — who, when quicksilver is freezing and blood is ceasing to be quick, will stand to have his face frozen, watching the walls of Quebec, though, so far as they are concerned, both honest and dishonest men all the world over have been in their beds nearly half a century, — or at least for that space travellers have visited Quebec only as they would read history. I shall never again wake up in a colder night than usual, but I shall think how rapidly the sentinels are relieving one another on the walls of Quebec, their quicksilver being all frozen, as if apprehensive that some hostile Wolfe may even then be scaling the Heights of Abraham, or some persevering Arnold about to issue from the wilderness ; some Malay or Japanese, perchance, coming round by the northwest coast, have chosen that moment to assault the citadel ! Why I should as soon expect to find the sentinels still relieving one another on the walls of Nineveh, which have so long been buried to the world . What a troublesome thing a wall is ! I thought it was to defend me, and not I it. Of course, if they had no wall they would not need to have any sentinels.

You might venture to advertise this farm as well fenced with substantial stone walls (saying nothing about the eight hundred Highlanders and Royal Irish who are required to keep them from toppling down); stock and tools to go with the land if desired. But it would not be wise for the seller to exhibit his farm-book.

Why should Canada, wild and unsettled as it is, impress us as an older country than the States, unless because her institutions are old? All things appeared to contend there, as I have implied, with a certain rust of antiquity, — such as forms on old armor and iron guns, — the rust of conventions and formalities. It is said that the metallic roofs of Montreal and Quebec keep sound and bright for forty years in some cases. But if the rust was not on the tinned roofs and spires, it was on the inhabitants and their institutions. Yet the work of burnishing goes briskly forward. I imagined that the government vessels at the wharves were laden with rot ten-stone and oxalic acid, — that is what the first ship from England in the spring comes freighted with, — and the hands of the colonial legislature are cased in wash leather. The principal exports must be *gunny* bags, verdigrease, and iron rust. Those who first built this fort, coming from Old France with the memory and tradition of feudal days and customs weighing on them, were unquestionably behind their age; and those who now inhabit and repair it are behind their ancestors or predecessors. Those old chevaliers thought that they could transplant the feudal system to America. It has been set out, but it has not thriven. Notwithstanding that Canada was settled first, and, unlike New England, for a long series of years enjoyed the fostering care of

the mother country, — notwithstanding that, as Charlevoix tells us, it had more of the ancient *noblesse* among its
eaily settlers than any other of the French colonies, and
perhaps than all the others together, — there are in both
the Canadas but 600,000 of French descent to-day, —
about half so many as the population of Massachusetts.
The whole population of both Canadas is but about
1,700,000 Canadians, English, Irish, Scotch, Indians,
and all, put together ! Samuel Laing, in his essay on
the Northmen, to whom especially, rather than the Sax-
ons, he refers the energy and indeed the excellence of
the English character, observes that, when they occupied
Scandinavia, "each man possessed his lot of land without reference to, or acknowledgment of, any other man,
— without any local chief to whom his military service
or other quit-rent for his land was due, — without tenure from, or duty or obligation to, any superior, real or
fictitious, except the general sovereign. The individual
settler held his land, as his descendants in Norway still
express it, by the same right as the king held his crown,
— by udal right, or adel, — that is, noble right." The
French have occupied Canada, not *udally*, or by noble
right, but *feudally*, or by ignoble right. They are a
nation of peasants.

It was evident that, both on account of the feudal
system and the aristocratic government, a private man
was not worth so much in Canada as in the United
States ; and, if your wealth in any measure consists in
manliness, in originality, and independence, you had
better stay here. How could a peaceable, freethinking
man live neighbor to the Forty-ninth Regiment? A New-
Englander would naturally be a bad citizen, probably a
rebel, there, — certainly if he were already a rebel at

home. I suspect that a poor man who is not servile is
a much rarer phenomenon there and in England than
in the Northern United States. An Englishman, methinks, — not to speak of other European nations, —
habitually regards himself merely as a constituent part
of the English nation; he is a member of the royal
regiment of Englishmen, and is proud of his company,
as he has reason to be proud of it. But an American,
— one who has made a tolerable use of his opportunities, — cares, comparatively, little about such things, and
is advantageously nearer to the primitive and the ulti-
mate condition of man in these respects. It is a government, that English one, — like most other European ones,
— that cannot afford to be forgotten, as you would naturally forget it; under which one cannot be wholesomely
neglected, and grow up a man and not an Englishman
merely, — cannot be a poet even without danger of being
made poet-laureate! Give me a country where it is the
most natural thing in the world for a government that
does not understand you to let you alone. One would
say that a true Englishman could speculate only within
bounds. (It is true the Americans have proved that
they, in more than one sense, can *speculate* without
bounds.) He has to pay his respects to so many things,
that, before he knows it, he *may* have paid away all he is
worth. What makes the United States government, on
the whole, more tolerable, — I mean for us lucky white
men, — is the fact that there is so much less of government with us. Here it is only once in a month or a
year that a man *needs* remember that institution; and
those who go to Congress can play the game of the
Kilkenny cats there without fatal consequences to those
who stay at home, — their term is so short: but in Canada

you are reminded of the government every day. It pa-
rades itself before you. It is not content to be the servant, but will be the master; and every day it goes out
to the Plains of Abraham or to the Champ de Mars and
exhibits itself and its tools. Everywhere there appeared
an attempt to make and to preserve trivial and otherwise transient distinctions. In the streets of Montreal
and Quebec you met not only with soldiers in red, and
shuffling priests in unmistakable black and white, with
Sisters of Charity gone into mourning for their deceased
relative, — not to mention the nuns of various orders
depending on the fashion of a tear, of whom you heard, —
but youths belonging to some seminary or other, wearing coats edged with white, who looked as if their ex-
panding hearts were already repressed with a piece of
tape. In short, the inhabitants of Canada appeared to
be suffering between two fires, — the soldiery and the
priesthood.

CHAPTER V.

THE SCENERY OF QUEBEC; AND THE RIVER ST. LAWRENCE.

ABOUT twelve o'clock this day, being in the Lower
Town, I looked up at the signal-gun by the flag-staff on
Cape Diamond, and saw a soldier up in the heavens
there making preparations to fire it, — both he and the
gun in bold relief against the sky. Soon after, being
warned by the boom of the gun to look up again, there
was only the cannon in the sky, the smoke just blowing

away from it, as if the soldier, having touched it off, had concealed himself for effect, leaving the sound to echo grandly from shore to shore, and far up and down the river. This answered the purpose of a dinner-horn.

There are no such restaurateurs in Quebec or Montreal as there are in Boston. I hunted an hour or two in vain in this town to find one, till I lost my appetite. In one house, called a restaurateur, where lunches were advertised, I found only tables covered with bottles and glasses innumerable, containing apparently a sample of every liquid that has been known since the earth dried up after the flood, but no scent of solid food did I perceive gross enough to excite a hungry mouse. In short, I saw nothing to tempt me there, but a large map of Canada against the wall. In another place I once more got as far as the bottles, and then asked for a bill of fare; was told to walk up stairs; had no bill of fare, nothing but fare. "Have you any pies or puddings?" I inquired, for I am obliged to keep my savageness in check by a low diet. "No, sir; we 've nice mutton-chop, roast beef, beef-steak, cutlets," and so on. A burly Englishman, who was in the midst of the siege of a piece of roast beef, and of whom I have never had a front view to this day, turned half round, with his mouth half full, and remarked, "You 'll find no pies nor puddings in Quebec, sir; they don't make any here." I found that it was even so, and therefore bought some musty cake and some fruit in the open market-place. This market-place by the water-side, where the old women sat by their tables in the open air, amid a dense crowd jabbering all languages, was the best place in Quebec to observe the people; and the ferry-boats, continually coming and going with their motley crews and cargoes, added much to the entertain-

ment. I also saw them getting water from the river,
for Quebec is supplied with water by cart and barrel.
This city impressed me as wholly foreign and French,
for I scarcely heard the sound of the English language
in the streets. More than three fifths of the inhabitants
are of French origin; and if the traveller did not visit
the fortifications particularly, he might not be reminded
that the English have any foothold here; and, in any
case, if he looked no farther than Quebec, they would
appear to have planted themselves in Canada only as
they have in Spain at Gibraltar; and he who plants
upon a rock cannot expect much increase. The novel
sights and sounds by the water-side made me think of
such ports as Boulogne, Dieppe, Rouen, and Havre de
Grace, which I have never seen; but I have no doubt
that they present similar scenes. I was much amused
from first to last with the sounds made by the charette
and caleche drivers. It was that part of their foreign
language that you heard the most of, — the French they
talked to their horses, — and which they talked the
loudest. It was a more novel sound to me than the
French of conversation. The streets resounded with the
cries, " *Qui donc !* " " *March tôt !* " I suspect that many
of our horses which came from Canada would prick up
their ears at these sounds. Of the shops, I was most
attracted by those where furs and Indian works were
sold, as containing articles of genuine Canadian manu-
facture. I have been told that two townsmen of mine,
who were interested in horticulture, travelling once in
Canada, and being in Quebec, thought it would be a
good opportunity to obtain seeds of the real Canada
crook-neck squash. So they went into a shop where
such things were advertised, and inquired for the same

The shopkeeper had the very thing they wanted. "But are you sure," they asked, "that these are the genuine Canada crook-neck?" "O yes, gentlemen," answered he, "they are a lot which I have received directly from Boston." I resolved that my Canada crook-neck seeds should be such as had grown in Canada.

Too much has not been said about the scenery of Quebec. The fortifications of Cape Diamond are omnipresent. They preside, they frown over the river and surrounding country. You travel ten, twenty, thirty miles up or down the river's banks, you ramble fifteen miles amid the hills on either side, and then, when you have long since forgotten them, perchance slept on them by the way, at a turn of the road or of your body, there they are still, with their geometry against the sky. The child that is born and brought up thirty miles distant, and has never travelled to the city, reads his country's history, sees the level lines of the citadel amid the cloud-built citadels in the western horizon, and is told that that is Quebec. No wonder if Jacques Cartier's pilot exclaimed in Norman French, *Que bec!* — "What a beak!" — when he saw this cape, as some suppose. Every modern traveller involuntarily uses a similar expression. Particularly it is said that its sudden apparition on turning Point Levi makes a memorable impression on him who arrives by water. The view from Cape Diamond has been compared by European travellers with the most remarkable views of a similar kind in Europe, such as from Edinburgh Castle, Gibraltar, Cintra, and others, and preferred by many. A main peculiarity in this, compared with other views which I have beheld, is that it is from the ramparts of a fortified city, and not from a solitary and majestic river cape alone that this

view is obtained. I associate the beauty of Quebec
with the steel-like and flashing air, which may be peculiar to that season of the year, in which the blue flowers
of the succory and some late golden-rods and buttercups
on the summit of Cape Diamond were almost my only
companions, — the former bluer than the heavens they
faced. Yet even I yielded in some degree to the influence of historical associations, and found it hard to
attend to the geology of Cape Diamond or the botany
of the Plains of Abraham. I still remember the harbor
far beneath me, sparkling like silver in the sun, — the
answering highlands of Point Levi on the southeast, —
the frowning Cap Tourmente abruptly bounding the seaward view far in the northeast, — the villages of Lorette
and Charlesbourg on the north, — and further west the
distant Val Cartier, sparkling with white cottages, hardly
removed by distance through the clear air, — not to mention a few blue mountains along the horizon in that direction. You look out from the ramparts of the citadel
beyond the frontiers of civilization. Yonder small
group of hills, according to the guide-book, forms "the
portal of the wilds which are trodden only by the feet
of the Indian hunters as far as Hudson's Bay." It is
but a few years since Bouchette declared that the country ten leagues north of the British capital of North
America was as little known as the middle of Africa.
Thus the citadel under my feet, and all historical associations, were swept away again by an influence from
the wilds and from nature, as if the beholder had read
her history, — an influence which, like the Great River
itself, flowed from the Arctic fastnesses and Western
forests with irresistible tide over all.

The most interesting object in Canada to me was the

River St. Lawrence, known far and wide, and for centuries, as the Great River. Cartier, its discoverer, sailed up it as far as Montreal in 1535, — nearly a century before the coming of the Pilgrims; and I have seen a pretty accurate map of it so far, containing the city of " Hochelaga " and the river " Saguenay," in Ortelius's *Theatrum Orbis Terrarum*, printed at Antwerp in 1575, — the first edition having appeared in 1570, — in which the famous cities of "Norumbega" and "Orsinora" stand on the rough-blocked continent where New England is to-day, and the fabulous but unfortunate Isle of Demons, and Frislant, and others, lie off and on in the unfrequented sea, some of them prowling near what is now the course of the Cunard steamers. In this ponderous folio of the " Ptolemy of his age," said to be the first general atlas published after the revival of the sciences in Europe, only one page of which is devoted to the topography of the *Novus Orbis*, the St. Lawrence is the only large river, whether drawn from fancy or from observation, on the east side of North America. It was famous in Europe before the other rivers of North America were heard of, notwithstanding that the mouth of the Mississippi is said to have been discovered first, and its stream was reached by Soto not long after; but the St. Lawrence had attracted settlers to its cold shores long before the Mississippi, or even the Hudson, was known to the world. Schoolcraft was misled by Gallatin into saying that Narvaez discovered the Mississippi. De Vega does *not* say so. The first explorers declared that the summer in that country was as warm as France, and they named one of the bays in the Gulf of St. Lawrence the Bay of Chaleur, or of warmth; but they said nothing about the winter being as cold as

Greenland.   In the manuscript account of Cartier's
second voyage, attributed by some to that navigator
himself, it is called "the greatest river, without comparison, that is known to have ever been seen." The
savages told him that it was the "*chemin du Canada*,"—
the highway to Canada, — "which goes so far that no
man had ever been to the end that they had heard." The
Saguenay, one of its tributaries, which the panorama
has made known to New England within three years, is
described by Cartier, in 1535, and still more particularly
by Jean Alphonse, in 1542, who adds, "I think that this
river comes from the sea of Cathay, for in this place
there issues a strong current, and there runs there a
terrible tide." The early explorers saw many whales
and other sea-monsters far up the St. Lawrence. Champlain, in his map, represents a whale spouting in the
harbor of Quebec, three hundred and sixty miles from
what is called the mouth of the river; and Charlevoix
takes his reader to the summit of Cape Diamond to see
the "porpoises, white as snow," sporting on the surface
of the harbor of Quebec.   And Boucher says in 1664,
"from there (Tadoussac) to Montreal is found a great
quantity of *Marsouins blancs*." Several whales have been
taken pretty high up the river since I was there. P. A.
Gosse, in his "Canadian Naturalist," p. 171 (London,
1840), speaks of "the white dolphin of the St. Lawrence (*Delphinus Canadensis*)," as considered different
from those of the sea.   "The Natural History Society
of Montreal offered a prize, a few years ago, for an essay
on the *Cetacea* of the St. Lawrence, which was, I believe, handed in." In Champlain's day it was commonly called "the Great River of Canada." More
than one nation has claimed it. In Ogilby's "America

of 1670," in the map *Novi Belgii*, it is called " De
Groote Rivier van Niew Nederlandt." It bears different names in different parts of its course, as it flows
through what were formerly the territories of different
nations. From the Gulf to Lake Ontario it is called at
present the St. Lawrence; from Montreal to the same
place it is frequently called the Cateraqui; and higher
up it is known successively as the Niagara, Detroit, St.
Clair, St. Mary's, and St. Louis rivers. Humboldt,
speaking of the Orinoco, says that this name is unknown
in the interior of the country; so likewise the tribes
that dwell about the sources of the St. Lawrence have
never heard the name which it bears in the lower part
of its course. It rises near another father of waters, —
the Mississippi, — issuing from a remarkable spring far up
in the woods, called Lake Superior, fifteen hundred miles
in circumference; and several other springs there are
thereabouts which feed it. It makes such a noise in its
tumbling down at one place as is heard all round the
world. Bouchette, the Surveyor-General of the Canadas, calls it "the most splendid river on the globe";
says that it is two thousand statute miles long (more
recent geographers make it four or five hundred miles
longer); that at the Rivière du Sud it is eleven miles
wide; at the Traverse, thirteen; at the Paps of Matane,
twenty-five; at the Seven Islands, seventy-three; and
at its mouth, from Cape Rosier to the Mingan Settlements in Labrador, near one hundred and five (?) miles
wide. According to Captain Bayfield's recent chart it
is about *ninety-six* geographical miles wide at the latter
place, measuring at right angles with the stream. It has
much the largest estuary, regarding both length and
breadth, of any river on the globe. Humboldt says

that the river Plate, which has the broadest estuary of
the South American rivers, is ninety-two geographical
miles wide at its mouth; also he found the Orinoco to
be more than three miles wide at five hundred and sixty
miles from its mouth; but he does not tell us that ships
of six hundred tons can sail up it so far, as they can up
the St. Lawrence to Montreal,—an equal distance. If he
had described a fleet of such ships at anchor in a city's
port so far inland, we should have got a very different
idea of the Orinoco.   Perhaps Charlevoix describes the
St. Lawrence truly as the most *navigable* river in the
world.   Between Montreal and Quebec it averages
about two miles wide.   The tide is felt as far up as
Three Rivers, four hundred and thirty-two miles, which
is as far as from Boston to Washington.   As far up as
Cap aux Oyes, sixty or seventy miles below Quebec,
Kalm found a great part of the plants near the shore to
be marine, as glass-wort (*Salicornia*), seaside pease
(*Pisum maritimum*), sea-milkwort (*Glaux*), beach-grass
(*Psamma arenarium*), seaside plantain (*Plantago mari-
tima*), the sea-rocket (*Bunias cakile*), &c.

The geographer Guyot observes that the Maranon is
three thousand miles long, and gathers its waters from
a surface of a million and a half square miles; that the
Mississippi is also three thousand miles long, but its
basin covers only from eight to nine hundred thousand
square miles; that the St. Lawrence is eighteen hundred miles long, and its basin covers more than a million
square miles (Darby says five hundred thousand); and
speaking of the lakes, he adds, "These vast fresh-water
seas, together with the St. Lawrence, cover a surface of
nearly one hundred thousand square miles, and it has
been calculated that they contain about one half of all

the fresh water on the surface of our planet." But all
these calculations are necessarily very rude and inaccu-
rate. Its tributaries, the Ottawa, St. Maurice, and Saguenay, are great rivers themselves. The latter is said
to be more than one thousand (?) feet deep at its mouth,
while its cliffs rise perpendicularly an equal distance
above its surface. Pilots say there are no soundings till
one hundred and fifty miles up the St. Lawrence. The
greatest sounding in the river, given on Bayfield's chart
of the gulf and river, is two hundred and twenty-eight
fathoms. McTaggart, an engineer, observes that " the
Ottawa is larger than all the rivers in Great Britain,
were they running in one." The traveller Grey writes:
" A dozen Danubes, Rhines, Taguses, and Thameses
would be nothing to twenty miles of fresh water in
breadth (as where he happened to be), from ten to
forty fathoms in depth." And again: " There is not
perhaps in the whole extent of this immense continent
so fine an approach to it as by the river St. Lawrence.
In the Southern States you have, in general, a level
country for many miles inland; here you are introduced
at once into a majestic scenery, where everything is on
a grand scale, — mountains, woods, lakes, rivers, preci-
pices, waterfalls."

We have not yet the data for a minute comparison of
the St. Lawrence with the South American rivers; but
it is obvious that, taking it in connection with its lakes,
its estuary, and its falls, it easily bears off the palm
from all the rivers on the globe; for though, as Bouchette observes, it may not carry to the ocean a greater
volume of water than the Amazon and Mississippi, its
surface and cubic mass are far greater than theirs. But,
unfortunately, this noble river is closed by ice from the

beginning of December to the middle of April. The arrival of the first vessel from England when the ice breaks up is, therefore, a great event, as when the salmon, shad, and alewives come up a river in the spring to relieve the famishing inhabitants on its banks. Who can say what would have been the history of this continent if, as has been suggested, this river had emptied into the sea where New York stands!

After visiting the Museum and taking one more look at the wall, I made haste to the Lord Sydenham steamer, which at five o'clock was to leave for Montreal. I had already taken a seat on deck, but finding that I had still an hour and a half to spare, and remembering that large map of Canada which I had seen in the parlor of the restaurateur in my search after pudding, and realizing that I might never see the like out of the country, I returned thither, asked liberty to look at the map, rolled up the mahogany table, put my handkerchief on it, stood on it, and copied all I wanted before the maid came in and said to me standing on the table, "Some gentlemen want the room, sir"; and I retreated without having broken the neck of a single bottle, or my own, very thankful and willing to pay for all the solid food I had got. We were soon abreast of Cap Rouge, eight miles above Quebec, after we got underway. It was in this place, then called "*Fort du France Roy*," that the Sieur de Roberval with his company, having sent home two of his three ships, spent the winter of 1542 – 43. It appears that they fared in the following manner (I translate from the original) : "Each mess had only two loaves, weighing each a pound, and half a pound of beef. They ate pork for dinner, with half a pound of butter, and beef for supper, with about two handfuls of beans,

without butter. Wednesdays, Fridays, and Saturdays
they ate salted cod, and sometimes green, for dinner,
with butter; and porpoise and beans for supper. Monsieur Roberval administered good justice, and punished
each according to his offence. One, named Michel Gail-
lon, was hung for theft; John of Nantes was put in
irons and imprisoned for his fault; and others were likewise put in irons; and many were whipped, both men
and women; by which means they lived in peace and
tranquillity." In an account of a voyage up this river,
printed in the Jesuit Relations in the year 1664, it is
said: "It was an interesting navigation for us in ascend-
ing the river from Cap Tourment to Quebec, to see on
this side and on that, for the space of eight leagues, the
farms and the houses of the company, built by our
French, all along these shores. On the right, the
seigniories of Beauport, of Notre Dames des Anges;
and on the left, this beautiful Isle of Orleans." The
same traveller names among the fruits of the country
observed at the Isles of Richelieu, at the head of Lake
St. Peter, "kinds (*des espèces*) of little apples or haws
(*semelles*), and of pears, which only ripen with the
frost."

Night came on before we had passed the high banks.
We had come from Montreal to Quebec in one night.
The return voyage, against the stream, takes but an
hour longer. Jacques Cartier, the first white man who
is known to have ascended this river, thus speaks of his
voyage from what is now Quebec to the foot of Lake
St. Peter, or about half-way to Montreal: "From the
said day, the 19th, even to the 28th of the said month,
[September, 1535] we had been navigating up the said
river without losing hour or day, during which time we

had seen and found as much country and lands as level as we could desire, full of the most beautiful trees in the world," which he goes on to describe. But we merely slept and woke again to find that we had passed through all that country which he was eight days in sailing through. He must have had a troubled sleep. We were not long enough on the river to realize that it had length; we got only the impression of its breadth, as if we had passed over a lake a mile or two in breadth and several miles long, though we might thus have slept through a European kingdom. Being at the head of Lake St. Peter, on the above-mentioned 28th of September, dealing with the natives, Cartier says: "We inquired of them by signs if this was the route to Hochelaga [Montreal]; and they answered that it was, and that there were yet three days' journeys to go there." He finally arrived at Hochelaga on the 2d of October.

When I went on deck at dawn we had already passed through Lake St. Peter, and saw islands ahead of us. Our boat advancing with a strong and steady pulse over the calm surface, we felt as if we were permitted to be awake in the scenery of a dream. Many vivacious Lombardy poplars along the distant shores gave them a novel and lively, though artificial, look, and contrasted strangely with the slender and graceful elms on both shores and islands. The church of Varennes, fifteen miles from Montreal, was conspicuous at a great distance before us, appearing to belong to, and rise out of, the river; and now, and before, Mount Royal indicated where the city was. We arrived about seven o'clock, and set forth immediately to ascend the mountain, two miles distant, going across lots in spite of numerous signs threatening the severest penalties to trespassers, past

an old building known as the Mac Tavish property, —
Simon Mac Tavish, I suppose, whom Silliman refers to
as "in a sense the founder of the Northwestern Company." His tomb was behind in the woods, with a remarkably high wall and higher monument. The family
returned to Europe. He could not have imagined how
dead he would be in a few years, and all the more dead
and forgotten for being buried under such a mass of
gloomy stone, where not even memory could get at him
without a crowbar. Ah! poor man, with that last end
of his! However, he may have been the worthiest of
mortals for aught that I know. From the mountain-top
we got a view of the whole city; the flat, fertile, extensive island; the noble sea of the St. Lawrence swelling
into lakes; the mountains about St. Hyacinth, and in
Vermont and New York; and the mouth of the Ottawa
in the west, overlooking that St. Ann's where the voyageur sings his "parting hymn," and bids adieu to civilization, — a name, thanks to Moore's verses, the most suggestive of poetic associations of any in Canada. We,
too, climbed the hill which Cartier, first of white men,
ascended, and named Mont-real, (the 3d of October,
O. S., 1535,) and, like him, "we saw the said river as
far as we could see, *grand, large, et spacieux*, going to
the southwest," toward that land whither Donnacona
had told the discoverer that he had been a month's journey from Canada, where there grew "*force Canelle et
Girofle*," much cinnamon and cloves, and where also, as
the natives told him, were three great lakes and afterward *une mer douce*, — a sweet sea, — *de laquelle n'est
mention avoir vu le bout*, of which there is no mention
to have seen the end. But instead of an Indian town
far in the interior of a new world, with guides **to**

show us where the river came from, we found a splendid and bustling stone-built city of white men, and only
a few squalid Indians offered to sell us baskets at the
Lachine Railroad Depot, and Hochelaga is, perchance,
but the fancy name of an engine company or an eating-
house.

We left Montreal Wednesday, the 2d of October, late
in the afternoon. In the La Prairie cars the Yankees
made themselves merry, imitating the cries of the charette-drivers to perfection, greatly to the amusement of
some French-Canadian travellers, and they kept it up
all the way to Boston. I saw one person on board the
boat at St. John's, and one or two more elsewhere in
Canada, wearing homespun gray great-coats, or capotes,
with conical and comical hoods, which fell back between
their shoulders like small bags, ready to be turned up
over the head when occasion required, though a hat
usurped that place now. They looked as if they would
be convenient and proper enough as long as the coats
were new and tidy, but would soon come to have a beg-
garly and unsightly look, akin to rags and dust-holes.
We reached Burlington early in the morning, where the
Yankees tried to pass off their Canada coppers, but the
news-boys knew better. Returning through the Green
Mountains, I was reminded that I had not seen in Canada such brilliant autumnal tints as I had previously
seen in Vermont. Perhaps there was not yet so great
and sudden a contrast with the summer heats in the former country as in these mountain valleys. As we were
passing through Ashburnham, by a new white house
which stood at some distance in a field, one passenger
exclaimed, so that all in the car could hear him, "There,
there's not so good a house as that in all Canada!"

I did not much wonder at his remark, for there is a neatness, as well as evident prosperity, a certain elastic easiness of circumstances, so to speak, when not rich, about a New England house, as if the proprietor could at least afford to make repairs in the spring, which the Canadian houses do not suggest. Though of stone, they are no better constructed than a stone barn would be with us; the only building, except the chateau, on which money and taste are expended, being the church. In Canada an ordinary New England house would be mistaken for the chateau, and while every village here contains at least several gentlemen or " squires," *there* there is but one to a seigniory.

I got home this Thursday evening, having spent just one week in Canada and travelled eleven hundred miles. The whole expense of this journey, including two guide-books and a map, which cost one dollar twelve and a half cents, was twelve dollars seventy-five cents. I do not suppose that I have seen all British America ; that could not be done by a cheap excursion, unless it were a cheap excursion to the Icy Sea, as seen by Hearne or McKenzie, and then, no doubt, some interesting features would be omitted. I wished to go a little way behind that word *Canadense*, of which naturalists make such frequent use ; and I should like still right well to make a longer excursion on foot through the wilder parts of Canada, which perhaps might be called *Iter Canadense*.

ANTI-SLAVERY AND REFORM PAPERS.

SLAVERY IN MASSACHUSETTS.*

I LATELY attended a meeting of the citizens of Concord, expecting, as one among many, to speak on the subject of slavery in Massachusetts; but I was surprised and disappointed to find that what had called my townsmen together was the destiny of Nebraska, and not of Massachusetts, and that what I had to say would be entirely out of order. I had thought that the house was on fire, and not the prairie; but though several of the citizens of Massachusetts are now in prison for attempting to rescue a slave from her own clutches, not one of the speakers at that meeting expressed regret for it, not one even referred to it. It was only the disposition of some wild lands a thousand miles off, which appeared to concern them. The inhabitants of Concord are not prepared to stand by one of their own bridges, but talk only of taking up a position on the highlands beyond the Yellowstone River. Our Buttricks and Davises and Hosmers are retreating thither, and I fear that they will leave no Lexington Common between them and the enemy. There is not one slave in Nebraska; there are perhaps a million slaves in Massachusetts.

They who have been bred in the school of politics fail now and always to face the facts. Their measures are

* An Address, delivered at the Anti Slavery Celebration at Framingham, July 4th, 1854.

half measures and make-shifts merely. They put off the day of settlement indefinitely, and meanwhile the debt accumulates. Though the Fugitive Slave Law had not been the subject of discussion on that occasion, it was at length faintly resolved by my townsmen, at an adjourned meeting, as I learn, that the compromise compact of 1820 having been repudiated by one of the parties, "Therefore, ... the Fugitive Slave Law of 1850 must be repealed." But this is not the reason why an iniquitous law should be repealed. The fact which the politician faces is merely, that there is less honor among thieves than was supposed, and not the fact that they are thieves.

As I had no opportunity to express my thoughts at that meeting, will you allow me to do so here?

Again it happens that the Boston Court-House is full of armed men, holding prisoner and trying a MAN, to find out if he is not really a SLAVE. Does any one think that justice or God awaits Mr. Loring's decision? For him to sit there deciding still, when this question is already decided from eternity to eternity, and the unlettered slave himself, and the multitude around have long since heard and assented to the decision, is simply to make himself ridiculous. We may be tempted to ask from whom he received his commission, and who he is that received it; what novel statutes he obeys, and what precedents are to him of authority. Such an arbiter's very existence is an impertinence. We do not ask him to make up his mind, but to make up his pack.

I listen to hear the voice of a Governor, Commander-in-Chief of the forces of Massachusetts. I hear only the creaking of crickets and the hum of insects which now fill the summer air. The Governor's exploit is to review the troops on muster days. I have seen him on horseback, with his hat off, listening to a chaplain's prayer. It chances that that is all I have ever seen of a Governor. I think that I could manage to get along without one. If *he* is not of the least use to prevent my being kidnapped, pray of what important use is he likely to be to me? When freedom is most endangered, he dwells in the deepest obscurity. A distinguished clergyman told me that he chose the profession of a clergyman, because it afforded the most leisure for literary pursuits. I would recommend to him the profession of a governor.

Three years ago, also, when the Simms tragedy was acted, I said to myself, there is such an officer, if not such a man, as the Governor of Massachusetts, — what has he been about the last fortnight? Has he had as much as he could do to keep on the fence during this moral earthquake? It seemed to me that no keener satire could have been aimed at, no more cutting insult have been offered to that man, than just what happened, — the absence of all inquiry after him in that crisis. The worst and the most I chance to know of him is, that he did not improve that opportunity to make himself known, and worthily known. He could at least have *resigned* himself into fame. It appeared to be forgotten that there was such a man or such an office. Yet no doubt he was endeavoring to fill the gubernatorial chair all the while. He was no Governor of mine. He did not govern me.

But at last, in the present case, the Governor was heard from. After he and the United States government had perfectly succeeded in robbing a poor inno-

cent black man of his liberty for life, and, as far as
they could, of his Creator's likeness in his breast, he
made a speech to his accomplices, at a congratulatory
supper!

I have read a recent law of this State, making it pe-
nal for any officer of the " Commonwealth " to " detain
or aid in the . . . . detention," anywhere within its
limits, " of any person, for the reason that he is claimed
as a fugitive slave."   Also, it was a matter of notoriety
that a writ of replevin to take the fugitive out of the
custody of the United States Marshal could not be
served, for want of sufficient force to aid the officer.

I had thought that the Governor was, in some sense,
the executive officer of the State; that it was his business, as a Governor, to see that the laws of the State were
executed; while, as a man, he took care that he did not,
by so doing, break the laws of humanity; but when
there is any special important use for him, he is useless,
or worse than useless, and permits the laws of the State
to go unexecuted.   Perhaps I do not know what are the
duties of a Governor; but if to be a Governor requires
to subject one's self to so much ignominy without remedy, if it is to put a restraint upon my manhood, I
shall take care never to be Governor of Massachusetts.   I have not read far in the statutes of this Commonwealth.   It is not profitable reading.   They do not
always say what is true; and they do not always mean
what they say.   What I am concerned to know is, that
that man's influence and authority were on the side of
the slaveholder, and not of the slave, — of the guilty
and not of the innocent, — of injustice, and not of justice.   I never saw him of whom I speak; indeed, I did
not know that he was Governor until this event occurred

I heard of him and Anthony Burns at the same time, and thus, undoubtedly, most will hear of him. So far am I from being governed by him. I do not mean that it was anything to his discredit that I had not heard of him, only that I heard what I did. The worst I shall say of him is, that he proved no better than the majority of his constituents would be likely to prove. In my opinion, he was not equal to the occasion.

The whole military force of the State is at the service of a Mr. Suttle, a slaveholder from Virginia, to enable him to catch a man whom he calls his property; but not a soldier is offered to save a citizen of Massachusetts from being kidnapped! Is this what all these soldiers, all this *training*, has been for these seventy-nine years past? Have they been trained merely to rob Mexico and carry back fugitive slaves to their masters?

These very nights, I heard the sound of a drum in our streets. There were men *training* still; and for what? I could with an effort pardon the cockerels of Concord for crowing still, for they, perchance, had not been beaten that morning; but I could not excuse this rub-a-dub of the "trainers." The slave was carried back by exactly such as these; i. e. by the soldier, of whom the best you can say in this connection is, that he is a fool made conspicuous by a painted coat.

Three years ago, also, just a week after the authorities of Boston assembled to carry back a perfectly innocent man, and one whom they knew to be innocent, into slavery, the inhabitants of Concord caused the bells to be rung and the cannons to be fired, to celebrate their liberty, — and the courage and love of liberty of their ancestors who fought at the bridge. As if *those* three millions had fought for the right to be free themselves, but to hold in slavery three millions others. Now-a-days, men wear a fool's-cap, and call it a liberty-cap. I do not know but there are some, who, if they were tied to a whipping-post, and could but get one hand free, would use it to ring the bells and fire the cannons to celebrate *their* liberty. So some of my townsmen took the liberty to ring and fire. That was the extent of their freedom; and when the sound of the bells died away, their liberty died away also; when the powder was all expended, their liberty went off with the smoke.

The joke could be no broader, if the inmates of the prisons were to subscribe for all the powder to be used in such salutes, and hire the jailers to do the firing and ringing for them, while they enjoyed it through the grating.

This is what I thought about my neighbors.

Every humane and intelligent inhabitant of Concord, when he or she heard those bells and those cannons, thought not with pride of the events of the 19th of April, 1775, but with shame of the events of the 12th of April, 1851. But now we have half buried that old shame under a new one.

Massachusetts sat waiting Mr. Loring's decision, as if it could in any way affect her own criminality. Her crime, the most conspicuous and fatal crime of all, was permitting him to be the umpire in such a case. It was really the trial of Massachusetts. Every moment that she hesitated to set this man free, every moment that she now hesitates to atone for her crime, she is convicted. The Commissioner on her case is God; not Edward G. God, but simple God.

I wish my countrymen to consider, that whatever the

human law may be, neither an individual nor a nation can ever commit the least act of injustice against the obscurest individual, without having to pay the penalty for it. A government which deliberately enacts injustice, and persists in it, will at length even become the laughing-stock of the world.

Much has been said about American slavery, but I think that we do not even yet realize what slavery is. If I were seriously to propose to Congress to make mankind into sausages, I have no doubt that most of the members would smile at my proposition, and if any believed me to be in earnest, they would think that I proposed something much worse than Congress had ever done. But if any of them will tell me that to make a man into a sausage would be much worse, — would be any worse, — than to make him into a slave, — than it was to enact the Fugitive Slave Law, — I will accuse him of foolishness, of intellectual incapacity, of making a distinction without a difference. The one is just as sensible a proposition as the other.

I hear a good deal said about trampling this law under foot. Why, one need not go out of his way to do that. This law rises not to the level of the head or the reason; its natural habitat is in the dirt. It was born and bred, and has its life, only in the dust and mire, on a level with the feet; and he who walks with freedom, and does not with Hindoo mercy avoid treading on every venomous reptile, will inevitably tread on it, and so trample it under foot, — and Webster, its maker, with it, like the dirt-bug and its ball.

Recent events will be valuable as a criticism on the administration of justice in our midst, or, rather, as showing what are the true resources of justice in any

community. It has come to this, that the friends of
liberty, the friends of the slave, have shuddered when
they have understood that his fate was left to the legal
tribunals of the country to be decided. Free men have
no faith that justice will be awarded in such a case. The
judge may decide this way or that; it is a kind of accident, at best. It is evident that he is not a competent
authority in so important a case. It is no time, then,
to be judging according to his precedents, but to estab-
lish a precedent for the future. I would much rather
trust to the sentiment of the people. In their vote, you
would get something of some value, at least, however
small; but in the other case, only the trammelled judgment of an individual, of no significance, be it which
way it might.

It is, to some extent, fatal to the courts, when the people are compelled to go behind them. I do not wish
to believe that the courts were made for fair weather,
and for very civil cases merely; but think of leaving it
to any court in the land to decide whether more than
three millions of people, in this case, a sixth part of
a nation, have a right to be freemen or not? But it
has been left to the courts of *justice*, so called, — to the
Supreme Court of the land, — and, as you all know,
recognizing no authority but the Constitution, it has decided that the three millions are, and shall continue to
be slaves. Such judges as these are merely the inspec-
tors of a pick-lock and murderer's tools, to tell him
whether they are in working order or not, and there
they think that their responsibility ends. There was a
prior case on the docket, which they, as judges appointed
by God, had no right to skip; which having been justly
settled, they would have been saved from this humilia-
tion. It was the case of the murderer himself.

The law will never make men free ; it is men who have got to make the law free.   They are the lovers of law and order, who observe the law when the government breaks it.

Among human beings, the judge whose words seal the fate of a man furthest into eternity is not he who merely pronounces the verdict of the law, but he, whoever he may be, who, from a love of truth, and unprejudiced by any custom or enactment of men, utters a true opinion or *sentence* concerning him.   He it is that *sentences* him.   Whoever can discern truth has received his commission from a higher source than the chiefest justice in the world, who can discern only law.   He finds himself constituted judge of the judge. Strange that it should be necessary to state such simple truths !

I am more and more convinced that, with reference to any public question, it is more important to know what the country thinks of it, than what the city thinks.   The city does not *think* much.   On any moral question, I would rather have the opinion of Boxboro than of Boston and New York put together.   When the former speaks, I feel as if somebody *had* spoken, as if *humanity* was yet, and a reasonable being had asserted its rights, — as if some unprejudiced men among the country's hills had at length turned their attention to the subject, and by a few sensible words redeemed the reputation of the race.   When, in some obscure country town, the farmers come together to a special town-meeting, to express their opinion on some subject which is vexing the land, that, I think, is the true Congress, and the most respectable one that is ever assembled in the United States.

It is evident that there are, in this Commonwealth
at least, two parties, becoming more and more distinct,
— the party of the city, and the party of the country.
I know that the country is mean enough, but I am glad
to believe that there is a slight difference in her favor.
But as yet, she has few, if any organs, through which
to express herself. The editorials which she reads, like
the news, come from the seaboard. Let us, the inhabitants of the country, cultivate self-respect. Let us not
send to the city for aught more essential than our broad-
cloths and groceries; or, if we read the opinions of the
city, let us entertain opinions of our own.

Among measures to be adopted, I would suggest to
make as earnest and vigorous an assault on the press as
has already been made, and with effect, on the church.
The church has much improved within a few years; but
the press is almost, without exception, corrupt. I believe
that, in this country, the press exerts a greater and a
more pernicious influence than the church did in its
worst period. We are not a religious people, but we
are a nation of politicians. We do not care for the
Bible, but we do care for the newspaper. At any meeting of politicians, — like that at Concord the other evening, for instance, — how impertinent it would be to quote
from the Bible! how pertinent to quote from a newspaper or from the Constitution! The newspaper is a
Bible which we read every morning and every afternoon, standing and sitting, riding and walking. It is a
Bible which every man carries in his pocket, which lies
on every table and counter, and which the mail, and
thousands of missionaries, are continually dispersing. It
is, in short, the only book which America has printed,
and which America reads. So wide is its influence.

The editor is a preacher whom you voluntarily support.
Your tax is commonly one cent daily, and it costs nothing for pew hire.   But how many of these preachers
preach the truth?   I repeat the testimony of many an
intelligent foreigner, as well as my own convictions,
when I say, that probably no country was ever ruled by
so mean a class of tyrants as, with a few noble exceptions, are the editors of the periodical press in *this* country.   And as they live and rule only by their servility,
and appealing to the worse, and not the better, nature of
man, the people who read them are in the condition of
the dog that returns to his vomit.

The *Liberator* and the *Commonwealth* were the only
papers in Boston, as far as I know, which made themselves heard in condemnation of the cowardice and
meanness of the authorities of that city, as exhibited in
'51.   The other journals, almost without exception, by
their manner of referring to and speaking of the Fugitive Slave Law, and the carrying back of the slave
Simms, insulted the common sense of the country, at
least.   And, for the most part, they did this, one would
say, because they thought so to secure the approbation
of their patrons, not being aware that a sounder sentiment prevailed to any extent in the heart of the Commonwealth.   I am told that some of them have improved
of late; but they are still eminently time-serving.   Such
is the character they have won.

But, thank fortune, this preacher can be even more
easily reached by the weapons of the reformer than
could the recreant priest.   The free men of New England have only to refrain from purchasing and reading
these sheets, have only to withhold their cents, to kill
a score of them at once.   One whom I respect told me

that he purchased Mitchell's *Citizen* in the cars, and then threw it out the window. But would not his contempt have been more fatally expressed if he had not bought it?

Are they Americans? are they New-Englanders? are they inhabitants of Lexington and Concord and Framingham, who read and support the Boston *Post, Mail, Journal, Advertiser, Courier,* and *Times*? Are these the Flags of our Union? I am not a newspaper reader, and may omit to name the worst.

Could slavery suggest a more complete servility than some of these journals exhibit? Is there any dust which their conduct does not lick, and make fouler still with its slime? I do not know whether the Boston *Herald* is still in existence, but I remember to have seen it about the streets when Simms was carried off. Did it not act its part well, — serve its master faithfully? How could it have gone lower on its belly? How can a man stoop lower than he is low? do more than put his extremities in the place of the head he has? than make his head his lower extremity? When I have taken up this paper with my cuffs turned up, I have heard the gurgling of the sewer through every column. I have felt that I was handling a paper picked out of the public gutters, a leaf from the gospel of the gambling-house, the groggery, and the brothel, harmonizing with the gospel of the Merchants' Exchange.

The majority of the men of the North, and of the South and East and West, are not men of principle. If they vote, they do not send men to Congress on errands of humanity; but while their brothers and sisters are being scourged and hung for loving liberty, while — I might here insert all that slavery implies and is,

— it is the mismanagement of wood and iron and stone and gold which concerns them. Do what you will, O Government, with my wife and children, my mother and brother, my father and sister, I will obey your commands to the letter. It will indeed grieve me if you hurt them, if you deliver them to overseers to be hunted by hounds or to be whipped to death ; but, nevertheless, I will peaceably pursue my chosen calling on this fair earth, until perchance, one day, when I have put on mourning for them dead, I shall have persuaded you to relent. Such is the attitude, such are the words of Massachusetts.

Rather than do thus, I need not say what match I would touch, what system endeavor to blow up ; but as I love my life, I would side with the light, and let the dark earth roll from under me, calling my mother and my brother to follow.

I would remind my countrymen, that they are to be men first, and Americans only at a late and convenient hour. No matter how valuable law may be to protect your property, even to keep soul and body together, if it do not keep you and humanity together.

I am sorry to say, that I doubt if there is a judge in Massachusetts who is prepared to resign his office, and get his living innocently, whenever it is required of him to pass sentence under a law which is merely contrary to the law of God. I am compelled to see that they put themselves, or rather, are by character, in this respect, exactly on a level with the marine who discharges his musket in any direction he is ordered to. They are just as much tools, and as little men. Certainly, they are not the more to be respected, because their master enslaves their understandings and consciences, instead of their bodies.

The judges and lawyers, — simply as such, I mean, — and all men of expediency, try this case by a very low and incompetent standard.   They consider, not whether the Fugitive Slave Law is right, but whether it is what they call *constitutional*.   Is virtue constitutional, or vice?   Is equity constitutional, or iniquity?   In important moral and vital questions, like this, it is just as impertinent to ask whether a law is constitutional or not, as to ask whether it is profitable or not.   They persist in being the servants of the worst of men, and not the servants of humanity.   The question is, not whether you or your grandfather, seventy years ago, did not enter into an agreement to serve the Devil, and that service is not accordingly now due; but whether you will not now, for once and at last, serve God, — in spite of your own past recreancy, or that of your ancestor, — by obeying that eternal and only just CONSTITUTION, which He, and not any Jefferson or Adams, has written in your being.

The amount of it is, if the majority vote the Devil to be God, the minority will live and behave accordingly, — and obey the successful candidate, trusting that, some time or other, by some Speaker's casting-vote, perhaps, they may reinstate God.   This is the highest principle I can get out or invent for my neighbors.   These men act as if they believed that they could safely slide down a hill a little way — or a good way — and would surely come to a place, by and by, where they could begin to slide up again.   This is expediency, or choosing that course which offers the slightest obstacles to the feet, that is, a down-hill one.   But there is no such thing as accomplishing a righteous reform by the use of "expediency."   There is no such thing as sliding up hill.   In morals, the only sliders are backsliders.

Thus we steadily worship Mammon, both school and state and church, and on the seventh day curse God with a tintamar from one end of the Union to the other.

Will mankind never learn that policy is not morality, — that it never secures any moral right, but considers merely what is expedient? chooses the available candidate, — who is invariably the Devil, — and what right have his constituents to be surprised, because the Devil does not behave like an angel of light? What is wanted is men, not of policy, but of probity, — who recognize a higher law than the Constitution, or the decision of the majority. The fate of the country does not depend on how you vote at the polls, — the worst man is as strong as the best at that game; it does not depend on what kind of paper you drop into the ballot-box once a year, but on what kind of man you drop from your chamber into the street every morning.

What should concern Massachusetts is not the Nebraska Bill, nor the Fugitive Slave Bill, but her own slaveholding and servility. Let the State dissolve her union with the slaveholder. She may wriggle and hesitate, and ask leave to read the Constitution once more; but she can find no respectable law or precedent which sanctions the continuance of such a Union for an instant.

Let each inhabitant of the State dissolve his union with her, as long as she delays to do her duty.

The events of the past month teach me to distrust Fame. I see that she does not finely discriminate, but coarsely hurrahs. She considers not the simple heroism of an action, but only as it is connected with its apparent consequences. She praises till she is hoarse the easy exploit of the Boston tea party, but will be com-

paratively silent about the braver and more disinterest-
edly heroic attack on the Boston Court-House, simply
because it was unsuccessful!

Covered with disgrace, the State has sat down coolly
to try for their lives and liberties the men who attempted to do its duty for it. And this is called *justice!*
They who have shown that they can behave particularly
well may perchance be put under bonds for *their good
behavior.* They whom truth requires at present to plead
guilty are, of all the inhabitants of the State, pre-emi-
nently innocent. While the Governor, and the Mayor,
and countless officers of the Commonwealth are at large,
the champions of liberty are imprisoned.

Only they are guiltless, who commit the crime of contempt of such a court. It behooves every man to see
that his influence is on the side of justice, and let the
courts make their own characters. My sympathies in
this case are wholly with the accused, and wholly
against their accusers and judges. Justice is sweet and
musical; but injustice is harsh and discordant. The
judge still sits grinding at his organ, but it yields no
music, and we hear only the sound of the handle. He
believes that all the music resides in the handle, and the
crowd toss him their coppers the same as before.

Do you suppose that that Massachusetts which is now
doing these things, — which hesitates to crown these men,
some of whose lawyers, and even judges, perchance, may
be driven to take refuge in some poor quibble, that they
may not wholly outrage their instinctive sense of justice,
— do you suppose that she is anything but base and
servile? that she is the champion of liberty?

Show me a free state, and a court truly of justice,
and I will fight for them, if need be; but show me

Massachusetts, and I refuse her my allegiance, and express contempt for her courts.

The effect of a good government is to make life more valuable, — of a bad one, to make it less valuable. We can afford that railroad, and all merely material stock, should lose some of its value, for that only compels us to live more simply and economically ; but suppose that the value of life itself should be diminished! How can we make a less demand on man and nature, how live more economically in respect to virtue and all noble qualities, than we do? I have lived for the last month, — and I think that every man in Massachusetts capable of the sentiment of patriotism must have had a similar experience, — with the sense of having suffered a vast and indefinite loss. I did not know at first what ailed me. At last it occurred to me that what I had lost was a country. I had never respected the government near to which I lived, but I had foolishly thought that I might manage to live here, minding my private affairs, and forget it. For my part, my old and worthiest pursuits have lost I cannot say how much of their attraction, and I feel that my investment in life here is worth many per cent less since Massachusetts last deliberately sent back an innocent man, Anthony Burns, to slavery. I dwelt before, perhaps, in the illusion that my life passed somewhere only *between* heaven and hell, but now I cannot persuade myself that I do not dwell *wholly within* hell. The site of that political organization called Massachusetts is to me morally covered with volcanic scoriæ and cinders, such as Milton describes in the infernal regions. If there is any hell more unprincipled than our rulers, and we, the ruled, I feel curious to see it. Life itself being worth less, all things with it, which minister to it, are worth less. Suppose you have a small library, with pictures to adorn the walls, — a garden laid out around, — and contemplate scientific and literary pursuits, and discover all at once that your villa, with all its contents, is located in hell, and that the justice of the peace has a cloven foot and a forked tail, — do not these things suddenly lose their value in your eyes?

I feel that, to some extent, the State has fatally interfered with my lawful business. It has not only interrupted me in my passage through Court Street on errands of trade, but it has interrupted me and every man on his onward and upward path, on which he had trusted soon to leave Court Street far behind. What right had it to remind me of Court Street? I have found that hollow which even I had relied on for solid.

I am surprised to see men going about their business as if nothing had happened. I say to myself, "Unfortunates! they have not heard the news." I am surprised that the man whom I just met on horseback should be so earnest to overtake his newly bought cows running away, — since all property is insecure, and if they do not run away again, they may be taken away from him when he gets them. Fool! does he not know that his seed-corn is worth less this year, — that all beneficent harvests fail as you approach the empire of hell? No prudent man will build a stone house under these circumstances, or engage in any peaceful enterprise which it requires a long time to accomplish. Art is as long as ever, but life is more interrupted and less available for a man's proper pursuits. It is not an era of repose. We have used up all our inherited freedom. If we would save our lives, we must fight for them.

I walk toward one of our ponds: but what signifies the

beauty of nature when men are base? We walk to
lakes to see our serenity reflected in them; when we are
not serene, we go not to them. Who can be serene in a
country where both the rulers and the ruled are without
principle? The remembrance of my country spoils my
walk. My thoughts are murder to the State, and involuntarily go plotting against her.

But it chanced the other day that I scented a white
water-lily, and a season I had waited for had arrived.
It is the emblem of purity. It bursts up so pure and
fair to the eye, and so sweet to the scent, as if to show
us what purity and sweetness reside in, and can be extracted from, the slime and muck of earth. I think I
have plucked the first one that has opened for a mile.
What confirmation of our hopes is in the fragrance of
this flower! I shall not so soon despair of the world for
it, notwithstanding slavery, and the cowardice and want
of principle of Northern men. It suggests what kind
of laws have prevailed longest and widest, and still prevail, and that the time may come when man's deeds will
smell as sweet. Such is the odor which the plant emits.
If Nature can compound this fragrance still annually,
I shall believe her still young and full of vigor, her integrity and genius unimpaired, and that there is virtue
even in man, too, who is fitted to perceive and love it.
It reminds me that Nature has been partner to no Missouri Compromise. I scent no compromise in the fragrance of the water-lily. It is not a *Nymphæa* Doug-
LASSII. In it, the sweet, and pure, and innocent are
wholly sundered from the obscene and baleful. I do not
scent in this the time-serving irresolution of a Massachusetts Governor, nor of a Boston Mayor. So behave
that the odor of your actions may enhance the general

sweetness of the atmosphere, that when we behold or
scent a flower, we may not be reminded how inconsistent your deeds are with it; for all odor is but one form
of advertisement of a moral quality, and if fair actions
had not been performed, the lily would not smell sweet.
The foul slime stands for the sloth and vice of man, the
decay of humanity; the fragrant flower that springs from
it, for the purity and courage which are immortal.

Slavery and servility have produced no sweet-scented
flower annually, to charm the senses of men, for they
have no real life: they are merely a decaying and a
death, offensive to all healthy nostrils.   We do not complain that they *live*, but that they do not *get buried*.   Let
the living bury them; even they are good for manure.

PRAYERS.

Not with fond shekels of the tested gold,
Nor gems whose rates are either rich or poor,
As fancy values them : but with true prayers,
That shall be up at heaven, and enter there
Ere sunrise ; prayers from preserved souls,
From fasting maids, whose minds are dedicate
To nothing temporal.

SHAKESPEARE.

PYTHAGORAS said that the time when men are hon-
estest, is when they present themselves before the gods.
If we can overhear the prayer, we shall know the man.
But prayers are not made to be overheard, or to be printed, so that we seldom have the prayer otherwise than it
can be inferred from the man and his fortunes, which
are the answer to the prayer, and always accord with it.
Yet there are scattered about in the earth a few records
of these devout hours, which it would edify us to read,
could they be collected in a more catholic spirit than the
wretched and repulsive volumes which usurp that name.
Let us not have the prayers of one sect, nor of the
Christian Church, but of men in all ages and religions,
who have prayed well. The prayer of Jesus is, as it
deserves, become a form for the human race. Many
men have contributed a single expression, a single word
to the language of devotion, which is immediately caught
and stereotyped in the prayers of their church and na
tion. Among the remains of Euripides, we have this

prayer: "Thou God of all! infuse light into the souls of men, whereby they may be enabled to know what is the root from whence all their evils spring, and by what means they may avoid them." In the Phædrus of Plato, we find this petition in the mouth of Socrates: "O gracious Pan! and ye other gods who preside over this place! grant that I may be beautiful within; and that those external things which I have may be such as may best agree with a right internal disposition of mind; and that I may account him to be rich, who is wise and just." Wacic the Caliph, who died A. D. 845, ended his life, the Arabian historians tell us, with these words: "O thou whose kingdom never passes away, pity one whose dignity is so transient." But what led us to these remembrances was the happy accident which, in this undevout age, lately brought us acquainted with two or three diaries, which attest, if there be need of attestation, the eternity of the sentiment and its equality to itself through all the variety of expression. The first is the prayer of a deaf and dumb boy.

"When my long-attached friend comes to me, I have pleasure to converse with him, and I rejoice to pass my eyes over his countenance; but soon I am weary of spending my time causelessly and unimproved, and I desire to leave him (*but not in rudeness*), because I wish to be engaged in my business. But thou, O my Father, knowest I always delight to commune with thee in my lone and silent heart; I am never full of thee; I am never weary of thee; I am always desiring thee. I hunger with strong hope and affection for thee, and I thirst for thy grace and spirit.

"When I go to visit my friends, I must put on my best garments, and I must think of my manner to please them. I am tired to stay long, because my mind is not free, and they sometimes talk gossip with me. But, O my Father, thou visitest me in my work, and I can lift up my desires to thee, and my heart is cheered and at rest with thy presence, and I am always alone with thee, *and thou dost not steal my time by foolishness.* I always ask in my heart, Where can I find thee?"

The next is a voice out of a solitude as strict and sacred as that in which nature had isolated this eloquent mute.

"My Father, when I cannot be cheerful or happy, I can be true and obedient, and I will not forget that joy has been, and may still be. If there is no hour of solitude granted me, still I will commune with thee. If I may not search out and pierce my thought, so much the more may my living praise thee. At whatever price, I must be alone with thee; this must be the demand I make. These *duties* are not the life, but the means which enable us to show forth the life. So must I take up this cross, and bear it willingly. Why should I feel reproved when a busy one enters the room? I am not idle, though I sit with folded hands; but instantly I must seek some cover. For that shame I reprove myself. Are they only the valuable members of society who labor to dress and feed it? Shall we never ask the aim of all this hurry and foam, of this aimless activity? Let the purpose for which I live be always before me; let every thought and word go to confirm and illuminate that end; namely, that I must become near and dear to thee; that now I am beyond the reach of all but thee.

"How can we not be reconciled to thy will? I will know the joy of giving to my friend the dearest treasure I have. I know that sorrow comes not at once only. We cannot meet it, and say, now it is overcome, but again, and yet again its flood pours over us, and as full as at first.

> "If but this tedious battle could be fought,
> Like Sparta's heroes at one rocky pass,
> 'One day be spent in dying,' men had sought
> The spot and been cut down like mower's grass."

The next is all in metrical form. It is the aspiration
of a different mind, in quite other regions of power and
Joy, yet they all accord at last.

> " Great God, I ask thee for no meaner pelf
> Than that I may not disappoint myself,
> That in my action I may soar as high
> As I can now discern with this clear eye.
>
> " And next in value, which thy kindness lends,
> That I may greatly disappoint my friends,
> Howe'er they think or hope that it may be,
> They may not dream how thou 'st distinguished me.
>
> " That my weak hand may equal my firm faith,
> And my life practise more than my tongue saith;
> That my low conduct may not show,
> Nor my relenting lines,
> That I thy purpose did not know,
> Or overrated thy designs."

The last of the four orisons is written in a singularly
calm and healthful spirit, and contains this petition : —

" My Father! I now come to thee with a desire to thank
thee for the continuance of our love, the one for the other.
I feel that without thy love in me, I should be alone here in
the flesh. I cannot express my gratitude for what thou hast
been and continuest to be to me. But thou knowest what
my feelings are. When naught on earth seemeth pleasant
to me, thou dost make thyself known to me, and teach
me that which is needful for me, and dost cheer my travels
on.   I know that thou hast not created me and placed
me here on earth, amidst its toils and troubles, and the follies
of those around me, and told me to be like thyself, when I
see so little of thee here to profit by ; thou hast not done this,
and then left me to myself, a poor, weak man, scarcely able
to earn my bread. No ; thou art my Father, and I will love
thee, for thou didst first love me, and lovest me still. We
will ever be parent and child. Wilt thou give me strength
to persevere in this great work of redemption. Wilt thou

show me the true means of accomplishing it. . . . . I thank thee for the knowledge that I have attained of thee by thy sons who have been before me, and especially for him who brought me so perfect a type of thy goodness and love to men. . . . . I know that thou wilt deal with me as I deserve. I place myself, therefore in thy hand, knowing that thou wilt keep me from all harm so long as I consent to live under thy protecting care."

Let these few scattered leaves, which a chance, as men say, but which to us shall be holy, brought under our eye nearly at the same moment, stand as an example of innumerable similar expressions which no mortal witness has reported, and be a sign of the times. Might they be suggestion to many a heart of yet higher secret experiences which are ineffable ! But we must not tie up the rosary on which we have strung these few white beads, without adding a pearl of great price from that book of prayer, the " Confessions of Saint Augustine."

" And being admonished to reflect upon myself, I entered into the very inward parts of my soul, by thy conduct; and I was able to do it, because now thou wert become my helper. I entered and discerned with the eye of my soul (such as it was), even beyond my soul and mind itself the Light unchangeable. Not this vulgar light which all flesh may look upon, nor as it were a greater of the same kind, as though the brightness of this should be manifold greater and with its greatness take up all space. Not such was this light, but other, yea, far other from all these. Neither was it so above my understanding, as oil swims above water, or as the heaven is above the earth. But it is above me, because it made me; and I am under it, because I was made by it. He that knows truth or verity, knows what that Light is, and he that knows it, knows eternity, and it is known by charity. O eternal Verity ! and true Charity ! and dear Eternity ! thou art my God, to thee do I sigh day and night. Thee when I first knew, thou liftedst me up that I might see there was what I might see, and that I was not yet such as to see. And thou didst beat back my weak sight upon myself, shooting out beams upon me after a vehement manner, and I even trembled between love and horror, and I found myself to be far off, and even in the very region of dissimilitude from thee."

CIVIL DISOBEDIENCE.*

I HEARTILY accept the motto, — "That government is best which governs least"; and I should like to see it acted up to more rapidly and systematically. Carried out, it finally amounts to this, which also I believe, — "That government is best which governs not at all"; and when men are prepared for it, that will be the kind of government which they will have. Government is at best but an expedient; but most governments are usually, and all governments are sometimes, inexpedient. The objections which have been brought against a standing army, and they are many and weighty, and deserve to prevail, may also at last be brought against a standing government. The standing army is only an arm of the standing government. The government itself, which is only the mode which the people have chosen to execute their will, is equally liable to be abused and perverted before the people can act through it. Witness the present Mexican war, the work of comparatively a few individuals using the standing government as their tool; for, in the outset, the people would not have consented to this measure.

This American government, — what is it but a tradition, though a recent one, endeavoring to transmit itself unimpaired to posterity, but each instant losing some

* Æsthetic Papers, No. I. Boston, 1849.

of its integrity ? It has not the vitality and force of a
single living man ; for a single man can bend it to his
will.   It is a sort of wooden gun to the people themselves.
But it is not the less necessary for this; for the people must
have some complicated machinery or other, and hear its
din, to satisfy that idea of government which they have.
Governments show thus how successfully men can be
imposed on, even impose on themselves, for their own
advantage.   It is excellent, we must all allow.   Yet this
government never of itself furthered any enterprise, but
by the alacrity with which it got out of its way.   *It* does
not keep the country free.   *It* does not settle the West.
It does not educate.   The character inherent in the
American people has done all that has been accomplished ; and it would have done somewhat more, if the
government had not sometimes got in its way.   For
government is an expedient by which men would fain
succeed in letting one another alone ; and, as has been
said, when it is most expedient, the governed are most
let alone by it.   Trade and commerce, if they were not
made of India-rubber, would never manage to bounce
over the obstacles which legislators are continually putting in their way ; and, if one were to judge these men
wholly by the effects of their actions and not partly by
their intentions, they would deserve to be classed and
punished with those mischievous persons who put ob-
structions on the railroads.

But, to speak practically and as a citizen, unlike those
who call themselves no-government men, I ask for, not
at once no government, but *at once* a better government.
Let every man make known what kind of government
would command his respect, and that will be one step
toward obtaining it.

After all, the practical reason why, when the power is once in the hands of the people, a majority are permitted, and for a long period continue, to rule, is not because they are most likely to be in the right, nor because this seems fairest to the minority, but because they are physically the strongest. But a government in which the majority rule in all cases cannot be based on justice, even as far as men understand it. Can there not be a government in which majorities do not virtually decide right and wrong, but conscience? — in which majorities decide only those questions to which the rule of expediency is applicable? Must the citizen ever for a moment, or in the least degree, resign his conscience to the legislator? Why has every man a conscience, then? I think that we should be men first, and subjects afterward. It is not desirable to cultivate a respect for the law, so much as for the right. The only obligation which I have a right to assume, is to do at any time what I think right. It is truly enough said, that a corporation has no conscience; but a corporation of conscientious men is a corporation *with* a conscience. Law never made men a whit more just; and, by means of their respect for it, even the well-disposed are daily made the agents of injustice. A common and natural result of an undue respect for law is, that you may see a file of soldiers, colonel, captain, corporal, privates, powder-monkeys, and all, marching in admirable order over hill and dale to the wars, against their wills, ay, against their common sense and consciences, which makes it very steep marching indeed, and produces a palpitation of the heart. They have no doubt that it is a damnable business in which they are concerned; they are all peaceably inclined. Now, what are they? Men

at all? or small movable forts and magazines, at the
service of some unscrupulous man in power? Visit the
Navy-Yard, and behold a marine, such a man as an
American government can make, or such as it can make
a man with its black arts, — a mere shadow and reminiscence of humanity, a man laid out alive and standing,
and already, as one may say, buried under arms with
funeral accompaniments, though it may be, —

> "Not a drum was heard, not a funeral note,
>   As his corse to the rampart we hurried;
> Not a soldier discharged his farewell shot
>   O'er the grave where our hero we buried."

The mass of men serve the state thus, not as men
mainly, but as machines, with their bodies. They are
the standing army, and the militia, jailers, constables,
posse comitatus, &c. In most cases there is no free exer-
cise whatever of the judgment or of the moral sense;
but they put themselves on a level with wood and earth
and stones; and wooden men can perhaps be manu-
factured that will serve the purpose as well. Such command no more respect than men of straw or a lump of dirt.
They have the same sort of worth only as horses and
dogs. Yet such as these even are commonly esteemed
good citizens. Others, — as most legislators, politicians,
lawyers, ministers, and office-holders, — serve the state
chiefly with their heads; and, as they rarely make any
moral distinctions, they are as likely to serve the Devil,
without *intending* it, as God. A very few, as heroes,
patriots, martyrs, reformers in the great sense, and *men*,
serve the state with their consciences also, and so necessarily resist it for the most part; and they are commonly
treated as enemies by it. A wise man will only be
useful as a man, and will not submit to be " clay," and

" stop a hole to keep the wind away," but leave that office to his dust at least : —

> " I am too high-born to be propertied,
> To be a secondary at control,
> Or useful serving-man and instrument
> To any sovereign state throughout the world."

He who gives himself entirely to his fellow-men appears to them useless and selfish ; but he who gives himself partially to them is pronounced a benefactor and philanthropist.

How does it become a man to behave toward this American government to-day ? I answer, that he cannot without disgrace be associated with it. I cannot for an instant recognize that political organization as *my* government which is the *slave's* government also.

All men recognize the right of revolution ; that is, the right to refuse allegiance to, and to resist, the government, when its tyranny or its inefficiency are great and unendurable. But almost all say that such is not the case now. But such was the case, they think, in the Revolution of '75. If one were to tell me that this was a bad government because it taxed certain foreign commodities brought to its ports, it is most probable that I should not make an ado about it, for I can do without them. All machines have their friction ; and possibly this does enough good to counterbalance the evil. At any rate, it is a great evil to make a stir about it. But when the friction comes to have its machine, and oppression and robbery are organized, I say, let us not have such a machine any longer. In other words, when a sixth of the population of a nation which has undertaken to be the refuge of liberty are slaves, and a whole country is unjustly overrun and conquered by a foreign army, and

subjected to military law, I think that it is not too soon
for honest men to rebel and revolutionize.   What makes
this duty the more urgent is the fact, that the country so
overrun is not our own, but ours is the invading army.

Paley, a common authority with many on moral questions, in his chapter on the "Duty of Submission to
Civil Government," resolves all civil obligation into expediency ; and he proceeds to say, " that so long as the
interest of the whole society requires it, that is, so long
as the established government cannot be resisted or
changed without public inconveniency, it is the will of
God that the established government be obeyed, and no
longer. . . . . This principle being admitted, the justice
of every particular case of resistance is reduced to a
computation of the quantity of the danger and grievance
on the one side, and of the probability and expense of
redressing it on the other."   Of this, he says, every man
shall judge for himself.   But Paley appears never to
have contemplated those cases to which the rule of expediency does not apply, in which a people, as well as
an individual, must do justice, cost what it may.   If I
have unjustly wrested a plank from a drowning man,
I must restore it to him though I drown myself.   This,
according to Paley, would be inconvenient.   But he
that would save his life, in such a case, shall lose it
This people must cease to hold slaves, and to make war
on Mexico, though it cost them their existence as a people.

In their practice, nations agree with Paley ; but does
any one think that Massachusetts does exactly what is
right at the present crisis ?

    " A drab of state, a cloth-o'-silver slut,
       To have her train borne up, and her soul trail in the dirt."

Practically speaking, the opponents to a reform in Massachusetts are not a hundred thousand politicians at the South, but a hundred thousand merchants and farmers here, who are more interested in commerce and agriculture than they are in humanity, and are not prepared to do justice to the slave and to Mexico, *cost what it may.* I quarrel not with far-off foes, but with those who, near at home, co-operate with, and do the bidding of, those far away, and without whom the latter would be harmless. We are accustomed to say, that the mass of men are unprepared; but improvement is slow, because the few are not materially wiser or better than the many. It is not so important that many should be as good as you, as that there be some absolute goodness somewhere; for that will leaven the whole lump. There are thousands who are *in opinion* opposed to slavery and to the war, who yet in effect do nothing to put an end to them; who, esteeming themselves children of Washington and Franklin, sit down with their hands in their pockets, and say that they know not what to do, and do nothing; who even postpone the question of freedom to the question of free-trade, and quietly read the prices-current along with the latest advices from Mexico, after dinner, and, it may be, fall asleep over them both. What is the price-current of an honest man and patriot to-day? They hesitate, and they regret, and sometimes they petition; but they do nothing in earnest and with effect. They will wait, well disposed, for others to remedy the evil, that they may no longer have it to regret. At most, they give only a cheap vote, and a feeble countenance and God-speed, to the right, as it goes by them. There are nine hundred and ninety-nine patrons of virtue to one virtuous man. But it is easier to deal with the real possessor of a thing than with the temporary guardian of it.

All voting is a sort of gaming, like checkers or back-gammon, with a slight moral tinge to it, a playing with right and wrong, with moral questions; and betting naturally accompanies it. The character of the voters is not staked. I cast my vote, perchance, as I think right; but I am not vitally concerned that that right should prevail. I am willing to leave it to the majority. Its obligation, therefore, never exceeds that of expediency. Even voting *for the right* is *doing* nothing for it. It is only expressing to men feebly your desire that it should prevail. A wise man will not leave the right to the mercy of chance, nor wish it to prevail through the power of the majority. There is but little virtue in the action of masses of men. When the majority shall at length vote for the abolition of slavery, it will be because they are indifferent to slavery, or because there is but little slavery left to be abolished by their vote. *They* will then be the only slaves. Only *his* vote can hasten the abolition of slavery who asserts his own freedom by his vote.

I hear of a convention to be held at Baltimore, or elsewhere, for the selection of a candidate for the Presidency, made up chiefly of editors, and men who are politicians by profession; but I think, what is it to any independent, intelligent, and respectable man what decision they may come to? Shall we not have the advantage of his wisdom and honesty, nevertheless? Can we not count upon some independent votes? Are there not many individuals in the country who do not attend conventions? But no: I find that the respectable man, so called, has immediately drifted from his position, and

despairs of his country, when his country has more reason to despair of him.   He forthwith adopts one of the
candidates thus selected as ᵗʰe only *available* one, thus
proving that he is himself *available* for any purposes of
the demagogue.   His vote is of no more worth than that
of any unprincipled foreigner or hireling native, who
may have been bought.   O for a man who is a *man*,
and, as my neighbor says, has a bone in his back which
you cannot pass your hand through !   Our statistics are
at fault : the population has been returned too large.
How many *men* are there to a square thousand miles in
this country ?   Hardly one.   Does not America offer
any inducement for men to settle here ?   The American
has dwindled into an Odd Fellow, — one who may be
known by the development of his organ of gregarious-
ness, and a manifest lack of intellect and cheerful self-
reliance ; whose first and chief concern, on coming into
the world, is to see that the Almshouses are in good
repair ; and, before yet he has lawfully donned the virile
garb, to collect a fund for the support of the widows
and orphans that may be ; who, in short, ventures to
live only by the aid of the Mutual Insurance company,
which has promised to bury him decently.

It is not a man's duty, as a matter of course, to devote
nimself to the eradication of any, even the most enormous wrong ; he may still properly have other concerns
to engage him ; but it is his duty, at least, to wash his
hands of it, and, if he gives it no thought longer, not to
give it practically his support.   If I devote myself to
other pursuits and contemplations, I must first see, at
least, that I do not pursue them sitting upon another
man's shoulders.   I must get off him first, that he may
pursue his contemplations too.   See what gross incon-

sistency is tolerated. I have heard some of my townsmen say, " I should like to have them order me out to
help put down an insurrection of the slaves, or to march
to Mexico; — see if I would go "; and yet these very
men have each, directly by their allegiance, and so
indirectly, at least, by their money, furnished a substitute. The soldier is applauded who refuses to serve
in an unjust war by those who do not refuse to sustain
the unjust government which makes the war; is applauded by those whose own act and authority he disregards
and sets at naught; as if the State were penitent to that
degree that it hired one to scourge it while it sinned, but
not to that degree that it left off sinning for a moment.
Thus, under the name of Order and Civil Government,
we are all made at last to pay homage to and support
our own meanness. After the first blush of sin comes its
indifference ; and from immoral it becomes, as it were,
unmoral, and not quite unnecessary to that life which
we have made.

The broadest and most prevalent error requires the
most disinterested virtue to sustain it. The slight reproach to which the virtue of patriotism is commonly
liable, the noble are most likely to incur. Those who,
while they disapprove of the character and measures of
a government, yield to it their allegiance and support,
are undoubtedly its most conscientious supporters, and
so frequently the most serious obstacles to reform.
Some are petitioning the State to dissolve the Union, to
disregard the requisitions of the President. Why do
they not dissolve it themselves, — the union between
themselves and the State, — and refuse to pay their
quota into its treasury? Do not they stand in the same
relation to the State, that the State does to the Union?

And have not the same reasons prevented the State from resisting the Union, which have prevented them from resisting the State?

How can a man be satisfied to entertain an opinion merely, and enjoy *it*? Is there any enjoyment in it, if his opinion is that he is aggrieved? If you are cheated out of a single dollar by your neighbor, you do not rest satisfied with knowing that you are cheated, or with saying that you are cheated, or even with petitioning him to pay you your due; but you take effectual steps at once to obtain the full amount, and see that you are never cheated again. Action from principle, the perception and the performance of right, changes things and relations; it is essentially revolutionary, and does not consist wholly with anything which was. It not only divides states and churches, it divides families; ay, it divides the *individual*, separating the diabolical in him from the divine.

Unjust laws exist: shall we be content to obey them, or shall we endeavor to amend them, and obey them until we have succeeded, or shall we transgress them at once? Men generally, under such a government as this, think that they ought to wait until they have persuaded the majority to alter them. They think that, if they should resist, the remedy would be worse than the evil. But it is the fault of the government itself that the remedy *is* worse than the evil. *It* makes it worse. Why is it not more apt to anticipate and provide for reform? Why does it not cherish its wise minority? Why does it cry and resist before it is hurt? Why does it not encourage its citizens to be on the alert to point out its faults, and *do* better than it would have them? Why does it always crucify Christ, and excommunicate

Copernicus and Luther, and pronounce Washington and Franklin rebels?

One would think, that a deliberate and practical denial of its authority was the only offence never contemplated by government; else, why has it not assigned its definite, its suitable and proportionate penalty? If a man who has no property refuses but once to earn nine shillings for the State, he is put in prison for a period unlimited by any law that I know, and determined only by the discretion of those who placed him there; but if he should steal ninety times nine shillings from the State, he is soon permitted to go at large again.

If the injustice is part of the necessary friction of the machine of government, let it go, let it go: perchance it will wear smooth, — certainly the machine will wear out. If the injustice has a spring, or a pulley, or a rope, or a crank, exclusively for itself, then perhaps you may consider whether the remedy will not be worse than the evil; but if it is of such a nature that it requires you to be the agent of injustice to another, then, I say, break the law. Let your life be a counter friction to stop the machine. What I have to do is to see, at any rate, that I do not lend myself to the wrong which I condemn.

As for adopting the ways which the State has provided for remedying the evil, I know not of such ways. They take too much time, and a man's life will be gone. I have other affairs to attend to. I came into this world, not chiefly to make this a good place to live in, but to live in it, be it good or bad. A man has not everything to do, but something; and because he cannot do *everything*, it is not necessary that he should do *something* wrong. It is not my business to be petitioning the Governor or the Legislature any more than it is theirs to petition me; and,

If they should not hear my petition, what should I do then? But in this case the State has provided no way: its very Constitution is the evil. This may seem to be harsh and stubborn and unconciliatory; but it is to treat with the utmost kindness and consideration the only spirit that can appreciate or deserves it. So is all change for the better, like birth and death, which convulse the body.

I do not hesitate to say, that those who call themselves Abolitionists should at once effectually withdraw their support, both in person and property, from the government of Massachusetts, and not wait till they constitute a majority of one, before they suffer the right to prevail through them. I think that it is enough if they have God on their side, without waiting for that other one. Moreover, any man more right than his neighbors constitutes a majority of one already.

I meet this American government, or its representative, the State government, directly, and face to face, once a year — no more — in the person of its tax-gatherer; this is the only mode in which a man situated as I am necessarily meets it; and it then says distinctly, Recognize me; and the simplest, the most effectual, and, in the present posture of affairs, the indispensablest mode of treating with it on this head, of expressing your little satisfaction with and love for it, is to deny it then. My civil neighbor, the tax-gatherer, is the very man I have to deal with, — for it is, after all, with men and not with parchment that I quarrel, — and he has voluntarily chosen to be an agent of the government. How shall he ever know well what he is and does as an officer of the government, or as a man, until he is obliged to consider whether he shall treat me, his neighbor, for whom he

has respect, as a neighbor and well-disposed man, or as
a maniac and disturber of the peace, and see if he can
get over this obstruction to his neighborliness without a
ruder and more impetuous thought or speech corresponding with his action.   I know this well, that if one thousand, if one hundred, if ten men whom I could name, —
if ten *honest* men only, — ay, if *one* HONEST man, in this
State of Massachusetts, *ceasing to hold slaves*, were actually to withdraw from this copartnership, and be locked
up in the county jail therefor, it would be the abolition
of slavery in America.   For it matters not how small
the beginning may seem to be : what is once well done is
done forever.   But we love better to talk about it : that
we say is our mission.   Reform keeps many scores of
newspapers in its service, but not one man.   If my esteemed neighbor, the State's ambassador, who will devote
his days to the settlement of the question of human
rights in the Council Chamber, instead of being threat-
ened with the prisons of Carolina, were to sit down the
prisoner of Massachusetts, that State which is so anxious
to foist the sin of slavery upon her sister, — though at
present she can discover only an act of inhospitality to
be the ground of a quarrel with her, — the Legislature
would not wholly waive the subject the following winter.

Under a government which imprisons any unjustly,
the true place for a just man is also a prison.   The
proper place to-day, the only place which Massachusetts
has provided for her freer and less desponding spirits,
is in her prisons, to be put out and locked out of the
State by her own act, as they have already put themselves out by their principles.   It is there that the
fugitive slave, and the Mexican prisoner on parole,
and the Indian come to plead the wrongs of his race.

should find them; on that separate, but more free and honorable ground, where the State places those who are not *with* her, but *against* her, — the only house in a slave State in which a free man can abide with honor. If any think that their influence would be lost there, and their voices no longer afflict the ear of the State, that they would not be as an enemy within its walls, they do not know by how much truth is stronger than error, nor how much more eloquently and effectively he can combat injustice who has experienced a little in his own person. Cast your whole vote, not a strip of paper merely, but your whole influence. A minority is powerless while it conforms to the majority; it is not even a minority then; but it is irresistible when it clogs by its whole weight. If the alternative is to keep all just men in prison, or give up war and slavery, the State will not hesitate which to choose. If a thousand men were not to pay their tax-bills this year, that would not be a violent and bloody measure, as it would be to pay them, and enable the State to commit violence and shed innocent blood. This is, in fact, the definition of a peaceable revolution, if any such is possible. If the tax-gatherer, or any other public officer, asks me, as one has done, " But what shall I do?" my answer is, "If you really wish to do anything, resign your office." When the subject has refused allegiance, and the officer has resigned his office, then the revolution is accomplished. But even suppose blood should flow. Is there not a sort of blood shed when the conscience is wounded? Through this wound a man's real manhood and immortality flow out, and he bleeds to an everlasting death. I see this blood flowing now.

I have contemplated the imprisonment of the offender, rather than the seizure of his goods, — though both will serve the same purpose, — because they who assert the purest right, and consequently are most dangerous to a corrupt State, commonly have not spent much time in accumulating property. To such the State renders comparatively small service, and a slight tax is wont to appear exorbitant, particularly if they are obliged to earn it by special labor with their hands. If there were one who lived wholly without the use of money, the State itself would hesitate to demand it of him. But the rich man, — not to make any invidious comparison, — is always sold to the institution which makes him rich. Absolutely speaking, the more money, the less virtue; for money comes between a man and his objects, and obtains them for him; and it was certainly no great virtue to obtain it. It puts to rest many questions which he would otherwise be taxed to answer; while the only new question which it puts is the hard but superfluous one, how to spend it. Thus his moral ground is taken from under his feet. The opportunities of living are diminished in proportion as what are called the "means" are increased. The best thing a man can do for his culture when he is rich is to endeavor to carry out those schemes which he entertained when he was poor. Christ answered the Herodians according to their condition. "Show me the tribute-money," said he; — and one took a penny out of his pocket; — if you use money which has the image of Cæsar on it, and which he has made current and valuable, that is, *if you are men of the State*, and gladly enjoy the advantages of Cæsar's government, then pay him back some of his own when he demands it; "Render therefore to Cæsar that which is Cæsar's, and to God those things which are God's," — leaving them no wiser than before as to which was which; for they did not wish to know.

When I converse with the freest of my neighbors, I perceive that, whatever they may say about the magnitude and seriousness of the question, and their regard for the public tranquillity, the long and the short of the matter is, that they cannot spare the protection of the existing government, and they dread the consequences to their property and families of disobedience to it. For my own part, I should not like to think that I ever rely on the protection of the State. But, if I deny the authority of the State when it presents its tax-bill, it will soon take and waste all my property, and so harass me and my children without end. This is hard. This makes it impossible for a man to live honestly, and at the same time comfortably, in outward respects. It will not be worth the while to accumulate property; that would be sure to go again. You must hire or squat somewhere, and raise but a small crop, and eat that soon. You must live within yourself, and depend upon yourself always tucked up and ready for a start, and not have many affairs. A man may grow rich in Turkey even, if he will be in all respects a good subject of the Turkish government. Confucius said: "If a state is governed by the principles of reason, poverty and misery are subjects of shame; if a state is not governed by the principles of reason, riches and honors are the subjects of shame." No: until I want the protection of Massachusetts to be extended to me in some distant Southern port, where my liberty is endangered, or until I am bent solely on building up an estate at home by peaceful enterprise, I can afford to refuse allegiance to Massachusetts, and her right to my property and life. It costs me less in every sense to incur the penalty of disobedience to the State, than it would to obey. I should feel as if I were worth less in that case

Some years ago, the State met me in behalf of the Church, and commanded me to pay a certain sum toward the support of a clergyman whose preaching my father attended, but never I myself. "Pay," it said, "or be locked up in the jail." I declined to pay. But, unfortunately, another man saw fit to pay it. I did not see why the schoolmaster should be taxed to support the priest, and not the priest the schoolmaster; for I was not the State's schoolmaster, but I supported myself by voluntary subscription. I did not see why the lyceum should not present its tax-bill, and have the State to back its demand, as well as the Church. However, at the request of the selectmen, I condescended to make some such statement as this in writing: — " Know all men by these presents, that I, Henry Thoreau, do not wish to be regarded as a member of any incorporated society which I have not joined." This I gave to the town clerk; and he has it. The State, having thus learned that I did not wish to be regarded as a member of that church, has never made a like demand on me since; though it said that it must adhere to its original presumption that time. If I had known how to name them, I should then have signed off in detail from all the societies which I never signed on to; but I did not know where to find a complete list.

I have paid no poll-tax for six years. I was put into a jail once on this account, for one night; and, as I stood considering the walls of solid stone, two or three feet thick, the door of wood and iron, a foot thick, and the iron grating which strained the light, I could not help being struck with the foolishness of that institution which treated me as if I were mere flesh and blood and bones, to be locked up. I wondered that it should have concluded at length that this was the best use it could put me to, and had never thought to avail itself of my services in some way. I saw that, if there was a wall of stone between me and my townsmen, there was a still more difficult one to climb or break through, before they could get to be as free as I was. I did not for a moment feel confined, and the walls seemed a great waste of stone and mortar. I felt as if I alone of all my townsmen had paid my tax. They plainly did not know how to treat me, but behaved like persons who are underbred. In every threat and in every compliment there was a blunder; for they thought that my chief desire was to stand the other side of that stone wall. I could not but smile to see how industriously they locked the door on my meditations, which followed them out again without let or hindrance, and *they* were really all that was dangerous. As they could not reach me, they had resolved to punish my body; just as boys, if they cannot come at some person against whom they have a spite, will abuse his dog. I saw that the State was half-witted, that it was timid as a lone-woman with her silver spoons, and that it did not know its friends from its foes, and I lost all my remaining respect for it, and pitied it.

Thus the State never intentionally confronts a man's sense, intellectual or moral, but only his body, his senses. It is not armed with superior wit or honesty, but with superior physical strength. I was not born to be forced. I will breathe after my own fashion. Let us see who is the strongest. What force has a multitude? They only can force me who obey a higher law than I. They force me to become like themselves. I do not hear of *men* being *forced* to live this way or that by masses of men. What sort of life were that to live? When I meet a government which says to me, "Your money or your life," why should I be in haste to give it my money? It may be in a great strait, and not know what to do: I cannot help that. It must help itself; do as I do. It is not worth the while to snivel about it. I am not responsible for the successful working of the machinery of society. I am not the son of the engineer. I perceive that, when an acorn and a chestnut fall side by side, the one does not remain inert to make way for the other, but both obey their own laws, and spring and grow and flourish as best they can, till one, perchance, overshadows and destroys the other. If a plant cannot live according to its nature, it dies; and so a man.

The night in prison was novel and interesting enough. The prisoners in their shirt-sleeves were enjoying a chat and the evening air in the doorway, when I entered. But the jailer said, " Come, boys, it is time to lock up"; and so they dispersed, and I heard the sound of their steps returning into the hollow apartments. My room-mate was introduced to me by the jailer, as " a first-rate fellow and a clever man." When the door was locked, he showed me where to hang my hat, and how he managed matters there. The rooms were whitewashed once a month; and this one, at least, was the whitest, most simply furnished, and probably the neatest apartment in the town. He naturally wanted to know where I came from, and what brought me there; and, when I had told him, I asked him in my turn how he came there, presuming him to be an honest man, of course; and, as the world goes, I believe he was. " Why," said he, " they accuse me of burning a barn; but I never did it." As near as I could discover, he had probably gone to bed in a barn when drunk, and smoked his pipe there; and so a barn was burnt. He had the reputation of being a clever man, had been there some three months waiting for his trial to come on, and would have to wait as much longer; but he was quite domesticated and contented, since he got his board for nothing, and thought that he was well treated.

He occupied one window, and I the other; and I saw, that, if one stayed there long, his principal business would be to look out the window. I had soon read all the tracts that were left there, and examined where former prisoners had broken out, and where a grate had been sawed off, and heard the history of the various occupants of that room; for I found that even here there was a history and a gossip which never circulated beyond the walls of the jail. Probably this is the only house in the town where verses are composed, which are afterward printed in a circular form, but not published. I was shown quite a long list of verses which were composed by some young men who had been detected in an attempt to escape, who avenged themselves by singing them.

I pumped my fellow-prisoner as dry as I could, for fear I should never see him again; but at length he showed me which was my bed, and left me to blow out the lamp.

It was like travelling into a far country, such as I had never expected to behold, to lie there for one night. It seemed to me that I never had heard the town-clock strike before, nor the evening sounds of the village; for we slept with the windows open, which were inside the grating. It was to see my native village in the light of the Middle Ages, and our Concord was turned into a Rhine stream, and visions of knights and castles passed before me. They were the voices of old burghers that I heard in the streets. I was an involuntary spectator and auditor of whatever was done and said in the kitchen of the adjacent village-inn, — a wholly new and rare experience to me. It was a closer view of my native town. I was fairly inside of it. I never had seen its institutions before. This is one of its peculiar institutions; for it is a shire town. I began to comprehend what its inhabitants were about.

In the morning, our breakfasts were put through the hole in the door, in small oblong-square tin pans, made to fit, and holding a pint of chocolate, with brown bread, and an iron spoon. When they called for the vessels again, I was green enough to return what bread I had left; but my comrade seized it, and said that I should lay that up for lunch or dinner. Soon after he was let out to work at haying in a neighboring field, whither he went every day, and would not be back till noon; so he bade me good-day, saying that he doubted if he should see me again.

When I came out of prison, — for some one interfered, and paid that tax, — I did not perceive that great changes had taken place on the common, such as he observed who went in a youth, and emerged a tottering and gray-headed man; and yet a change had to my eyes come over the scene, — the town, and State, and country, — greater than any that mere time could effect. I saw yet more distinctly the State in which I lived. I saw to what extent the people among whom I lived could be trusted as good neighbors and friends; that their friendship was for summer weather only; that they did not greatly propose to do right; that they were a distinct race from me by their prejudices and superstitions, as the Chinamen and Malays are; that, in their sacrifices to humanity, they ran no risks, not even to their property; that, after all, they were not so noble but they treated the thief as he had treated them, and hoped, by a certain outward observance and a few prayers, and by walking in a particular straight though useless path from time to time, to save their souls. This may be to judge my neighbors harshly; for I believe that many of them are not aware that they have such an institution as the jail in their village.

It was formerly the custom in our village, when a poor debtor came out of jail, for his acquaintances to salute him, looking through their fingers, which were crossed to represent the grating of a jail window, "How do ye do?" My neighbors did not thus salute me, but first looked at me, and then at one another, as if I had returned from a long journey. I was put into jail as I was going to the shoemaker's to get a shoe which was mended. When I was let out the next morning, I proceeded to finish my errand, and having put on my mended shoe, joined a huckleberry party, who were impatient to put themselves under my conduct; and in half an hour, — for the horse was soon tackled, — was in the midst of a huckleberry field, on one of our highest hills, two miles off, and then the State was nowhere to be seen.

This is the whole history of " My Prisons."

I have never declined paying the highway tax, because I am as desirous of being a good neighbor as I am of being a bad subject; and, as for supporting schools, I am doing my part to educate my fellow-countrymen now. It is for no particular item in the tax-bill that I refuse to pay it. I simply wish to refuse allegiance to the State, to withdraw and stand aloof from it effectually. I do not care to trace the course of my dollar, if I could, till it buys a man or a musket to shoot one with, — the dollar is innocent, — but I am concerned to trace the effects of my allegiance. In fact, I quietly declare war with the State, after my fashion, though I will still make what use and get what advantage of her I can, as is usual in such cases.

If others pay the tax which is demanded of me, from a sympathy with the State, they do but what they have already done in their own case, or rather they abet injustice to a greater extent than the State requires. If they pay the tax from a mistaken interest in the individual taxed, to save his property, or prevent his going to jail, it is because they have not considered wisely how far they let their private feelings interfere with the public good.

This, then, is my position at present. But one cannot be too much on his guard in such a case, lest his action be biassed by obstinacy, or an undue regard for the opinions of men. Let him see that he does only what belongs to himself and to the hour.

I think sometimes, Why, this people mean well; they are only ignorant; they would do better if they knew how: why give your neighbors this pain to treat you as they are not inclined to? But I think again, this is no reason why I should do as they do, or permit others to suffer much greater pain of a different kind. Again, I sometimes say to myself, When many millions of men, without heat, without ill will, without personal feeling of any kind, demand of you a few shillings only, without the possibility, such is their constitution, of retracting or altering their present demand, and without the possibility, on your side, of appeal to any other millions, why expose yourself to this overwhelming brute force? You do not resist cold and hunger, the winds and the waves, thus obstinately; you quietly submit to a thousand similar necessities. You do not put your head into the fire. But just in proportion as I regard this as not wholly a brute force, but partly a human force, and consider that I have relations to those millions as to so many millions of men, and not of mere brute or inanimate things, I see that appeal is possible, first and instantaneously, from them to the Maker of them, and, secondly, from them to themselves. But, if I put my head deliberately into the fire, there is no appeal to fire or to the Maker of fire, and I have only myself to blame. If I could convince myself that I have any right to be satisfied with men as they are, and to treat them accordingly, and not according, in some respects, to my requisitions and expectations of what they and I ought to be, then, like a good Mussulman and fatalist, I should endeavor to be satisfied with things as they are, and say it is the will of God. And, above all, there is this difference between resisting this and a purely brute or natural force, that I can resist this with some effect; but I cannot expect like Orpheus, to change the nature of the rocks and trees and beasts.

I do not wish to quarrel with any man or nation. I do not wish to split hairs, to make fine distinctions, or set myself up as better than my neighbors. I seek rather, I may say, even an excuse for conforming to the laws of the land. I am but too ready to conform to them. Indeed, I have reason to suspect myself on this head; and each year, as the tax-gatherer comes round, I find myself disposed to review the acts and position of the general and State governments, and the spirit of the people, to discover a pretext for conformity.

> " We must affect our country as our parents
> And if at any time we alienate
> Our love or industry from doing it honor,
> We must respect effects and teach the soul
> Matter of conscience and religion,
> And not desire of rule or benefit.''

I believe that the State will soon be able to take all my work of this sort out of my hands, and then I shall be no better a patriot than my fellow-countrymen. Seen from a lower point of view, the Constitution, with all its faults, is very good; the law and the courts are very respectable; even this State and this American government are, in many respects, very admirable and rare things, to be thankful for, such as a great many have described them; but seen from a point of view a little higher, they are what I have described them; seen from a higher still, and the highest, who shall say what they are, or that they are worth looking at or thinking of at all?

However, the government does not concern me much, and I shall bestow the fewest possible thoughts on it. It is not many moments that I live under a government,

even in this world.   If a man is thought-free, fancy-
free, imagination-free, that which *is not* never for a long
time appearing *to be* to him, unwise rulers or reformers
cannot fatally interrupt him.

I know that most men think differently from myself;
ut those whose lives are by profession devoted to the
study of these or kindred subjects, content me as little as
any.   Statesmen and legislators, standing so completely
within the institution, never distinctly and nakedly behold it.   They speak of moving society, but have no
resting-place without it.   They may be men of a certain
experience and discrimination, and have no doubt invented ingenious and even useful systems, for which we
sincerely thank them ; but all their wit and usefulness
lie within certain not very wide limits.   They are wont
to forget that the world is not governed by policy and
expediency.   Webster never goes behind government,
and so cannot speak with authority about it.   His words
are wisdom to those legislators who contemplate no
essential reform in the existing government ; but for
thinkers, and those who legislate for all time, he never
once glances at the subject.   I know of those whose
serene and wise speculations on this theme would soon
reveal the limits of his mind's range and hospitality.
Yet, compared with the cheap professions of most reformers, and the still cheaper wisdom and eloquence of
politicians in general, his are almost the only sensible
and valuable words, and we thank Heaven for him.
Comparatively, he is always strong, original, and, above
all, practical.   Still his quality is not wisdom, but prudence.   The lawyer's truth is not Truth, but consistency,
or a consistent expediency.   Truth is always in harmony
with herself, and is not concerned chiefly to reveal the

justice that may consist with wrong-doing. He well deserves to be called, as he has been called, the Defender of the Constitution. There are really no blows to be given by him but defensive ones. He is not a leader, but a follower. His leaders are the men of '87. " I have never made an effort," he says, " and never propose to make an effort; I have never countenanced an effort, and never mean to countenance an effort, to disturb the arrangement as originally made, by which the various States came into the Union." Still thinking of the sanction which the Constitution gives to slavery, he says, " Because it was a part of the original compact, — let it stand." Notwithstanding his special acuteness and ability, he is unable to take a fact out of its merely political relations, and behold it as it lies absolutely to be disposed of by the intellect, — what, for instance, it behooves a man to do here in America to-day with regard to slavery, but ventures, or is driven, to make some such desperate answer as the following, while professing to speak absolutely, and as a private man, — from which what new and singular code of social duties might be inferred? " The manner," says he, " in which the governments of those States where slavery exists are to regulate it, is for their own consideration, under their responsibility to their constituents, to the general laws of propriety, humanity, and justice, and to God. Associations formed elsewhere, springing from a feeling of humanity, or any other cause, have nothing whatever to do with it. They have never received any encouragement from me, and they never will." *

They who know of no purer sources of truth, who

* These extracts have been inserted since the Lecture was read.

have traced up its stream no higher, stand, and wisely
stand, by the Bible and the Constitution, and drink at it
there with reverence and humility ; but they who behold
where it comes trickling into this lake or that pool, gird
up their loins once more, and continue their pilgrimage
toward its fountain-head.

No man with a genius for legislation has appeared in
America. They are rare in the history of the world.
There are orators, politicians, and eloquent men, by the
thousand; but the speaker has not yet opened his mouth
to speak, who is capable of settling the much-vexed
questions of the day. We love eloquence for its own
sake, and not for any truth which it may utter, or any
heroism it may inspire. Our legislators have not yet
learned the comparative value of free-trade and of freedom, of union, and of rectitude, to a nation. They have
no genius or talent for comparatively humble questions
of taxation and finance, commerce and manufactures and
agriculture. If we were left solely to the wordy wit of
legislators in Congress for our guidance, uncorrected by
the seasonable experience and the effectual complaints
of the people, America would not long retain her rank
among the nations. For eighteen hundred years, though
perchance I have no right to say it, the New Testament
has been written ; yet where is the legislator who has
wisdom and practical talent enough to avail himself of
the light which it sheds on the science of legislation ?

The authority of government, even such as I am willing to submit to, — for I will cheerfully obey those who
know and can do better than I, and in many things even
those who neither know nor can do so well, — is still an
impure one: to be strictly just, it must have the sanction
and consent of the governed. It can have no pure right

over my person and property but what I concede to it.
The progress from an absolute to a limited monarchy,
from a limited monarchy to a democracy, is a progress
toward a true respect for the individual.   Even the
Chinese philosopher was wise enough to regard the individual as the basis of the empire.   Is a democracy, such
as we know it, the last improvement possible in government?   Is it not possible to take a step further towards
recognizing and organizing the rights of man?   There
will never be a really free and enlightened State, until
the State comes to recognize the individual as a higher
and independent power, from which all its own power
and authority are derived, and treats him accordingly. I
please myself with imagining a State at last which can
afford to be just to all men, and to treat the individual
with respect as a neighbor; which even would not think
it inconsistent with its own repose, if a few were to live
aloof from it, not meddling with it, nor embraced by it,
who fulfilled all the duties of neighbors and fellow-men.
A State which bore this kind of fruit, and suffered it to
drop off as fast as it ripened, would prepare the way for
a still more perfect and glorious State, which also I have
imagined, but not yet anywhere seen.

A PLEA FOR CAPTAIN JOHN BROWN.*

I TRUST that you will pardon me for being here. I do not wish to force my thoughts upon you, but I feel forced myself. Little as I know of Captain Brown, I would fain do my part to correct the tone and the statements of the newspapers, and of my countrymen generally, respecting his character and actions. It costs us nothing to be just. We can at least express our sympathy with, and admiration of, him and his companions, and that is what I now propose to do.

First, as to his history. I will endeavor to omit, as much as possible, what you have already read. I need not describe his person to you, for probably most of you have seen and will not soon forget him. I am told that his grandfather, John Brown, was an officer in the Revolution; that he himself was born in Connecticut about the beginning of this century, but early went with his father to Ohio. I heard him say that his father was a contractor who furnished beef to the army there, in the war of 1812; that he accompanied him to the camp, and assisted him in that employment, seeing a good deal of military life, — more, perhaps, than if he had been a soldier; for he was often present at the councils of the officers. Especially, he learned by experience how armies are supplied

* Read to the citizens of Concord, Mass., Sunday Evening, October 30, 1859.

and maintained in the field, — a work which, he observed, requires at least as much experience and skill as to lead them in battle.   He said that few persons had any conception of the cost, even the pecuniary cost, of firing a single bullet in war.   He saw enough, at any rate, to disgust him with a military life; indeed, to excite in him a great abhorrence of it; so much so, that though he was tempted by the offer of some petty office in the army, when he was about eighteen, he not only declined that, but he also refused to train when warned, and was fined for it.   He then resolved that he would never have anything to do with any war, unless it were a war for liberty.

When the troubles in Kansas began, he sent several of his sons thither to strengthen the party of the Free State men, fitting them out with such weapons as he had; telling them that if the troubles should increase, and there should be need of him, he would follow, to assist them with his hand and counsel.   This, as you all know, he soon after did; and it was through his agency, far more than any other's, that Kansas was made free.

For a part of his life he was a surveyor, and at one time he was engaged in wool-growing, and he went to Europe as an agent about that business.   There, as everywhere, he had his eyes about him, and made many original observations.   He said, for instance, that he saw why the soil of England was so rich, and that of Germany (I think it was) so poor, and he thought of writing to some of the crowned heads about it.   It was because in England the peasantry live on the soil which they cultivate, but in Germany they are gathered into villages, at night. It is a pity that he did not make a book of his observations.

I should say that he was an old-fashioned man in

respect for the Constitution, and his faith in the permanence of this Union. Slavery he deemed to be wholly opposed to these, and he was its determined foe.

He was by descent and birth a New England farmer, a man of great common-sense, deliberate and practical as that class is, and tenfold more so. He was like the best of those who stood at Concord Bridge once, on Lexington Common, and on Bunker Hill, only he was firmer and higher principled than any that I have chanced to hear of as there. It was no abolition lecturer that converted him. Ethan Allen and Stark, with whom he may in some respects be compared, were rangers in a lower and less important field. They could bravely face their country's foes, but he had the courage to face his country herself, when she was in the wrong. A Western writer says, to account for his escape from so many perils, that he was concealed under a "rural exterior"; as if, in that prairie land, a hero should, by good rights, wear a citizen's dress only.

He did not go to the college called Harvard, good old Alma Mater as she is. He was not fed on the pap that is there furnished. As he phrased it, "I know no more of grammar than one of your calves." But he went to the great university of the West, where he sedulously pursued the study of Liberty, for which he had early betrayed a fondness, and having taken many degrees, he finally commenced the public practice of Humanity in Kansas, as you all know. Such were *his humanities* and not any study of grammar. He would have left a Greek accent slanting the wrong way, and righted up a falling man.

He was one of that class of whom we hear a great deal, but, for the most part, see nothing at all, — the

Puritans. It would be in vain to kill him. He died lately in the time of Cromwell, but he reappeared here. Why should he not? Some of the Puritan stock are said to have come over and settled in New England. They were a class that did something else than celebrate their forefathers' day, and eat parched corn in remembrance of that time. They were neither Democrats nor Republicans, but men of simple habits, straightforward, prayerful; not thinking much of rulers who did not fear God, not making many compromises, nor seeking after available candidates.

"In his camp," as one has recently written, and as I have myself heard him state, "he permitted no profanity; no man of loose morals was suffered to remain there, unless, indeed, as a prisoner of war. 'I would rather,' said he, 'have the small-pox, yellow-fever, and cholera, all together in my camp, than a man without principle. . . . . It is a mistake, sir, that our people make, when they think that bullies are the best fighters, or that they are the fit men to oppose these Southerners. Give me men of good principles, — God-fearing men, — men who respect themselves, and with a dozen of them I will oppose any hundred such men as these Buford ruffians.'" He said that if one offered himself to be a soldier under him, who was forward to tell what he could or would do, if he could only get sight of the enemy, he had but little confidence in him.

He was never able to find more than a score or so of recruits whom he would accept, and only about a dozen, among them his sons, in whom he had perfect faith. When he was here, some years ago, he showed to a few a little manuscript book, — his "orderly book" I think he called it, — containing the names of his company in Kansas, and the rules by which they bound themselves; and he stated that several of them had already sealed the contract with their blood. When some one remarked that, with the addition of a chaplain, it would have been a perfect Cromwellian troop, he observed that he would have been glad to add a chaplain to the list, if he could have found one who could fill that office worthily. It is easy enough to find one for the United States army. I believe that he had prayers in his camp morning and evening, nevertheless.

He was a man of Spartan habits, and at sixty was scrupulous about his diet at your table, excusing himself by saying that he must eat sparingly and fare hard, as became a soldier, or one who was fitting himself for difficult enterprises, a life of exposure.

A man of rare common-sense and directness of speech, as of action; a transcendentalist above all, a man of ideas and principles, — that was what distinguished him. Not yielding to a whim or transient impulse, but carrying out the purpose of a life. I noticed that he did not overstate anything, but spoke within bounds. I remember, particularly, how, in his speech here, he referred to what his family had suffered in Kansas, without ever giving the least vent to his pent-up fire. It was a volcano with an ordinary chimney-flue. Also referring to the deeds of certain Border Ruffians, he said, rapidly paring away his speech, like an experienced soldier, keeping a reserve of force and meaning, "They had a perfect right to be hung." He was not in the least a rhetorician, was not talking to Buncombe or his constituents anywhere, had no need to invent anything but to tell the simple truth, and communicate his own resolution; therefore he appeared incomparably strong,

and eloquence in Congress and elsewhere seemed to me
at a discount.   It was like the speeches of Cromwell
compared with those of an ordinary king.

As for his tact and prudence, I will merely say, that
at a time when scarcely a man from the Free States
was able to reach Kansas by any direct route, at least
without having his arms taken from him, he, carrying
what imperfect guns and other weapons he could collect,
openly and slowly drove an ox-cart through Missouri,
apparently in the capacity of a surveyor, with his surveying compass exposed in it, and so passed unsuspected,
and had ample opportunity to learn the designs of the
enemy.   For some time after his arrival he still followed
the same profession.   When, for instance, he saw a knot
of the ruffians on the prairie, discussing, of course, the single topic which then occupied their minds, he would, perhaps, take his compass and one of his sons, and proceed to
run an imaginary line right through the very spot on
which that conclave had assembled, and when he came
up to them, he would naturally pause and have some talk
with them, learning their news, and, at last, all their
plans perfectly; and having thus completed his real sur-
vey he would resume his imaginary one, and run on his
line till he was out of sight.

When I expressed surprise that he could live in Kansas at all, with a price set upon his head, and so large a
number, including the authorities, exasperated against
him, he accounted for it by saying, "It is perfectly well
understood that I will not be taken."   Much of the time
for some years he has had to skulk in swamps, suffering
from poverty and from sickness, which was the consequence of exposure, befriended only by Indians and
few whites.   But though it might be known that he

was lurking in a particular swamp, his foes commonly did not care to go in after him. He could even come out into a town where there were more Border Ruffians than Free State men, and transact some business, without delaying long, and yet not be molested; for, said he, "No little handful of men were willing to undertake it, and a large body could not be got together in season."

As for his recent failure, we do not know the facts about it. It was evidently far from being a wild and desperate attempt. His enemy, Mr. Vallandigham, is compelled to say, that "it was among the best planned and executed conspiracies that ever failed."

Not to mention his other successes, was it a failure, or did it show a want of good management, to deliver from bondage a dozen human beings, and walk off with them by broad daylight, for weeks if not months, at a leisurely pace, through one State after another, for half the length of the North, conspicuous to all parties, with a price set upon his head, going into a court-room on his way and telling what he had done, thus convincing Missouri that it was not profitable to try to hold slaves in his neighborhood? — and this, not because the government menials were lenient, but because they were afraid of him.

Yet he did not attribute his success, foolishly, to "his star," or to any magic. He said, truly, that the reason why such greatly superior numbers quailed before him was, as one of his prisoners confessed, because they *lacked a cause,* — a kind of armor which he and his party never lacked. When the time came, few men were found willing to lay down their lives in defence of what they knew to be wrong; they did not like that this should be their last act in this world

But to make haste to *his* last act, and its effects.

The newspapers seem to ignore, or perhaps are really ingorant of the fact, that there are at least as many as two or three individuals to a town throughout the North who think much as the present speaker does about him and his enterprise. I do not hesitate to say that they are an important and growing party. We aspire to be something more than stupid and timid chattels, pretending to read history and our Bibles, but desecrating every house and every day we breathe in. Perhaps anxious politicians may prove that only seventeen white men and five negroes were concerned in the late enterprise; but their very anxiety to prove this might suggest to themselves that all is not told. Why do they still dodge the truth? They are so anxious because of a dim consciousness of the fact, which they do not distinctly face, that at least a million of the free inhabitants of the United States would have rejoiced if it had succeeded. They at most only criticise the tactics. Though we wear no crape, the thought of that man's position and probable fate is spoiling many a man's day here at the North for other thinking. If any one who has seen him here can pursue successfully any other train of thought, I do not know what he is made of. If there is any such who gets his usual allowance of sleep, I will warrant him to fatten easily under any circumstances which do not touch his body or purse. I put a piece of paper and a pencil under my pillow, and when I could not sleep, I wrote in the dark.

On the whole, my respect for my fellow-men, except as one may outweigh a million, is not being increased these days. I have noticed the cold-blooded way in which newspaper writers and men generally speak of this event, as if an ordinary malefactor, though one of unusual "pluck," — as the Governor of Virginia is reported to have said, using the language of the cock-pit, "the gamest man he ever saw," — had been caught, and were about to be hung. He was not dreaming of his foes when the governor thought he looked so brave. It turns what sweetness I have to gall, to hear, or hear of, the remarks of some of my neighbors. When we heard at first that he was dead, one of my townsmen observed that "he died as the fool dieth"; which, pardon me, for an instant suggested a likeness in him dying to my neighbor living. Others, craven-hearted, said disparagingly, that "he threw his life away," because he resisted the government. Which way have they thrown *their* lives, pray? — such as would praise a man for attacking singly an ordinary band of thieves or murderers. I hear another ask, Yankee-like, "What will he gain by it?" as if he expected to fill his pockets by this enterprise. Such a one has no idea of gain but in this worldly sense. If it does not lead to a "surprise" party, if he does not get a new pair of boots, or a vote of thanks, it must be a failure. "But he won't gain anything by it." Well, no, I don't suppose he could get four-and-sixpence a day for being hung, take the year round; but then he stands a chance to save a considerable part of his soul, — and *such* a soul! — when *you* do not. No doubt you can get more in your market for a quart of milk than for a quart of blood, but that is not the market that heroes carry their blood to.

Such do not know that like the seed is the fruit, and that, in the moral world, when good seed is planted, good fruit is inevitable, and does not depend on our watering and cultivating; that when you plant, or bury, a hero in his field, a crop of heroes is sure to spring up. This is a seed of such force and vitality, that it does not ask our leave to germinate.

The momentary charge at Balaclava, in obedience to a blundering command, proving what a perfect machine the soldier is, has, properly enough, been celebrated by a poet laureate; but the steady, and for the most part successful, charge of this man, for some years, against the legions of Slavery, in obedience to an infinitely higher command, is as much more memorable than that, as an intelligent and conscientious man is superior to a machine.   Do you think that that will go unsung?

"Served him right," — "A dangerous man," — "He is undoubtedly insane."   So they proceed to live their sane, and wise, and altogether admirable lives, reading their Plutarch a little, but chiefly pausing at that feat of Putnam, who was let down into a wolf's den; and in this wise they nourish themselves for brave and patriotic deeds some time or other.   The Tract Society could afford to print that story of Putnam.   You might open the district schools with the reading of it, for there is nothing about Slavery or the Church in it; unless it occurs to the reader that some pastors are *wolves* in sheep's clothing.   "The American Board of Commissioners for Foreign Missions" even, might dare to protest against *that* wolf.   I have heard of boards, and of American boards, but it chances that I never heard of this particular lumber till lately.   And yet I hear of Northern men, and women, and children, by families, buying a "life membership" in such societies as these. A life-membership in the grave!   You can get buried cheaper than that.

Our foes are in our midst and all about us.   There is

hardly a house but is divided against itself, for our foe is
the all but universal woodenness of both head and heart,
the want of vitality in man, which is the effect of our vice;
and hence are begotten fear, superstition, bigotry, perse-
cution, and slavery of all kinds. We are mere figure-
heads upon a hulk, with livers in the place of hearts.
The curse is the worship of idols, which at length changes
the worshipper into a stone image himself; and the
New-Englander is just as much an idolater as the Hindoo. This man was an exception, for he did not set up
even a political graven image between him and his God.

A church that can never have done with excommuni-
cating Christ while it exists! Away with your broad
and flat churches, and your narrow and tall churches!
Take a step forward, and invent a new style of out-
houses. Invent a salt that will save you, and defend
our nostrils.

The modern Christian is a man who has consented to
say all the prayers in the liturgy, provided you will let
him go straight to bed and sleep quietly afterward. All
his prayers begin with "Now I lay me down to sleep,"
and he is forever looking forward to the time when he
shall go to his "*long* rest." He has consented to perform certain old-established charities, too, after a fashion,
but he does not wish to hear of any new-fangled ones; he
does n't wish to have any supplementary articles added
to the contract, to fit it to the present time. He shows
the whites of his eyes on the Sabbath, and the blacks all
the rest of the week. The evil is not merely a stagnation of blood, but a stagnation of spirit. Many, no
doubt, are well disposed, but sluggish by constitution and
by habit, and they cannot conceive of a man who is act
uated by higher motives than they are. Accordingly

they pronounce this man insane, for they know that *they* could never act as he does, as long ás they are themselves.

We dream of foreign countries, of other times and races of men, placing them at a distance in history or space; but let some significant event like the present occur in our midst, and we discover, often, this distance and this strangeness between us and our nearest neighbors. *They* are our Austrias, and Chinas, and South Sea Islands. Our crowded society becomes well spaced all at once, clean and handsome to the eye, — a city of magnificent distances. We discover why it was that we never got beyónd compliments and surfaces with them before; we become aware of as many versts between us and them as there are between a wandering Tartar and a Chinese town. The thoughtful man becomes a hermit in the thoroughfares of the market-place. Impassable seas suddenly find their level between us, or dumb steppes stretch themselves out there. It is the difference of constitution, of intelligence, and faith, and not streams and mountains, that make the true and impassable boundaries between individuals and between states. None but the like-minded can come plenipotentiary to our court.

I read all the newspapers I could get within a week after this event, and I do not remember in them a single expression of sympathy for these men. I have since seen one noble statement, in a Boston paper, not editorial Some voluminous sheets decided not to print the full report of Brown's words to the exclusion of other matter. It was as if a publisher should reject the manuscript of the New Testament, and print Wilson's last speech. The same journal which contained this pregnant news, was chiefly filled, in parallel columns, with the reports of the political conventions that were being held. But the descent to them was too steep. They should have been spared this contrast, — been printed in an extra, at least. To turn from the voices and deeds of earnest men to the *cackling* of political conventions! Office-seekers and speech-makers, who do not so much as lay an honest egg, but wear their breasts bare upon an egg of chalk! Their great game is the game of straws, or rather that universal aboriginal game of the platter, at which the Indians cried *hub, bub!* Exclude the reports of religious and political conventions, and publish the words of a living man.

But I object not so much to what they have omitted, as to what they have inserted. Even the *Liberator* called it "a misguided, wild, and apparently insane — effort." As for the herd of newspapers and magazines, I do not chance to know an editor in the country who will deliberately print anything which he knows will ultimately and permanently reduce the number of his subscribers. They do not believe that it would be expedient. How then can they print truth? If we do not say pleasant things, they argue, nobody will attend to us. And so they do like some travelling auctioneers, who sing an obscene song, in order to draw a crowd around them. Republican editors, obliged to get their sentences ready for the morning edition, and accustomed to look at everything by the twilight of politics, express no admiration, nor true sorrow even, but call these men "deluded fanatics," — "mistaken men," — "insane," or "crazed." It suggests what a *sane* set of editors we are blessed with, *not* "mistaken men"; who know very well on which side their bread is buttered, at least.

A man does a brave and humane deed, and

all sides, we hear people and parties declaring, "I did n't do it, nor countenance *him* to do it, in any conceivable way. It can't be fairly inferred from my past career." I, for one, am not interested to hear you define your position. I don't know that I ever was, or ever shall be. I think it is mere egotism, or impertinent at this time. Ye need n't take so much pains to wash your skirts of him. No intelligent man will ever be convinced that he was any creature of yours. He went and came, as he himself informs us, "under the auspices of John Brown and nobody else." The Republican party does not perceive how many his *failure* will make to vote more correctly than they would have them. They have counted the votes of Pennsylvania & Co., but they have not correctly counted Captain Brown's vote. He has taken the wind out of their sails, — the little wind they had, — and they may as well lie to and repair.

What though he did not belong to your clique! Though you may not approve of his method or his principles, recognize his magnanimity. Would you not like to claim kindredship with him in that, though in no other thing he is like, or likely, to you? Do you think that you would lose your reputation so? What you lost at the spile, you would gain at the bung.

If they do not mean all this, then they do not speak the truth, and say what they mean. They are simply at their old tricks still.

"It was always conceded to him," *says one who calls him crazy,* "that he was a conscientious man, very modest in his demeanor, apparently inoffensive, until the subject of Slavery was introduced, when he would exhibit a feeling of indignation unparalleled."

The slave-ship is on her way, crowded with its dying

victims; new cargoes are being added in mid-ocean a small crew of slaveholders, countenanced by a large body of passengers, is smothering four millions under the hatches, and yet the politician asserts that the only proper way by which deliverance is to be obtained, is by "the quiet diffusion of the sentiments of humanity," without any "outbreak." As if the sentiments of humanity were ever found unaccompanied by its deeds, and you could disperse them, all finished to order, the pure article, as easily as water with a watering-pot, and so lay the dust. What is that that I hear cast overboard? The bodies of the dead that have found deliverance. That is the way we are "diffusing" humanity, and its sentiments with it.

Prominent and influential editors, accustomed to deal with politicians, men of an infinitely lower grade, say, in their ignorance, that he acted "on the principle of revenge." They do not know the man. They must enlarge themselves to conceive of him. I have no doubt that the time will come when they will begin to see him as he was. They have got to conceive of a man of faith and of religious principle, and not a politician or an Indian; of a man who did not wait till he was personally interfered with or thwarted in some harmless business before he gave his life to the cause of the oppressed.

If Walker may be considered the representative of the South, I wish I could say that Brown was the representative of the North. He was a superior man. He did not value his bodily life in comparison with ideal things. He did not recognize unjust human laws, but resisted them as he was bid. For once we are lifted out of the trivialness and dust of politics into the region of truth and manhood. No man in America has ever stood up

so persistently and effectively for the dignity of human
nature, knowing himself for a man, and the equal of
any and all governments.   In that sense he was the most
American of us all.   He needed no babbling lawyer,
making false issues, to defend him.   He was more than
a match for all the judges that American voters, or office-
holders of whatever grade, can create.   He could not
have been tried by a jury of his peers, because his peers
did not exist.   When a man stands up serenely against
the condemnation and vengeance of mankind, rising
above them literally *by a whole body*, — even though he
were of late the vilest murderer, who has settled that
matter with himself, — the spectacle is a sublime one, —
did n't ye know it, ye *Liberators*, ye *Tribunes*, ye *Republicans?* — and we become criminal in comparison.
Do yourselves the honor to recognize him.   He needs
none of your respect.

As for the Democratic journals, they are not human
enough to affect me at all.   I do not feel indignation at
anything they may say.

I am aware that I anticipate a little, — that he was still,
at the last accounts, alive in the hands of his foes;
but that being the case, I have all along found myself
thinking and speaking of him as physically dead.

I do not believe in erecting statues to those who still
live in our hearts, whose bones have not yet crumbled
in the earth around us, but I would rather see the statue
of Captain Brown in the Massachusetts State-House
yard, than that of any other man whom I know.   I rejoice that I live in this age, that I am his contemporary.

What a contrast, when we turn to that political party
which is so anxiously shuffling him and his plot out of
its way, and looking around for some available slave

holder, perhaps, to be its candidate, at least for one who will execute the Fugitive Slave Law, and all those other unjust laws which he took up arms to annul!

Insane! A father and six sons, and one son-in-law, and several more men besides, — as many at least as twelve disciples, — all struck with insanity at once; while the same tyrant holds with a firmer gripe than ever his four millions of slaves, and a thousand sane editors, his abettors, are saving their country and their bacon! Just as insane were his efforts in Kansas. Ask the tyrant who is his most dangerous foe, the sane man or the insane? Do the thousands who know him best, who have rejoiced at his deeds in Kansas, and have afforded him material aid there, think him insane? Such a use of this word is a mere trope with most who persist in using it, and I have no doubt that many of the rest have already in silence retracted their words.

Read his admirable answers to Mason and others. How they are dwarfed and defeated by the contrast! On the one side, half-brutish, half-timid questioning; on the other, truth, clear as lightning, crashing into their obscene temples. They are made to stand with Pilate, and Gesler, and the Inquisition. How ineffectual their speech and action! and what a void their silence! They are but helpless tools in this great work. It was no human power that gathered them about this preacher.

What have Massachusetts and the North sent a few *sane* representatives to Congress for, of late years? — to declare with effect what kind of sentiments? All their speeches put together and boiled down, — and probably they themselves will confess it, — do not match for manly directness and force, and for simple truth, the few casual remarks of crazy John Brown, on the floor of the Harper's Ferry engine-house, — that man whom you are about to hang, to send to the other world, though not to represent *you* there.   No, he was not our representative in any sense.   He was too fair a specimen of a man to represent the like of us.   Who, then, *were* his constituents?   If you read his words understandingly you will find out.   In his case there is no idle eloquence, no made, nor maiden speech, no compliments to the oppressor.   Truth is his inspirer, and earnestness the polisher of his sentences.   He could afford to lose his Sharpe's rifles, while he retained his faculty of speech, — a Sharpe's rifle of infinitely surer and longer range.

And the New York *Herald* reports the conversation *verbatim /* It does not know of what undying words it is made the vehicle.

I have no respect for the penetration of any man who can read the report of that conversation, and still call the principal in it insane.   It has the ring of a saner sanity than an ordinary discipline and habits of life, than an ordinary organization, secure.   Take any sentence of it, — " Any questions that I can honorably answer, I will ; not otherwise.   So far as I am myself concerned, I have told everything truthfully.   I value my word, sir." The few who talk about his vindictive spirit, while they really admire his heroism, have no test by which to detect a noble man, no amalgam to combine with his pure gold.   They mix their own dross with it.

It is a relief to turn from these slanders to the testimony of his more truthful, but frightened jailers and hangmen.   Governor Wise speaks far more justly and appreciatingly of him than any Northern editor, or politician, or public personage, that I chance to have heard from. I know that you can afford to hear him again on this subject. He says : " They are themselves mistaken who take him to be a madman. . . . . He is cool, collected, and indomitable, and it is but just to him to say, that he was humane to his prisoners. . . . . And he inspired me with great trust in his integrity as a man of truth. He is a fanatic, vain and garrulous," (I leave that part to Mr. Wise,) " but firm, truthful, and intelligent. His men, too, who survive, are like him. . . . . Colonel Washington says that he was the coolest and firmest man he ever saw in defying danger and death. With one son dead by his side, and another shot through, he felt the pulse of his dying son with one hand, and held his rifle with the other, and commanded his men with the utmost composure, encouraging them to be firm, and to sell their lives as dear as they could. Of the three white prisoners, Brown, Stephens, and Coppic, it was hard to say which was most firm."

Almost the first Northern men whom the slaveholder has learned to respect !

The testimony of Mr. Vallandigham, though less valuable, is of the same purport, that " it is vain to underrate either the man or his conspiracy. . . . . He is the farthest possible removed from the ordinary ruffian, fanatic, or madman."

" All is quiet at Harper's Ferry," say the journals. What is the character of that calm which follows when the law and the slaveholder prevail ? I regard this event as a touchstone designed to bring out, with glaring distinctness, the character of this government. We needed to be thus assisted to see it by the light of history. It needed to see itself. When a government puts forth its strength on the side of injustice, as ours tc maintain slavery and kill the liberators of the slave, it reveals itself a merely brute force, or worse, a demoniacal force.   It is the head of the Plug-Uglies.   It is more manifest than ever that tyranny rules.   I see this government to be effectually allied with France and Austria in oppressing mankind.   There sits a tyrant holding fettered four millions of slaves ; here comes their heroic liberator.   This most hypocritical and diabolical government looks up from its seat on the gasping four millions, and inquires with an assumption of innocence : " What do you assault me for ?   Am I not an honest man ?   Cease agitation on this subject, or I will make a slave of you, too, or else hang you."

We talk about a *representative* government ; but what a monster of a government is that where the noblest faculties of the mind, and the *whole* heart, are not *represented*.   A semi-human tiger or ox, stalking over the earth, with its heart taken out and the top of its brain shot away.   Heroes have fought well on their stumps when their legs were shot off, but I never heard of any good done by such a government as that.

The only government that I recognize, — and it matters not how few are at the head of it, or how small its army, — is that power that establishes justice in the land, never that which establishes injustice.   What shall we think of a government to which all the truly brave and just men in the land are enemies, standing between it and those whom it oppresses ?   A government that pretends to be Christian and crucifies a million Christs every day !

Treason !   Where does such treason take its rise ?   I cannot help thinking of you as you deserve, ye governments. Can you dry up the fountains of thought ?   High treason, when it is resistance to tyranny here below, has its origin in, and is first committed by, the power that makes and forever recreates man. When you have caught and hung all these human rebels, you have accomplished nothing but your own guilt, for you have not struck at the fountain-head. You presume to contend with a foe against whom West Point cadets and rifled cannon *point* not. Can all the art of the cannon-founder tempt matter to turn against its maker? Is the form in which the founder thinks he casts it more essential than the constitution of it and of himself?

The United States have a coffle of four millions of slaves. They are determined to keep them in this condition; and Massachusetts is one of the confederated overseers to prevent their escape. Such are not all the inhabitants of Massachusetts, but such are they who rule and are obeyed here. It was Massachusetts, as well as Virginia, that put down this insurrection at Harper's Ferry. She sent the marines there, and she will have *to pay the penalty of her sin.*

Suppose that there is a society in this State that out of its own purse and magnanimity saves all the fugitive slaves that run to us, and protects our colored fellow-citizens, and leaves the other work to the government, so-called. Is not that government fast losing its occupation, and becoming contemptible to mankind? If private men are obliged to perform the offices of government, to protect the weak and dispense justice, then the government becomes only a hired man, or clerk, to perform menial or indifferent services. Of course, that is but the shadow of a government whose existence necessitates a Vigilant Committee. What should we think of the Oriental Cadi even, behind whom worked in secret a vigilant committee? But such is the character of our Northern States generally; each has its Vigilant Committee. And, to a certain extent, these crazy governments recognize and accept this relation. They say, virtually, " We'll be glad to work for you on these terms, only don't make a noise about it." And thus the government, its salary being insured, withdraws into the back shop, taking the Constitution with it, and bestows most of its labor on repairing that. When I hear it at work sometimes, as I go by, it reminds me, at best, of those farmers who in winter contrive to turn a penny by following the coopering business. And what kind of spirit is their barrel made to hold? They speculate in stocks, and bore holes in mountains, but they are not competent to lay out even a decent highway. The only *free* road, the Underground Railroad, is owned and managed by the Vigilant Committee. *They* have tunnelled under the whole breadth of the land. Such a government is losing its power and respectability as surely as water runs out of a leaky vessel, and is held by one that can contain it.

I hear many condemn these men because they were so few. When were the good and the brave ever in a majority? Would you have had him wait till that time came? — till you and I came over to him? The very fact that he had no rabble or troop of hirelings about him would alone distinguish him from ordinary heroes. His company was small indeed, because few could be found worthy to pass muster. Each one who there laid down his life for the poor and oppressed was a picked man, culled out of many thousands, if not millions; apparently a man of principle, of rare courage, and devoted humanity; ready to sacrifice his life at any moment for the benefit of his fellow-man. It may be doubted if there were as many more their equals in these respects in all the country; — I speak of his followers only; — for their leader, no doubt, scoured the land far and wide, seeking to swell his troop. These alone were ready to step between the oppressor and the oppressed. Surely they were the very best men you could select to be hung. That was the greatest compliment which this country could pay them. They were ripe for her gallows. She has tried a long time, she has hung a good many, but never found the right one before.

When I think of him, and his six sons, and his son-in-law, not to enumerate the others, enlisted for this fight, proceeding coolly, reverently, humanely to work, for months if not years, sleeping and waking upon it, summering and wintering the thought, without expecting any reward but a good conscience, while almost all America stood ranked on the other side, — I say again that it affects me as a sublime spectacle. If he had had any journal advocating "*his cause,*" any organ, as the phrase is, monotonously and wearisomely playing the same old tune, and then passing round the hat, it would have been fatal to his efficiency. If he had acted in any way so as to be let alone by the government, he might have been suspected. It was the fact that the tyrant must give place to him, or he to the tyrant, that distinguished him from all the reformers of the day that I know.

It was his peculiar doctrine that a man has a perfect right to interfere by force with the slaveholder, in order to rescue the slave. I agree with him. They who are continually shocked by slavery have some right to be shocked by the violent death of the slaveholder, but no others. Such will be more shocked by his life than by

his death. I shall not be forward to think him mistaken
in his method who quickest succeeds to liberate the slave.
I speak for the slave when I say, that I prefer the philanthropy of Captain Brown to that philanthropy which
neither shoots me nor liberates me. At any rate, I do
not think it is quite sane for one to spend his whole
life in talking or writing about this matter, unless he is
continuously inspired, and I have not done so. A man
may have other affairs to attend to. I do not wish to
kill nor to be killed, but I can foresee circumstances in
which both these things would be by me unavoidable.
We preserve the so-called peace of our community by
deeds of petty violence every day. Look at the police-
man's billy and handcuffs! Look at the jail! Look at
the gallows! Look at the chaplain of the regiment!
We are hoping only to live safely on the outskirts of
this provisional army. So we defend ourselves and our
hen-roosts, and maintain slavery. I know that the mass
of my countrymen think that the only righteous use that
can be made of Sharpe's rifles and revolvers is to fight
duels with them, when we are insulted by other nations,
or to hunt Indians, or shoot fugitive slaves with them, or
the like. I think that for once the Sharpe's rifles and
the revolvers were employed in a righteous cause. The
tools were in the hands of one who could use them.

The same indignation that is said to have cleared the
temple once will clear it again. The question is not
about the weapon, but the spirit in which you use it.
No man has appeared in America, as yet, who loved his
fellow-man so well, and treated him so tenderly. He
lived for him. He took up his life and he laid it down
for him. What sort of violence is that which is encouraged, not by soldiers, but by peaceable citizens, not

so much by laymen as by ministers of the Gospel, not so much by the fighting sects as by the Quakers, and not so much by Quaker men as by Quaker women?

This event advertises me that there is such a fact as death, — the possibility of a man's dying. It seems as if no man had ever died in America before; for in order to die you must first have lived. I don't believe in the hearses, and palls, and funerals that they have had. There was no death in the case, because there had been no life; they merely rotted or sloughed off, pretty much as they had rotted or sloughed along. No temple's veil was rent, only a hole dug somewhere. Let the dead bury their dead. The best of them fairly ran down like a clock. Franklin, — Washington, — they were let off without dying; they were merely missing one day. I hear a good many pretend that they are going to die; or that they have died, for aught that I know. Nonsense! I'll defy them to do it. They haven't got life enough in them. They'll deliquesce like fungi, and keep a hundred eulogists mopping the spot where they left off. Only half a dozen or so have died since the world began. Do you think that you are going to die, sir? No! there's no hope of you. You haven't got your lesson yet. You've got to stay after school. We make a needless ado about capital punishment, — taking lives, when there is no life to take. *Memento mori!* We don't understand that sublime sentence which some worthy got sculptured on his gravestone once. We've interpreted it in a grovelling and snivelling sense we've wholly forgotten how to die.

But be sure you do die nevertheless. Do your work, and finish it. If you know how to begin, you will know when to end.

These men, in teaching us how to die, have at the same time taught us how to live. If this man's acts and words do not create a revival, it will be the severest possible satire on the acts and words that do. It is the best news that America has ever heard. It has already quickened the feeble pulse of the North, and infused more and more generous blood into her veins and heart, than any number of years of what is called commercial and political prosperity could. How many a man who was lately contemplating suicide has now something to live for!

One writer says that Brown's peculiar monomania made him to be "dreaded by the Missourians as a super natural being." Sure enough, a hero in the midst of us cowards is always so dreaded. He is just that thing. He shows himself superior to nature. He has a spark of divinity in him.

> " Unless above himself he can
> Erect himself, how poor a thing is man! "

Newspaper editors argue also that it is a proof of his *insanity* that he thought he was appointed to do this work which he did, — that he did not suspect himself for a moment! They talk as if it were impossible that a man could be " divinely appointed " in these days to do any work whatever; as if vows and religion were out of date as connected with any man's daily work; as if the agent to abolish slavery could only be somebody appointed by the President, or by some political party. They talk as if a man's death were a failure, and his continued life, be it of whatever character, were a success.

When I reflect to what a cause this man devoted himself, and how religiously, and then reflect to what cause his judges and all who condemn him so angrily and fluently devote themselves, I see that they are as far apart as the heavens and earth are asunder.

The amount of it is, our " *leading men* " are a harmless kind of folk, and they know *well enough* that *they* were not divinely appointed, but elected by the votes of their party.

Who is it whose safety requires that Captain Brown be hung? Is it indispensable to any Northern man? Is there no resource but to cast this man also to the Minotaur? If you do not wish it, say so distinctly. While these things are being done, beauty stands veiled and music is a screeching lie. Think of him, — of his rare qualities! — such a man as it takes ages to make, and ages to understand; no mock hero, nor the representative of any party. A man such as the sun may not rise upon again in this benighted land. To whose making went the costliest material, the finest adamant; sent to be the redeemer of those in captivity; and the only use to which you can put him is to hang him at the end of a rope! You who pretend to care for Christ crucified, consider what you are about to do to him who offered himself to be the savior of four millions of men.

Any man knows when he is justified, and all the wits in the world cannot enlighten him on that point. The murderer always knows that he is justly punished; but when a government takes the life of a man without the consent of his conscience, it is an audacious government, and is taking a step towards its own dissolution. Is it not possible that an individual may be right and a government wrong? Are laws to be enforced simply because they were made? or declared by any number of men to be good, if they are *not* good ? Is there any necessity for a man's being a tool to perform a deed of which his better nature disapproves ? Is it the intention of law-makers that *good* men shall be hung ever? Are judges to interpret the law according to the letter, and not the spirit ? What right have *you* to enter into a compact with yourself that you *will* do thus or so, against the light within you ? Is it for *you* to *make up* your mind, — to form any resolution whatever, — and not accept the convictions that are forced upon you, and which ever pass your understanding ? I do not believe in lawyers, in that mode of attacking or defending a man, because you descend to meet the judge on his own ground, and, in cases of the highest importance, it is of no consequence whether a man breaks a human law or not. Let lawyers decide trivial cases. Business men may arrange that among themselves. If they were the interpreters of the everlasting laws which rightfully bind man, that would be another thing. A counterfeiting law-factory, standing half in a slave land and half in a free ! What kind of laws for free men can you expect from that ?

I am here to plead his cause with you. I plead not for his life, but for his character, — his immortal life ; and so it becomes your cause wholly, and is not his in the least. Some eighteen hundred years ago Christ was crucified ; this morning, perchance, Captain Brown was hung. These are the two ends of a chain which is not without its links. He is not Old Brown any longer ; he is an angel of light.

I see now that it was necessary that the bravest and humanest man in all the country should be hung. Perhaps he saw it himself. I *almost fear* that I may yet hear of his deliverance, doubting if a prolonged life it *any* life, can dc as much good as his death.

" Misguided " ! " Garrulous " ! " Insane " ! " Vindictive " ! Sc ye write in your easy-chairs, and thus he wounded responds from the floor of the Armory, clear as a cloudless sky, true as the voice of nature is : " No man sent me here ; it was my own prompting and that of my Maker.   I acknowledge no master in human form."

And in what a sweet and noble strain he proceeds, addressing his captors, who stand over him : " I think, my friends, you are guilty of a great wrong against God and humanity, and it would be perfectly right for any one to interfere with you so far as to free those you wilfully and wickedly hold in bondage."

And, referring to his movement : " It is, in my opinion, the greatest service a man can render to God."

" I pity the poor in bondage that have none to help them ; that is why I am here ; not to gratify any personal ..nimosity, revenge, or vindictive spirit.   It is my sympathy with the oppressed and the wronged, that are as good as you, and as precious in the sight of God."

You don't know your testament when you see it.

" I want you to understand that I respect the rights of the poorest and weakest of colored people, oppressed by the slave power, just as much as I do those of the most wealthy and powerful."

" I wish to say, furthermore, that you had better, all you people at the South, prepare yourselves for a settlement of that question, that must come up for settlement sooner than you are prepared for it.   The sooner you are prepared the better.   You may dispose of me very easily.   I am nearly disposed of now ; but this question is still to be settled, — this negro question, I mean; the end of that is not yet."

I foresee the time when the painter will paint that scene, no longer going to Rome for a subject; the poet will sing it; the historian record it; and, with the Landing of the Pilgrims and the Declaration of Independence, it will be the ornament of some future national gallery, when at least the present form of slavery shall be no more here. We shall then be at liberty to weep for Captain Brown. Then, and not till then, we will take our revenge.

PARADISE (TO BE) REGAINED.*

["Democratic Review," New York, November, 1843.]

WE learn that Mr. Etzler is a native of Germany, and originally published his book in Pennsylvania, ten or twelve years ago; and now a second English edition, from the original American one, is demanded by his readers across the water, owing, we suppose, to the recent spread of Fourier's doctrines. It is one of the signs of the times. We confess that we have risen from reading this book with enlarged ideas, and grander conceptions of our duties in this world. It did expand us a little. It is worth attending to, if only that it entertains large questions. Consider what Mr. Etzler proposes:

"Fellow-men! I promise to show the means of creating a paradise within ten years, where everything desirable for human life may be had by every man in superabundance, without labor, and without pay; where the whole face of nature shall be changed into the most beautiful forms, and man may live in the most magnificent palaces, in all imaginable refinements of luxury, and in the most delightful gardens; where he may accomplish, without labor, in one year, more than hitherto could be done in thousands' of years; may level mountains, sink

---

* The Paradise within the Reach of all Men, without Labor, by Powers of Nature and Machinery. An Address to all intelligent Men. In Two Parts. By J. A. Etzler. Part First. Second English Edition. London. 1842. pp. 55.

valleys, create lakes, drain lakes and swamps, and in-
tersect the land everywhere with beautiful canals, and
roads for transporting heavy loads of many thousand
tons, and for travelling one thousand miles in twenty-
four hours; may cover the ocean with floating islands
movable in any desired direction with immense power
and celerity, in perfect security, and with all comforts
and luxuries, bearing gardens and palaces, with thousands of families, and provided with rivulets of sweet
water; may explore the interior of the globe, and travel
from pole to pole in a fortnight; provide himself with
means, unheard of yet, for increasing his knowledge of
the world, and so his intelligence; lead a life of con
tinual happiness, of enjoyments yet unknown; free
himself from almost all the evils that afflict mankind,
except death, and even put death far beyond the common
period of human life, and finally render it less afflicting.
Mankind may thus live in and enjoy a new world, far
superior to the present, and raise themselves far higher
in the scale of being."

It would seem from this and various indications beside, that there is a transcendentalism in mechanics as
well as in ethics.   While the whole field of the one
reformer lies beyond the boundaries of space, the other
is pushing his schemes for the elevation of the race to its
utmost limits.   While one scours the heavens, the other
sweeps the earth.   One says he will reform himself, and
then nature and circumstances will be right.   Let us not
obstruct ourselves, for that is the greatest friction.   It is
of little importance though a cloud obstruct the view of
the astronomer compared with his own blindness.   The
other will reform nature and circumstances, and then
man will be right.   Talk no more vaguely, says he, of

reforming the world, — I will reform the globe itself.
What matters it whether I remove this humor out of my
flesh, or this pestilent humor from the fleshy part of the
globe? Nay, is not the latter the more generous course?
At present the globe goes with a shattered constitution
in its orbit. Has it not asthma, and ague, and fever,
and dropsy, and flatulence, and pleurisy, and is it not
afflicted with vermin? Has it not its healthful laws
counteracted, and its vital energy which will yet redeem
it? No doubt the simple powers of nature, properly
directed by man, would make it healthy and a paradise;
as the laws of man's own constitution but wait to be
obeyed, to restore him to health and happiness. Our
panaceas cure but few ails, our general hospitals are
private and exclusive. We must set up another Hygeia
than is now worshipped. Do not the quacks even direct
small doses for children, larger for adults, and larger still
for oxen and horses? Let us remember that we are to
prescribe for the globe itself.

This fair homestead has fallen to us, and how little
have we done to improve it, how little have we cleared
and hedged and ditched! We are too inclined to go
hence to a " better land," without lifting a finger, as our
farmers are moving to the Ohio soil; but would it not be
more heroic and faithful to till and redeem this New England soil of the world? The still youthful energies of
the globe have only to be directed in their proper channel. Every gazette brings accounts of the untutored
freaks of the wind, — shipwrecks and hurricanes which
the mariner and planter accept as special or general
providences; but they touch our consciences, they remind
us of our sins. Another deluge would disgrace mankind.
We confess we never had much respect for that an-

tediluvian race. A throughbred business man cannot enter heartily upon the business of life without first looking into his accounts. How many things are now at
loose ends. Who knows which way the wind will blow
to-morrow? Let us not succumb to nature. We will
marshal the clouds and restrain tempests; we will bottle
up pestilent exhalations; we will probe for earthquakes,
grub them up, and give vent to the dangerous gas; we
will disembowel the volcano, and extract its poison, take
its seed out. We will wash water, and warm fire, and
cool ice, and underprop the earth. We will teach birds
to fly, and fishes to swim, and ruminants to chew the
cud. It is time we had looked into these things.

And it becomes the moralist, too, to inquire what man
might do to improve and beautify the system ; what to
make the stars shine more brightly, the sun more cheery
and joyous, the moon more placid and content. Could
he not heighten the tints of flowers and the melody of
birds? Does he perform his duty to the inferior races?
Should he not be a god to them? What is the part of
magnanimity to the whale and the beaver? Should we
not fear to exchange places with them for a day, lest by
their behavior they should shame us? Might we not
treat with magnanimity the shark and the tiger, not
descend to meet them on their own level, with spears of
sharks' teeth and bucklers of tiger's skin? We slander
the hyena; man is the fiercest and cruellest animal. Ah!
he is of little faith; even the erring comets and meteors
would thank him, and return his kindness in their kind.

How meanly and grossly do we deal with nature!
Could we not have a less gross labor? What else do
these fine inventions suggest, — magnetism, the daguerreotype, electricity? Can we not do more than cut

and trim the forest, — can we not assist in its interior
economy, in the circulation of the sap ?   Now we work
superficially and violently.   We do not suspect how
much might be done to improve our relation to animated
nature even; what kindness and refined courtesy there
might be.

There are certain pursuits which, if not wholly poetic
and true, do at least suggest a nobler and finer relation to
nature than we know. The keeping of bees, for instance,
is a very slight interference.   It is like directing the
sunbeams.   All nations, from the remotest antiquity,
have thus fingered nature.   There are Hymettus and
Hybla, and how many bee-renowned spots beside ?
There is nothing gross in the idea of these little herds, —
their hum like the faintest low of kine in the meads.   A
pleasant reviewer has lately reminded us that in some
places they are led out to pasture where the flowers are
most abundant.   " Columella tells us," says he, " that
the inhabitants of Arabia sent their hives into Attica to
benefit by the later-blowing flowers."   Annually are the
hives, in immense pyramids, carried up the Nile in boats,
and suffered to float slowly down the stream by night,
resting by day, as the flowers put forth along the banks ;
and they determine the richness of any locality, and so
the profitableness of delay, by the sinking of the boat in
the water.   We are told, by the same reviewer, of a
man in Germany, whose bees yielded more honey than
those of his neighbors, with no apparent advantage ; but
at length he informed them, that he had turned his hives
one degree more to the east, and so his bees, having two
hours the start in the morning, got the first sip of honey.
True, there is treachery and selfishness behind all this ;
but these things suggest to the poetic mind what might
be done.

Many examples there are of a grosser interference, yet not without their apology. We saw last summer, on the side of a mountain, a dog employed to churn for a farmer's family, travelling upon a horizontal wheel, and though he had sore eyes, an alarming cough, and withal a demure aspect, yet their bread did get buttered for all that. Undoubtedly, in the most brilliant successes, the first rank is always sacrificed. Much useless travelling of horses, *in extenso*, has of late years been improved for man's behoof, only two forces being taken advantage of, — the gravity of the horse, which is the centripetal, and his centrifugal inclination to go ahead. Only these two elements in the calculation. And is not the creature's whole economy better economized thus? Are not all finite beings better pleased with motions relative than absolute? And what is the great globe itself but such a wheel, — a larger treadmill, — so that our horse's freest steps over prairies are oftentimes balked and rendered of no avail by the earth's motion on its axis? But here he is the central agent and motive-power; and, for variety of scenery, being provided with a window in front, do not the ever-varying activity and fluctuating energy of the creature himself work the effect of the most varied scenery on a country road? It must be confessed that horses at present work too exclusively for men, rarely men for horses; and the brute degenerates in man's society.

It will be seen that we contemplate a time when man's will shall be law to the physical world, and he shall no longer be deterred by such abstractions as time and space, height and depth, weight and hardness, but shall indeed be the lord of creation. " Well," says the faithless reader, " ' life is short, but art is long '; where

is the power that will effect all these changes ? ' This
it is the very object of Mr. Etzler's volume to show. At
present, he would merely remind us that there are innumerable and immeasurable powers already existing in
nature, unimproved on a large scale, or for generous and
universal ends, amply sufficient for these purposes. He
would only indicate their existence, as a surveyor makes
known the existence of a water-power on any stream ;
but for their application he refers us to a sequel to this
book, called the "Mechanical System." A few of the
most obvious and familiar of these powers are, the Wind,
the Tide, the Waves, the Sunshine. Let us consider
their value.

First, there is the power of the Wind, constantly ex-
erted over the globe. It appears from observation of a
sailing-vessel, and from scientific tables, that the average
power of the wind is equal to that of one horse for every
one hundred square feet. We do not attach much value
to this statement of the comparative power of the wind
and horse, for no common ground is mentioned on which
they can be compared. Undoubtedly, each is incomparably
excellent in its way, and every general comparison made
for such practical purposes as are contemplated, which
gives a preference to the one, must be made with some
unfairness to the other. The scientific tables are, for the
most part, true only in a tabular sense. We suspect
that a loaded wagon, with a light sail, ten feet square,
would not have been blown so far by the end of the
year, under equal circumstances, as a common racer or
dray horse would have drawn it. And how many crazy
structures on our globe's surface, of the same dimensions,
would wait for dry-rot if the traces of one horse were
hitched to them, even to their windward side ? Plainly,

this is not the principle of comparison. But even the steady and constant force of the horse may be rated as equal to his weight at least. Yet we should prefer to let the zephyrs and gales bear, with all their weight, upon our fences, than that Dobbin, with feet braced, should lean ominously against them for a season.

Nevertheless, here is an almost incalculable power at our disposal, yet how trifling the use we make of it. It only serves to turn a few mills, blow a few vessels across the ocean, and a few trivial ends besides. What a poor compliment do we pay to our indefatigable and energetic servant!

Men having discovered the power of falling water, which, after all, is comparatively slight, how eagerly do they seek out and improve these *privileges*? Let a difference of but a few feet in level be discovered on some stream near a populous town, some slight occasion for gravity to act, and the whole economy of the neighborhood is changed at once. Men do indeed speculate about and with this power as if it were the only privilege. But meanwhile this aerial stream is falling from far greater heights with more constant flow, never shrunk by drought, offering mill-sites wherever the wind blows; a Niagara in the air, with no Canada side; — only the application is hard.

There are the powers, too, of the Tide and Waves, constantly ebbing and flowing, lapsing and relapsing, but they serve man in but few ways. They turn a few tide-mills, and perform a few other insignificant and accidental services only. We all perceive the effect of the tide; how imperceptibly it creeps up into our harbors and rivers, and raises the heaviest navies as easily as the lightest chip. Everything that floats must yield to it.

But man, slow to take nature's constant hint of assistance, makes slight and irregular use of this power, in careening ships and getting them afloat when aground.

This power may be applied in various ways. A large body, of the heaviest materials that will float, may first be raised by it, and being attached to the end of a balance reaching from the land, or from a stationary support, fastened to the bottom, when the tide falls, the whole weight will be brought to bear upon the end of the balance. Also, when the tide rises, it may be made to exert a nearly equal force in the opposite direction. It can be employed wherever a *point d'appui* can be obtained.

Verily, the land would wear a busy aspect at the spring and neap tide, and these island ships, these *terræ infirmæ,* which realize the fables of antiquity, affect our imagination. We have often thought that the fittest locality for a human dwelling was on the edge of the land, that there the constant lesson and impression of the sea might sink deep into the life and character of the landsman, and perhaps impart a marine tint to his imagination. It is a noble word, that *mariner,* — one who is conversant with the sea. There should be more of what it signifies in each of us. It is a worthy country to belong to, — we look to see him not disgrace it. Perhaps we should be equally mariners and terreners, and even our Green Mountains need some of that sea-green to be mixed with them.

The computation of the power of the Waves is less satisfactory. While only the average power of the wind, and the average height of the tide, were taken before, now the extreme height of the waves is used, for they are made to rise ten feet above the level of the sea,

to which, adding ten more for depression, we have
twenty feet, or the extreme height of a wave. Indeed,
the power of the waves, which is produced by the wind
blowing obliquely and at disadvantage upon the water,
is made to be, not only three thousand times greater
than that of the tide, but one hundred times greater than
that of the wind itself, meeting its object at right angles.   Moreover, this power is measured by the area of
the vessel, and not by its length mainly, and it seems
to be forgotten that the motion of the waves is chiefly
undulatory, and exerts a power only within the limits
of a vibration, else the very continents, with their extensive coasts, would soon be set adrift.

Finally, there is the power to be derived from Sunshine, by the principle on which Archimedes contrived
his burning-mirrors, a multiplication of mirrors reflecting the rays of the sun upon the same spot, till the
requisite degree of heat is obtained.   The principal application of this power will be to the boiling of water and
production of steam.   So much for these few and more
obvious powers, already used to a trifling extent.   But
there are innumerable others in nature, not described
nor discovered.   These, however, will do for the present.   This would be to make the sun and the moon
equally our satellites.   For, as the moon is the cause
of the tides, and the sun the cause of the wind, which, in
turn, is the cause of the waves, all the work of this
planet would be performed by these far influences.

" We may store up water in some eminent pond, and
take out of this store, at any time, as much water through
the outlet as we want to employ, by which means the
original power may react for many days after it has
ceased. . . . . Such reservoirs of moderate elevation or

size need not be made artificially, but will be found
made by nature very frequently, requiring but little aid
for their completion. They require no regularity of
form. Any valley, with lower grounds in its vicinity,
would answer the purpose. Small crevices may be
filled up. Such places may be eligible for the beginning of enterprises of this kind."

The greater the height, of course, the less water required. But suppose a level and dry country; then
hill and valley, and "eminent pond," are to be constructed by main force; or, if the springs are unusually low,
then dirt and stones may be used, and the disadvantage arising from friction will be counterbalanced by
their greater gravity. Nor shall a single rood of dry
land be sunk in such artificial ponds as may be wanted,
but their surfaces "may be covered with rafts decked
with fertile earth, and all kinds of vegetables which may
grow there as well as anywhere else."

And, finally, by the use of thick envelopes retaining
the heat, and other contrivances, "the power of steam
caused by sunshine may react at will, and thus be rendered perpetual, no matter how often or how long the
sunshine may be interrupted."

Here is power enough, one would think, to accomplish somewhat. These are the Powers below. O ye
millwrights, ye engineers, ye operatives and speculators
of every class, never again complain of a want of power:
it is the grossest form of infidelity. The question is,
not how we shall execute, but what. Let us not use in
a niggardly manner what is thus generously offered.

Consider what revolutions are to be effected in agriculture. First, in the new country a machine is to move
along, taking out trees and stones to any required depth,

and piling them up in convenient heaps; then the same machine, " with a little alteration," is to plane the ground perfectly, till there shall be no hills nor valleys, making the requisite canals, ditches, and roads as it goes along. The same machine, " with some other little alterations," is then to sift the ground thoroughly, supply fertile soil from other places if wanted, and plant it; and finally the same machine, " with a little addition," is to reap and gather in the crop, thresh and grind it, or press it to oil, or prepare it any way for final use. For the description of these machines we are referred to " Etzler's Mechanical System," pages 11 to 27. We should be pleased to see that " Mechanical System." We have great faith in it. But we cannot stop for applications now.

Who knows but by accumulating the power until the end of the present century, using meanwhile only the smallest allowance, reserving all that blows, all that shines, all that ebbs and flows, all that dashes, we may have got such a reserved accumulated power as to run the earth off its track into a new orbit, some summer, and so change the tedious vicissitude of the seasons? Or, perchance, coming generations will not abide the dissolution of the globe, but, availing themselves of future inventions in aerial locomotion, and the navigation of space, the entire race may migrate from the earth, to settle some vacant and more western planet, it may be still healthy, perchance unearthy, not composed of dirt and stones, whose primary strata only are strewn, and where no weeds are sown. It took but little art, a simple application of natural laws, a canoe, a paddle, and a sail of matting, to people the isles of the Pacific, and a little more will people the shining isles of space. Do we not see in the firmament the lights carried along

the shore by night, as Columbus did? Let us not despair nor mutiny.

"The dwellings also ought to be very different from
what is known, if the full benefit of our means is to be enjoyed. They are to be of a structure for which we have
no name yet. They are to be neither palaces, nor temples, nor cities, but a combination of all, superior to
whatever is known.

"Earth may be baked into bricks, or even vitrified
stone by heat, — we may bake large masses of any size
and form, into stone and vitrified substance of the greatest durability, lasting even thousand of years, out of clayey
earth, or of stones ground to dust, by the application of
burning-mirrors. This is to be done in the open air,
without other preparation than gathering the substance,
grinding and mixing it with water and cement, moulding
or casting it, and bringing the focus of the burning-
mirrors of proper size upon the same."

The character of the architecture is to be quite different from what it ever has been hitherto; large solid
masses are to be baked or cast in one piece, ready shaped
in any form that may be desired. The building may,
therefore, consist of columns two hundred feet high and
upwards, of proportionate thickness, and of one entire
piece of vitrified substance; huge pieces are to be mould-
ed so as to join and hook on to each other firmly, by
proper joints and folds, and not to yield in any way without breaking.

"Foundries, of any description, are to be heated by
burning-mirrors, and will require no labor, except the
making of the first moulds and the superintendence for
gathering the metal and taking the finished articles away.'

Alas! in the present state of science, we must take the

finished articles away; but think not that man will always be the victim of circumstances.

The countryman who visited the city, and found the streets cluttered with bricks and lumber, reported that it was not yet finished; and one who considers the endless repairs and reforming of our houses might well wonder when they will be done.   But why may not the dwellings of men on this earth be built, once for all, of some durable material, some Roman or Etruscan masonry, which will stand, so that time shall only adorn and beautify them?   Why may we not finish the outward world for posterity, and leave them leisure to attend to the inner?   Surely, all the gross necessities and economies might be cared for in a few years.   All might be built and baked and stored up, during this, the term-time of the world, against the vacant eternity, and the globe go provisioned and furnished, like our public vessels, for its voyage through space, as through some Pacific Ocean, while we would "tie up the rudder and sleep before the wind," as those who sail from Lima to Manilla.

But, to go back a few years in imagination, think not that life in these crystal palaces is to bear any analogy to life in our present humble cottages.   Far from it.   Clothed, once for all, in some "flexible stuff," more durable than George Fox's suit of leather, composed of "fibres of vegetables," "glutinated" together by some "cohesive substances," and made into sheets, like paper, of any size or form, man will put far from him corroding care and the whole host of ills.

"The twenty-five halls in the inside of the square are to be each two hundred feet square and high; the forty corridors, each one hundred feet long and twenty wide; the eighty galleries, each from 1,000 to 1,250 feet long; about 7,000 private rooms, the whole surrounded and intersected by the grandest and most splendid colonnades imaginable; floors, ceilings, columns, with their various beautiful and fanciful intervals, all shining, and reflecting to infinity all objects and persons, with splendid lustre of all beautiful colors, and fanciful shapes and pictures.

"All galleries, outside and within the halls, are to be provided with many thousand commodious and most elegant vehicles, in which persons may move up and down like birds, in perfect security, and without exertion. .... Any member may procure himself all the common articles of his daily wants, by a short turn of some crank, without leaving his apartment.

"One or two persons are sufficient to direct the kitchen business. They have nothing else to do but to superintend the cookery, and to watch the time of the victuals being done, and then to remove them, with the table and vessels, into the dining-hall, or to the respective private apartments, by a slight motion of the hand at some crank..... *Any very extraordinary desire of any person may be satisfied by going to the place where the thing is to be had; and anything that requires a particular preparation in cooking or baking may be done by the person who desires it.*"

This is one of those instances in which the individual genius is found to consent, as indeed it always does, at last, with the universal. This last sentence has a certain sad and sober truth, which reminds us of the scripture of all nations. All expression of truth does at length take this deep ethical form. Here is hint of a place the most eligible of any in space, and of a servi-

tor, in comparison with whom all other helps dwindle
into insignificance. We hope to hear more of him anon,
for even a Crystal Palace would be deficient without his
invaluable services.

And as for the environs of the establishment : —

" There will be afforded the most enrapturing views
to be fancied, out of the private apartments, from the
galleries, from the roof, from its turrets and cupolas, —
gardens, as far as the eye can see, full of fruits and
flowers, arranged in the most beautiful order, with walks,
colonnades, aqueducts, canals, ponds, plains, amphithea-
tres, terraces, fountains, sculptural works, pavilions, gon-
dolas, places for public amusement, etc., to delight the
eye and fancy, the taste and smell. . . . . The walks
and roads are to be paved with hard vitrified large
plates, so as to be always clean from all dirt in any
weather or season. . . . .

" The walks may be covered with porticos adorned
with magnificent columns, statues, and sculptural works ;
all of vitrified substance, and lasting forever. At night
the roof, and the inside and outside of the whole square,
are illuminated by gas-light, which, in the maze of
many-colored crystal-like colonnades and vaultings, is
reflected with a brilliancy that gives to the whole a
lustre of precious stones, as far as the eye can see.
Such are the future abodes of men. . . . . Such is the
life reserved to true intelligence, but withheld from ignorance, prejudice, and stupid adherence to custom."

Thus is Paradise to be Regained, and that old and
stern decree at length reversed. Man shall no more
earn his living by the sweat of his brow. All labor
shall be reduced to " a short turn of some crank," and
" taking the finished articles away." But there is a

crank, — (), how hard to be turned! Could there not
be a crank upon a crank, — an infinitely small crank?
— we would fain inquire. No, — alas! not. But there
is a certain divine energy in every man, but sparingly
employed as yet, which may be called the crank within,
— the crank after all, — the prime mover in all machinery, — quite indispensable to all work. Would that
we might get our hands on its handle! In fact, no work
can be shirked. It may be postponed indefinitely, but
not infinitely. Nor can any really important work be
made easier by co-operation or machinery. Not one
particle of labor now threatening any man can be routed
without being performed. It cannot be hunted out of
the vicinity like jackals and hyenas. It will not run.
You may begin by sawing the little sticks, or you may
saw the great sticks first, but sooner or later you must
saw them both.

We will not be imposed upon by this vast application
of forces. We believe that most things will have to be
accomplished still by the application called Industry.
We are rather pleased after all to consider the small
private, but both constant and accumulated force, which
stands behind every spade in the field. This it is that
makes the valleys shine, and the deserts really bloom.
Sometimes, we confess, we are so degenerate as to reflect with pleasure on the days when men were yoked
liked cattle, and drew a crooked stick for a plough. After all, the great interests and methods were the same.

It is a rather serious objection to Mr. Etzler's schemes,
that they require time, men, and money, three very superfluous and inconvenient things for an honest and
well-disposed man to deal with. "The whole world,"
he tells us, "might therefore be really changed into a

paradise, within less than ten years, commencing from
the first year of an association for the purpose of con-
structing and applying the machinery." We are sensible of a startling incongruity when time and money are
mentioned in this connection. The ten years which are
proposed would be a tedious while to wait, if every man
were at his post and did his duty, but quite too short a
period, if we are to take time for it. But this fault is
by no means peculiar to Mr. Etzler's schemes. There
is far too much hurry and bustle, and too little patience
and privacy, in all our methods, as if something were to
be accomplished in centuries. The true reformer does
not want time, nor money, nor co-operation, nor advice.
What is time but the stuff delay is made of? And depend upon it, our virtue will not live on the interest of
our money. He expects no income, but outgoes; so
soon as we begin to count the cost, the cost begins.
And as for advice, the information floating in the atmosphere of society is as evanescent and unserviceable to him
as gossamer for clubs of Hercules. There is absolutely
no common sense; it is common nonsense. If we are
to risk a cent or a drop of our blood, who then shall advise
us? For ourselves, we are too young for experience.
Who is old enough? We are older by faith than by
experience. In the unbending of the arm to do the
deed there is experience worth all the maxims in the
world.

"It will now be plainly seen that the execution of
the proposals is not proper for individuals. Whether it
be proper for government at this time, before the subject has become popular, is a question to be decided; all
that is to be done is to step forth, after mature reflection,
to confess loudly one's conviction, and to constitute so-

cieties. Man is powerful but in union with many Nothing great, for the improvement of his own condition, or that of his fellow-men, can ever be effected by individual enterprise."

Alas! this is the crying sin of the age, this want of faith in the prevalence of a man. Nothing can be effected but by one man. He who wants help wants everything. True, this is the condition of our weakness, but it can never be the means of our recovery. We must first succeed alone, that we may enjoy our success together. We trust that the social movements which we witness indicate an aspiration not to be thus cheaply satisfied. In this matter of reforming the world, we have little faith in corporations; not thus was it first formed.

But our author is wise enough to say, that the raw materials for the accomplishment of his purposes are " iron, copper, wood, earth chiefly, and a union of men whose eyes and understanding are not shut up by preconceptions." Ay, this last may be what we want mainly, — a company of " odd fellows " indeed.

" Small shares of twenty dollars will be sufficient," — in all, from " 200,000 to 300,000," — " to create the first establishment for a whole community of from 3,000 tc 4,000 individuals," — at the end of five years we shall have a principal of 200 millions of dollars, and so paradise will be wholly regained at the end of the tenth year But, alas, the ten years have already elapsed, and there are no signs of Eden yet, for want of the requisite funds to begin the enterprise in a hopeful manner. Yet it seems a safe investment. Perchance they could be hired at a low rate, the property being mortgaged for security, and, if necessary, it could be given up in any stage of the enterprise, without loss, with the fixtures.

But we see two main difficulties in the way First,
the successful application of the powers by machinery,
(we have not yet seen the " Mechanical System,") and,
secondly, which is infinitely harder, the application of
man to the work by faith. This it is, we fear, which will
prolong the ten years to ten thousand at least. It will
take a power more than " 80,000 times greater than all
the men on earth could effect with their nerves," to persuade men to use that which is already offered them.
Even a greater than this physical power must be brought
to bear upon that moral power. Faith, indeed, is all the
reform that is needed; it is itself a reform. Doubtless,
we are as slow to conceive of Paradise as of Heaven, of
a perfect natural as of a perfect spiritual world. We
see how past ages have loitered and erred; "Is perhaps
our generation free from irrationality and error? Have
we perhaps reached now the summit of human wisdom,
and need no more to look out for mental or physical improvement?" Undoubtedly, we are never so visionary
as to be prepared for what the next hour may bring
forth.

      Μέλλει τὸ θεῖον δ᾿ ἔστι τοιοῦτον φύσει.

The Divine is about to be, and such is its nature. In
our wisest moments we are secreting a matter, which
like the lime of the shell-fish, incrusts us quite over, and
well for us if, like it, we cast our shells from time to
time, though they be pearl and of fairest tint. Let us
consider under what disadvantages Science has hitherto
labored before we pronounce thus confidently on her
progress.

Mr. Etzler is not one of the enlightened practical
men, the pioneers of the actual, who move with the slow,
deliberate tread of science, conserving the world; who

execute the dreams of the last century, though they have no dreams of their own ; yet he deals in the very raw but still solid material of all inventions. He has more of the practical than usually belongs to so bold a schemer, so resolute a dreamer. Yet his success is in theory, and not in practice, and he feeds our faith rather than contents our understanding. His book wants order, serenity, dignity, everything, — but it does not fail to impart what only man can impart to man of much importance, his own faith. It is true his dreams are not thrilling nor bright enough, and he leaves off to dream where he who dreams just before the dawn begins. His castles in the air fall to the ground, because they are not built lofty enough ; they should be secured to heaven's roof. After all, the theories and speculations of men concern us more than their puny accomplishment. It is with a certain coldness and languor that we loiter about the actual and so-called practical. How little do the most wonderful inventions of modern times detain us. They insult nature. Every machine, or particular application, seems a slight outrage against universal laws. How many fine inventions are there which do not clutter the ground ? We think that those only succeed which minister to our sensible and animal wants, which bake or brew, wash or warm, or the like. But are those of no account which are patented by fancy and imagination, and succeed so admirably in our dreams that they give the tone still to our waking thoughts ? Already nature is serving all those uses which science slowly derives on a much higher and grander scale to him that will be served by her. When the sunshine falls on the path of the poet, he enjoys all those pure benefits and pleasures which the arts slowly and partially realize from age to age. The winds which fan his cheek waft him the sum of that profit and happiness which their lagging inventions supply.

The chief fault of this book is, that it aims to secure the greatest degree of gross comfort and pleasure merely. It paints a Mahometan's heaven, and stops short with singular abruptness when we think it is drawing near to the precincts of the Christian's, — and we trust we have not made here a distinction without a difference. Undoubtedly if we were to reform this outward life truly and thoroughly, we should find no duty of the inner omitted. It would be employment for our whole nature; and what we should do thereafter would be as vain a question as to ask the bird what it will do when its nest is built and its brood reared. But a moral reform must take place first, and then the necessity of the other will be superseded, and we shall sail and plough by its force alone. There is a speedier way than the "Mechanical System" can show to fill up marshes, to drown the roar of the waves, to tame hyenas, secure agreeable environs, diversify the land, and refresh it with "rivulets of sweet water," and that is by the power of rectitude and true behavior. It is only for a little while, only occasionally, methinks, that we want a garden. Surely a good man need not be at the labor to level a hill for the sake of a prospect, or raise fruits and flowers, and construct floating islands, for the sake of a paradise. He enjoys better prospects than lie behind any hill. Where an angel travels it will be paradise all the way, but where Satan travels it will be burning marl and cinders. What says Veeshnoo Sarma? "He whose mind is at ease is possessed of all riches. Is it not the same to one whose foot is enclosed in a shoe, as if the whole surface of the earth were covered with leather?"

He who is conversant with the supernal powers will not worship these inferior deities of the wind, waves, tide, and sunshine.   But we would not disparage the importance of such calculations as we have described They are truths in physics, because they are true in ethics.   The moral powers no one would presume to calculate.   Suppose we could compare the moral with the physical, and say how many horse-power the force of love, for instance, blowing on every square foot of a man's soul, would equal.   No doubt we are well aware of this force ; figures would not increase our respect for it ; the sunshine is equal to but one ray of its heat.   The light of the sun is but the shadow of love.   " The souls of men loving and fearing God," says Raleigh, " receive influence from that divine light itself, whereof the sun's clarity, and that of the stars, is by Plato called but a shadow.   *Lumen est umbra Dei, Deus est Lumen Luminis.*   Light is the shadow of God's brightness, who is the light of light," and, we may add, the heat of heat. Love is the wind, the tide, the waves, the sunshine.   Its power is incalculable ; it is many horse-power.   It never ceases, it never slacks ; it can move the globe without a resting-place ; it can warm without fire ; it can feed without meat ; it can clothe without garments ; it can shelter without roof ; it can make a paradise within which will dispense with a paradise without.   But though the wisest men in all ages have labored to publish this force, and every human heart is, sooner or later, more or less, made to feel it, yet how little is actually applied to social ends. True, it is the motive-power of all successful social machinery ; but, as in physics, we have made the elements do only a little drudgery for us, steam to take the place of a few horses, wind of a few oars, water of a few cranks

and hand-mills; as the mechanical forces have not yet
been generously and largely applied to make the physical world answer to the ideal, so the power of love has
been but meanly and sparingly applied, as yet. It has
patented only such machines as the almshouse, the hospital, and the Bible Society, while its infinite wind is
still blowing, and blowing down these very structures
too, from time to time. Still less are we accumulating
its power, and preparing to act with greater energy at
a future time. Shall we not contribute our shares to
this enterprise, then?

HERALD OF FREEDOM.*

[From "The Dial," Boston, April, 1844.]

WE had occasionally, for several years, met with a number of this spirited journal, edited, as abolitionists need not to be informed, by Nathaniel P. Rogers, once a counsellor at law in Plymouth, still farther up the Merrimac, but now, in his riper years, come down the hills thus far, to be the Herald of Freedom to these parts. We had been refreshed not a little by the cheap cordial of his editorials, flowing like his own mountain-torrents, now clear and sparkling, now foaming and gritty, and always spiced with the essence of the fir and the Norway pine; but never dark nor muddy, nor threatening with smothered murmurs, like the rivers of the plain. The effect of one of his effusions reminds us of what the hydropathists say about the electricity in fresh spring-water, compared with that which has stood over night, to suit weak nerves. We do not know of another notable and public instance of such pure, youthful, and hearty indignation at all wrong. The Church itself must love it, if it have any heart, though he is said to have dealt rudely with its sanctity. His clean attachment to the right, however, sanctions the severest rebuke we have read.

* Herald of Freedom. Published weekly by the New Hampshire Anti-Slavery Society, Concord, N. H., Vol. X. No. 4.

Mr. Rogers seems to us to have occupied an honorable and manly position in these days, and in this country, making the press a living and breathing organ to reach the hearts of men, and not merely "fine paper and good type," with its civil pilot sitting aft, and magnanimously waiting for the news to arrive, — the vehicle of the earliest news, but the *latest intelligence*, — recording the indubitable and last results, the marriages and deaths, alone. This editor was wide awake, and standing on the beak of his ship; not as a scientific explorer under government, but a Yankee sealer rather, who makes those unexplored continents his harbors in which to refit for more adventurous cruises. He was a fund of news and freshness in himself, — had the gift of speech, and the knack of writing; and if anything important took place in the Granite State, we might be sure that we should hear of it in good season. No other paper that we know kept pace so well with one forward wave of the restless public thought and sentiment of New England, and asserted so faithfully and ingenuously the largest liberty in all things. There was beside more unpledged poetry in his prose than in the verses of many an accepted rhymer; and we were occasionally advertised by a mellow hunter's note from his trumpet, that, unlike most reformers, his feet were still where they should be, on the turf, and that he looked out from a serener natural life into the turbid arena of politics. Nor was slavery always a sombre theme with him, but invested with the colors of his wit and fancy, and an evil to be abolished by other means than sorrow and bitterness of complaint. He will fight this fight with what cheer may be.

But to speak of his composition. It is a genuine **Yan**

kee style, without fiction, — real guessing and calculating to some purpose, and reminds us occasionally, as
does all free, brave, and original writing, of its great
master in these days, Thomas Carlyle. It has a life
above grammar, and a meaning which need not be
parsed to be understood. But like those same mountain-torrents, there is rather too much slope to his channel, and the rainbow sprays and evaporations go double-
quick-time to heaven, while the body of his water falls
headlong to the plain. We would have more pause and
deliberation, occasionally, if only to bring his tide to a
head, — more frequent expansions of the stream, — still,
bottomless, mountain tarns, perchance inland seas, and
at length the deep ocean itself.

Some extracts will show in what sense he was a poet
as well as a reformer. He thus raises the anti-slavery
"war-whoop" in New Hampshire, when an important
convention is to be held, sending the summons, —

"To none but the whole-hearted, fully-committed, cross-
the-Rubicon spirits. . . . . From rich 'old Cheshire,' from
Rockingham, with her horizon setting down away to the
salt sea. . . . . from where the sun sets behind Kearsarge, even
to where he rises gloriously over *Moses Norris's* own town of
Pittsfield, — and from Amoskeag to Ragged Mountains, —
Coos — Upper Coos, home of the everlasting hills, — send out
your bold advocates of human rights, wherever they lay, scattered by lonely lake, or Indian stream, or 'Grant' or 'Loca-
tion,' from the trout-haunted brooks of the Amoriscoggin,
and where the adventurous streamlet takes up its mountain
march for the St. Lawrence.

"Scattered and insulated men, wherever the light of
philanthropy and liberty has beamed in upon your solitary
spirits, come down to us like your streams and clouds;
and our own Grafton, all about among your dear hills, and

your mountain-flanked valleys. — whether you *home* along
the swift Ammonoosuck, the cold Pemigewassett, or the ox-
bowed Connecticut. . . . .

"We are slow, brethren, dishonorably slow, in a cause
like ours. Our feet should be as 'hinds' feet.' 'Liberty
lies bleeding.' The leaden-colored wing of slavery obscures
the land with its baleful shadow. Let us come together, and
inquire at the hand of the Lord, what is to be done."

And again; on occasion of a New England Convention, in the Second-Advent Tabernacle, in Boston, he
desires to try one more blast, as it were, "on Fabyan's
White Mountain horn."

"Ho, then, people of the Bay State, — men, women, and
children; children, women, and men, scattered friends of
the *friendless*, wheresoever ye inhabit, — if habitations ye
have, as such friends have not *always*, — along the sea-beat
border of Old Essex and the Puritan Landing, and up beyond sight of the sea-cloud, among the inland hills, where the
sun rises and sets upon the dry land, in that vale of the Connecticut, too fair for human content and too fertile for virtuous
industry, — where deepens the haughtiest of earth's streams,
on its seaward way, proud with the pride of old Massachusetts. Are there any friends of the friendless negro haunt-
ing such a valley as this? In God's name, I fear there are
none, or few; for the very scene looks apathy and oblivion to
the genius of humanity. I blow you the summons, though.
Come, if any of you are there.

"And gallant little Rhode Island; *transcendent* abolitionists of the tiny Commonwealth. I need not call you. You
are *called* the year round, and, instead of sleeping in your
tents, stand harnessed, and with trumpets in your hands, —
every one!

"Connecticut! yonder, the home of the Burleighs, the
Monroes, and the Hudsons, and the native land of old
George Benson! are you ready? 'All ready!'

"Maine here, off east, looking from my mountain post like

an everglade. Where is your Sam. Fessenden, who stood storm-proof 'gainst New Organization in '38 ? Has he too much name as a jurist and orator, to be found at a New England Convention in '43 ? God forbid. Come one and all of you from ' Down East ' to Boston, on the 30th, and let the sails of your coasters whiten all the sea-road. Alas ! there are scarce enough of you to man a fishing boat. Come up mighty in your fewness."

Such timely, pure, and unpremeditated expressions of a public sentiment, such publicity of genuine indignation and humanity, as abound everywhere in this journal, are the most generous gifts which a man can make.

THOMAS CARLYLE AND HIS WORKS.*

THOMAS CARLYLE is a Scotchman, born about fifty years ago, "at Ecclefechan, Annandale," according to one authority. "His parents 'good farmer people,' his father an elder in the Secession church there, and a man of strong native sense, whose words were said to 'nail a subject to the wall.'" We also hear of his "excellent mother," still alive, and of "her fine old covenanting accents, concerting with his transcendental tones." He seems to have gone to school at Annan, on the shore of the Solway Frith, and there, as he himself writes, "heard of famed professors, of high matters classical, mathematical, a whole Wonderland of Knowledge," from Edward Irving, then a young man "fresh from Edinburgh, with college prizes, ... come to see our schoolmaster, who had also been his." From this place, they say, you can look over into Wordsworth's country. Here first he may have become acquainted with Nature, with woods, such as are there, and rivers and brooks, some of whose names we have heard, and the last lapses of Atlantic billows. He got some of his education, too, more or less liberal, out of the University of Edinburgh, where, according to the same authority, he had to "support himself," partly by "private tuition, translations for the booksellers, &c.," and afterward, as we are glad to hear, "taught an academy in Dysart, at the same

* Graham's Magazine, Philadelphia, March, 1847.

time that Irving was teaching in Kirkaldy," the usual middle passage of a literary life. He was destined for the Church, but not by the powers that rule man's life; made his literary *début* in Fraser's Magazine, long ago; read here and there in English and French, with more or less profit, we may suppose, such of us at least as are not particularly informed, and at length found some words which spoke to his condition in the German language, and set himself earnestly to unravel that mystery, — with what success many readers know.

After his marriage he " resided partly at Comely Bank, Edinburgh; and for a year or two at Craigenputtock, a wild and solitary farm-house in the upper part of Dumfriesshire," at which last place, amid barren heather hills, he was visited by our countryman, Emerson. With Emerson he still corresponds. He was early intimate with Edward Irving, and continued to be his friend until the latter's death. Concerning this " freest, brotherliest, bravest human soul," and Carlyle's relation to him, those whom it concerns will do well to consult a notice of his death in Fraser's Magazine for 1835, reprinted in the Miscellanies. He also corresponded with Goethe. Latterly, we hear, the poet Sterling was his only intimate acquaintance in England.

He has spent the last quarter of his life in London, writing books; has the fame, as all readers know, of having made England acquainted with Germany, in late years, and done much else that is novel and remarkable in literature. He especially is the literary man of those parts. You may imagine him living in altogether a retired and simple way, with small family, in a quiet part of London, called Chelsea, a little out of the din of commerce, in " Cheyne Row," there, not far from the

Chelsea Hospital." "A little past this, and an old ivy-
clad church, with its buried generations lying around it,"
writes one traveller, "you come to an antique street running at right angles with the Thames, and, a few steps
from the river, you find Carlyle's name on the door."
'A Scotch lass ushers you into the second story front
chamber, which is the spacious workshop of the world
maker." Here he sits a long time together, with many
books and papers about him ; many new books, we have
been told, on the upper shelves, uncut, with the "author's
respects" in them ; in late months, with many manu-
scripts in an old English hand, and innumerable pamph-
lets, from the public libraries, relating to the Cromwellian
period ; now, perhaps, looking out into the street on brick
and pavement, for a change, and now upon some rod of
grass ground in the rear ; or, perchance, he steps over to
the British Museum, and makes that his studio for the
time.   This is the fore part of the day ; that is the way
with literary men commonly ; and then in the afternoon,
we presume, he takes a short run of a mile or so through
the suburbs out into the country ; we think he would run
that way, though so short a trip might not take him to
very sylvan or rustic places.   In the mean while, people
are calling to *see* him, from various quarters, few very
worthy of being *seen* by him ; "distinguished travellers
from America," not a few ; to all and sundry of whom he
gives freely of his yet unwritten rich and flashing solilo-
quy, in exchange for whatever they may have to offer ;
speaking his English, as they say, with a "broad Scotch
accent," talking, to their astonishment and to ours, very
much as he writes, a sort of Carlylese, his discourse
"coming to its climaxes, ever and anon, in long, deep
chest-shaking bursts of laughter."

He goes to Scotland sometimes, to visit his native heath-clad hills, having some interest still in the earth there; such names as Craigenputtock and Ecclefechan, which we have already quoted, stand for habitable places there to him; or he rides to the seacoast of England in his vacations, upon his horse Yankee, bought by the sale of his books here, as we have been told.

How, after all, he gets his living; what proportion of his daily bread he earns by day-labor or job-work with his pen, what he inherits, what steals, — questions whose answers are so significant, and not to be omitted in his biography, — we, alas! are unable to answer here. It may be worth the while to state that he is not a Reformer in our sense of the term, — eats, drinks, and sleeps, thinks and believes, professes and practises, not according to the New England standard, nor to the Old English wholly. Nevertheless, we are told that he is a sort of lion in certain quarters there, "an amicable centre for men of the most opposite opinions," and "listened to as an oracle," "smoking his perpetual pipe."

A rather tall, gaunt figure, with intent face, dark hair and complexion, and the air of a student; not altogether well in body, from sitting too long in his workhouse, — he, born in the border country and descended from moss-troopers, it may be. We have seen several pictures of him here; one, a full-length portrait, with hat and overall, if it did not tell us much, told the fewest lies; another, we remember, was well said to have "too combed a look"; one other also we have seen in which we discern some features of the man we are thinking of; but the only ones worth remembering, after all, are those which he has unconsciously drawn of himself.

When we remember how these volumes came over to us, with their encouragement and provocation from month to month, and what commotion they created in many private breasts, we wonder that the country did not ring, from shore to shore, from the Atlantic to the Pacific, with its greeting; and the Boones and Crockets of the West make haste to hail him, whose wide humanity embraces them too. Of all that the packets have brought over to us, has there been any richer cargo than this? What else has been English news for so long a season? What else, of late years, has been England to us, — to us who read books, we mean? Unless we remembered it as the scene where the age of Wordsworth was spending itself, and a few younger muses were trying their wings, and from time to time, as the residence of Landor, Carlyle alone, since the death of Coleridge, has kept the promise of England. It is the best apology for all the bustle and the sin of commerce, that it has made us acquainted with the thoughts of this man. Commerce would not concern us much if it were not for such results as this. New England owes him a debt which she will be slow to recognize. His earlier essays reached us at a time when Coleridge's were the only recent words which had made any notable impression so far, and they found a field unoccupied by him, before yet any words of moment had been uttered in our midst. He had this advantage, too, in a teacher, that he stood near to his pupils; and he has no doubt afforded reasonable encouragement and sympathy to many an independent but solitary thinker.

It is remarkable, but on the whole, perhaps, not to be lamented, that the world is so unkind to a new book. Any distinguished traveller who comes to our shores is

likely to get more dinners and speeches of welcome than
he can well dispose of, but the best books, if noticed at
all, meet with coldness and suspicion, or, what is worse,
gratuitous, off-hand criticism.   It is plain that the reviewers, both here and abroad, do not know how to
dispose of this man.   They approach him too easily, as
if he were one of the men of letters about town, who
grace Mr. Somebody's administration, merely; but he
already belongs to literature, and depends neither on the
favor of reviewers, nor the honesty of booksellers, nor
the pleasure of readers for his success.   He has more to
impart than to receive from his generation.   He is another such a strong and finished workman in his craft as
Samuel Johnson was, and, like him, makes the literary
class respectable.   Since few are yet out of their appren-
ticeship, or, even if they learn to be able writers, are at
the same time able and valuable thinkers.   The aged
and critical eye, especially, is incapacitated to appreciate
the works of this author.   To such their meaning is im-
palpable and evanescent, and they seem to abound only
in obstinate mannerisms, Germanisms, and whimsical
ravings of all kinds, with now and then an unaccountably
true and sensible remark.   On the strength of this last,
Carlyle is admitted to have what is called genius.   We
hardly know an old man to whom these volumes are not
hopelessly sealed.   The language, they say, is foolishness and a stumbling-block to them; but to many a clear-
headed boy, they are plainest English, and despatched
with such hasty relish as his bread and milk.   The fathers wonder how it is that the children take to this diet
so readily, and digest it with so little difficulty.   They
shake their heads with mistrust at their free and easy
delight, and remark that " Mr. Carlyle is a very learned

man"; for they, too, not to be out of fashion, have got grammar and dictionary, if the truth were known, and with the best faith cudgelled their brains to get a little way into the jungle, and they could not but confess, as often as they found the clew, that it was as intricate as Blackstone to follow, if you read it honestly. But merely reading, even with the best intentions, is not enough: you must almost have written these books yourself. Only he who has had the good fortune to read them in the nick of time, in the most perceptive and recipient season of life, can give any adequate account of them.

Many have tasted of this well with an odd suspicion, as if it were some fountain Arethuse which had flowed under the sea from Germany, as if the materials of his books had lain in some garret there, in danger of being appropriated for waste-paper. Over what German ocean, from what Hercynian forest, he has been imported, piecemeal, into England, or whether he has now all arrived, we are not informed. This article is not invoiced in Hamburg nor in London. Perhaps it was contraband. However, we suspect that this sort of goods cannot be imported in this way. No matter how skilful the stevedore, all things being got into sailing trim, wait for a Sunday, and aft wind, and then weigh anchor, and run up the main-sheet, — straightway what of transcendent and permanent value is there resists the aft wind, and will doggedly stay behind that Sunday, — it does not travel Sundays; while biscuit and pork make headway, and sailors cry heave-yo! It must part company, if it open a seam. It is not quite safe to send out a venture in this kind, unless yourself go supercargo. Where a man goes, there he is; but the slightest virtue is immovable, — it is real estate, not personal; who would keep it, must consent to be bought and sold with it.

However, we need not dwell on this charge of a German extraction, it being generally admitted, by this time, that Carlyle is English, and an inhabitant of London. He has the English for his mother-tongue, though with a Scotch accent, or never so many accents, and thoughts also, which are the legitimate growth of native soil, to utter therewith. His style is eminently colloquial, and no wonder it is strange to meet with in a book. It is not literary or classical; it has not the music of poetry, nor the pomp of philosophy, but the rhythms and cadences of conversation endlessly repeated. It resounds with emphatic, natural, lively, stirring tones, muttering, rattling, exploding, like shells and shot, and with like execution. So far as it is a merit in composition, that the written answer to the spoken word, and the spoken word to a fresh and pertinent thought in the mind, as well as to the half thoughts, the tumultuary misgivings and expectancies, this author is, perhaps, not to be matched in literature.

He is no mystic, either, more than Newton or Arkwright or Davy, and tolerates none. Not one obscure line, or half line, did he ever write. His meaning lies plain as the daylight, and he who runs may read; indeed, only he who runs *can* read, and keep up with the meaning. It has the distinctness of picture to his mind, and he tells us only what he sees printed in largest English type upon the face of things. He utters substantial English thoughts in plainest English dialects; for it must be confessed, he speaks more than one of these. All the shires of England, and all the shires of Europe, are laid under contribution to his genius; for to be Eng-

lish does not mean to be exclusive and narrow, and
adapt one's self to the apprehension of his nearest neighbor only.   And yet no writer is more thoroughly Saxon.
In the translation of those fragments of Saxon poetry,
we have met with the same rhythm that occurs so often
in his poem on the French Revolution.   And if you
would know where many of those obnoxious Carlyleisms
and Germanisms came from, read the best of Milton's
prose, read those speeches of Cromwell which he has
brought to light, or go and listen once more to your
mother's tongue.   So much for his German extraction.

Indeed, for fluency and skill in the use of the English tongue, he is a master unrivalled.   His felicity
and power of expression surpass even his special merits as historian and critic.   Therein his experience has
not failed him, but furnished him with such a store of
winged, ay and legged words, as only a London life,
perchance, could give account of.   We had not understood the wealth of the language before.   Nature is ran-
sacked, and all the resorts and purlieus of humanity are
taxed, to furnish the fittest symbol for his thought.   He
does not go to the dictionary, the word-book, but to the
word-manufactory itself, and has made endless work
for the lexicographers.   Yes, he has that same English
for his mother-tongue that you have, but with him it is
no dumb, muttering, mumbling faculty, concealing the
thoughts, but a keen, unwearied, resistless weapon.   He
has such command of it as neither you nor I have ; and
it would be well for any who have a lost horse to advertise, or a town-meeting warrant, or a sermon, or a letter
to write, to study this universal letter-writer, for he
knows more than the grammar or the dictionary.

The style is worth attending to, as one of the most important features of the man which we at this distance can discern. It is for once quite equal to the matter. It can carry all its load, and never breaks down nor staggers. His books are solid and workmanlike, as all that England does ; and they are graceful and readable also. They tell of huge labor done, well done, and all the rubbish swept away, like the bright cutlery which glitters in shop windows, while the coke and ashes, the turnings, filings, dust, and borings lie far away at Birmingham, unheard of. He is a masterly clerk, scribe, reporter, writer. He can reduce to writing most things, — gestures, winks, nods, significant looks, patois, brogue, accent, pantomime, and how much that had passed for silence before, does he represent by written words. The countryman who puzzled the city lawyer, requiring him to write, among other things, his call to his horses, would hardly have puzzled him ; he would have found a word for it, all right and classical, that would have started his team for him. Consider the ceaseless tide of speech forever flowing in countless cellars, garrets, *parlors ;* that of the French, says Carlyle, " only ebbs toward the short hours of night," and what a drop in the bucket is the printed word. Feeling, thought, speech, writing, and, we might add, poetry, inspiration, — for so the circle is completed ; how they gradually dwindle at length, passing through successive colanders, into your history and classics, from the roar of the ocean, the murmur of the forest, to the squeak of a mouse ; so much only parsed and spelt out, and punctuated, at last. The few who can talk like a book, they only get reported commonly. But this writer reports a new " Lieferung."

One wonders how so much, after all, was expressed in the old way, so much here depends. upon the emphasis,

tone, pronunciation, style, and spirit of the reading No
writer uses so profusely all the aids to intelligibility
which the printer's art affords. You wonder how others
had contrived to write so many pages without emphatic
or italicized words, they are so expressive, so natural, so
indispensable here, as if none had ever used the demon-
strative pronouns demonstratively before. In another's
sentences the thought, though it may be immortal, is as
it were embalmed, and does not *strike* you, but here it is
so freshly living, even the body of it not having passed
through the ordeal of death, that it stirs in the very extremities, and the smallest particles and pronouns are all
alive with it. It is not simple dictionary *it*, yours or
mine, but IT. The words did not come at the command
of grammar, but of a tyrannous, inexorable meaning; not
like standing soldiers, by vote of Parliament, but any able-
bodied countryman pressed into the service, for " Sire, it
is not a revolt, it is a revolution."

We have never heard him speak, but we should say
that Carlyle was a rare talker. He has broken the ice,
and streams freely forth like a spring torrent. He does
not trace back the stream of his thought, silently adventurous, up to its fountain-head, but is borne away with
it, as it rushes through his brain like a torrent to over-
whelm and fertilize. He holds a talk with you. His
audience is such a tumultuous mob of thirty thousand, as
assembled at the University of Paris, before printing
was invented. Philosophy, on the other hand, does not
talk, but write, or, when it comes personally before an
audience, lecture or read ; and therefore it must be read
to-morrow, or a thousand years hence. But the talker
must naturally be attended to at once ; he does not talk
on without an audience ; the winds do not long bear the

sound of his voice. Think of Carlyle reading his French Revolution to any audience. One might say it was never written, but spoken; and thereafter reported and printed, that those not within sound of his voice might know something about it. Some men read to you something which they have written in a dead *language*, of course, but it may be in a living *letter*, in a Syriac, or Roman, or Runic character. Men must *speak* English who can *write* Sanscrit; they must speak a modern language who write, perchance, an ancient and universal one. We do not live in those days when the learned used a learned language. There is no writing of Latin with Carlyle; but as Chaucer, with all reverence to Homer, and Virgil, and Messieurs the Normans, sung his poetry in the homely Saxon tongue, — and Locke has at least the merit of having done philosophy into English, — so Carlyle has done a different philosophy still further into English, and thrown open the doors of literature and criticism to the populace.

Such a style, — so diversified and variegated! It is like the face of a country; it is like a New England landscape, with farm-houses and villages, and cultivated spots, and belts of forests and blueberry-swamps round about, with the fragrance of shad-blossoms and violets on certain winds. And as for the reading of it, it is novel enough to the reader who has used only the diligence, and old line mail-coach. It is like travelling, sometimes on foot, sometimes in a gig tandem; sometimes in a full coach, over highways, mended and unmended, for which you will prosecute the town; on level roads, through French departments, by Simplon roads over the Alps, and now and then he hauls up for a relay, and yokes in an unbroken colt of a Pegasus for a leader, driving off by cart-paths, and across lots, by corduroy roads and gridiron bridges; and where the bridges are gone, not even a string-piece left, and the reader has to set his breast and swim. You have got an expert driver this time, who has driven ten thousand miles, and was never known to upset; can drive six in hand on the edge of a precipice, and touch the leaders anywhere with his snapper.

With wonderful art he grinds into paint for his picture all his moods and experiences, so that all his forces may be brought to the encounter. Apparently writing without a particular design or responsibility, setting down his soliloquies from time to time, taking advantage of all his humors, when at length the hour comes to declare himself, he puts down in plain English, without quotation marks, what he, Thomas Carlyle, is ready to defend in the face of the world, and fathers the rest, often quite as defensible, only more modest, or plain spoken, or insinuating, upon "Sauerteig," or some other gentleman long employed on the subject. Rolling his subject how many ways in his mind, he meets it now face to face, wrestling with it at arm's length, and striving to get it down, or throw it over his head; and if that will not do, or whether it will do or not, tries the back-stitch and side-hug with it, and downs it again, scalps it, draws and quarters it, hangs it in chains, and leaves it to the winds and dogs. With his brows knit, his mind made up, his will resolved and resistless, he advances, crashing his way through the host of weak, half-formed, *dilettante* opinions, honest and dishonest ways of thinking, with their standards raised, sentimentalities and conjectures, and tramples them all into dust. See how he prevails; you don't even hear the groans of the wounded and dying.   Certainly it is not so well worth the while to look through any man's eyes at history, for the time, as through his ; and his way of looking at things is fastest getting adopted by his generation.

It is not in man to determine what his style shall be. He might as well determine what his thoughts shall be. We would not have had him write always as in the chapter on Burns, and the Life of Schiller, and elsewhere.   No ; his thoughts were ever irregular and impetuous.   Perhaps as he grows older and writes more he acquires a truer expression ; it is in some respects manlier, freer, struggling up to a level with its fountain-head. We think it is the richest prose style we know of.

Who cares what a man's style is, so it is intelligible, — as intelligible as his thought.   Literally and really, the style is no more than the *stylus,* the pen he writes with ; and it is not worth scraping and polishing, and gilding, unless it will write his thoughts the better for it.   It is something for use, and not to look at.   The question for us is, not whether Pope had a fine style, wrote with a peacock's feather, but whether he uttered useful thoughts. Translate a book a dozen times from one language to another, and what becomes of its style ?   Most books would be worn out and disappear in this ordeal.   The pen which wrote it is soon destroyed, but the poem survives.   We believe that Carlyle has, after all, more readers, and is better known to-day for this very originality of style, and that posterity will have reason to thank him for emancipating the language, in some measure, from the fetters which a merely conservative, aimless, and pedantic literary class had imposed upon it, and setting an example of greater freedom and naturalness.   No man's thoughts are new, but the style of their expression is the never-failing novelty which cheers and refreshes men.   If we were to answer the question, whether the mass of men, as we know them, talk as the standard authors and reviewers write, or rather as this man writes, we should say that he alone begins to write their language at all, and that the former is, for the most part, the mere effigies of a language, not the best method of concealing one's thoughts even, but frequently a method of doing without thoughts at all.

In his graphic description of Richter's style, Carlyle describes his own pretty nearly ; and no doubt he first got his own tongue loosened at that fountain, and was inspired by it to equal freedom and originality.   "The language," as he says of Richter, "groans with indescribable metaphors and allusions to all things, human and divine, flowing onward, not like a river, but like an inundation ; circling in complex eddies, chafing and gurgling, now this way, now that"; but in Carlyle, "the proper current" never "sinks out of sight amid the boundless uproar."   Again: "His very language is Titanian, — deep, strong, tumultuous, shining with a thousand hues, fused from a thousand elements, and winding in labyrinthic mazes."

In short, if it is desirable that a man be eloquent, that he talk much, and address himself to his own age mainly, then this is not a bad style of doing it.   But if it is desired rather that he pioneer into unexplored regions of thought, and speak to silent centuries to come, then, indeed, we could wish that he had cultivated the style of Goethe more, that of Richter less ; not that Goethe's is the kind of utterance most to be prized by mankind, but it will serve for a model of the best that can be successfully cultivated.

But for style, and fine writing, and Augustan ages, that is but a poor style, and vulgar writing, and a degenerate age, which allows us to remember these things This man has something to communicate. Carlyle's are not, in the common sense, works of art in their origin and aim ; and yet, perhaps, no living English writer evinces an equal literary talent. They are such works of art only as the plough and corn-mill and steam-engine, — not as pictures and statues. Others speak with greater emphasis to scholars, as such, but none so earnestly and effectually to all who can read. Others give their advice, he gives his sympathy also. It is no small praise that he does not take upon himself the airs, has none of the whims, none of the pride, the nice vulgarities, the starched, impoverished isolation, and cold glitter of the spoiled children of genius. He does not need to husband his pearl, but excels by a greater humanity and sincerity.

He is singularly serious and untrivial. We are everywhere impressed by the rugged, unwearied, and rich sincerity of the man. We are sure that he never sacrificed one jot of his honest thought to art or whim, but to utter himself in the most direct and effectual way, — that is the endeavor. These are merits which will wear well. When time has worn deeper into the substance of these books, this grain will appear. No such sermons have come to us here out of England, in late years, as those of this preacher, — sermons to kings, and sermons to peasants, and sermons to all intermediate classes. It is in vain that John Bull, or any of his cousins, turns a deaf ear, and pretends not to hear them : nature will not soon be weary of repeating them. There are words less obviously true, more for the ages to hear, perhaps, but none so impossible for this age not to hear. What a cutting cimeter was that " Past and Present," going through heaps of silken stuffs, and glibly through the necks of men, too, without their knowing it, leaving no trace. He has the earnestness of a prophet. In an age of pedantry and dilettantism, he has no grain of these in his composition. There is nowhere else, surely, in recent readable English, or other books, such direct and effectual teaching, reproving, encouraging, stimulating, earnestly, vehemently, almost like Mahomet, like Luther; not looking behind him to see how his *Opera Omnia* will look, but forward to other work to be done. His writings are a gospel to the young of this generation; they will hear his manly, brotherly speech with responsive joy, and press forward to older or newer gospels.

We should omit a main attraction in these books, if we said nothing of their humor. Of this indispensable pledge of sanity, without some leaven, of which the abstruse thinker may justly be suspected of mysticism, fanaticism, or insanity, there is a superabundance in Carlyle. Especially the transcendental philosophy needs the leaven of humor to render it light and digestible. In his later and longer works it is an unfailing accompaniment, reverberating through pages and chapters, long sustained without effort. The very punctuation, the italics, the quotation-marks, the blank spaces and dashes, and the capitals, each and all are pressed into its service.

Carlyle's humor is vigorous and Titanic, and has more sense in it than the sober philosophy of many another. It is not to be disposed of by laughter and smiles merely; it gets to be too serious for that: only

they may laugh who are not hit by it.   For those who
love a merry jest, this is a strange kind of fun, — rather
too practical joking, if they understand it.   The pleasant
humor which the public loves is but the innocent pranks
of the ball-room, harmless flow of animal spirits, the light
plushy pressure of dandy pumps, in comparison.   But
when an elephant takes to treading on your corns, why
then you are lucky if you sit high, or wear cowhide.
His humor is always subordinate to a serious purpose,
though often the real charm for the reader is not so much
in the essential progress and final upshot of the chapter,
as in this indirect side-light illustration of every hue.   He
sketches first, with strong, practical English pencil, the
essential features in outline, black on white, more faithfully than Dryasdust would have done, telling us wisely
whom and what to mark, to save time, and then with
brush of camel's hair, or sometimes with more expe-
ditious swab, he lays on the bright and fast colors of his
humor everywhere.   One piece of solid work, be it
known, we have determined to do, about which let there
be no jesting, but all things else under the heavens, to
the right and left of that, are for the time fair game.   To
us this humor is not wearisome, as almost every other is.
Rabelais, for instance, is intolerable ; one chapter is better than a volume, — it may be sport to him, but it is
death to us.   A mere humorist, indeed, is a most unhappy man ; and his readers are most unhappy also.

Humor is not so distinct a quality as, for the purposes
of criticism, it is commonly regarded, but allied to every,
even the divinest faculty.   The familiar and cheerful
conversation about every hearthside, if it be analyzed,
will be found to be sweetened by this principle.   There
is not only a never-failing, pleasant, and earnest humor

kept up there, embracing the domestic affairs, the dinner,
and the scolding, but there is also a constant run upon
the neighbors, and upon Church and State, and to cherish
and maintain this, in a great measure, the fire is kept
burning, and the dinner provided. There will be neighbors, parties to a very genuine, even romantic friendship,
whose whole audible salutation and intercourse, abstain-
ing from the usual cordial expressions, grasping of hands,
or affectionate farewells, consists in the mutual play and
interchange of a genial and healthy humor, which excepts
nothing, not even themselves, in its lawless range. The
child plays continually, if you will let it, and all its life is
a sort of practical humor of a very pure kind, often of so
fine and ethereal a nature, that its parents, its uncles and
cousins, can in no wise participate in it, but must stand
aloof in silent admiration, and reverence even.   The
more quiet the more profound it is.   Even Nature is observed to have her playful moods or aspects, of which
man seems sometimes to be the sport.

But, after all, we could sometimes dispense with the
humor, though unquestionably incorporated in the blood,
if it were replaced by this author's gravity. We should
not apply to himself, without qualification, his remarks
on the humor of Richter. With more repose in his inmost being, his humor would become more thoroughly
genial and placid. Humor is apt to imply but a half
satisfaction at best. In his pleasantest and most genial
hour, man smiles but as the globe smiles, and the works
of nature. The fruits *dry* ripe, and much as we relish
some of them in their green and pulpy state, we lay up
for our winter store, not out of these, but the rustling
autumnal harvests. Though we never weary of this
vivacious wit, while we are perusing its work, yet when

we remember it from afar, we sometimes feel balked and disappointed, missing the security, the simplicity, and frankness, even the occasional magnanimity of acknowledged dulness and bungling. This never-failing success and brilliant talent become a reproach.

Besides, humor does not wear well. It is commonly enough said, that a joke will not bear repeating. The deepest humor will not keep. Humors do not circulate but stagnate, or circulate partially. In the oldest literature, in the Hebrew, the Hindoo, the Persian, the Chinese, it is rarely humor, even the most divine, which still survives, but the most sober and private, painful or joyous thoughts, maxims of duty, to which the life of all men may be referred. After time has sifted the literature of a people, there is left only their SCRIPTURE, for that is WRITING, *par excellence*. This is as true of the poets, as of the philosophers and moralists by profession; for what subsides in any of these is the moral only, to reappear as dry land at some remote epoch.

We confess that Carlyle's humor is rich, deep, and variegated, in direct communication with the backbone and risible muscles of the globe, — and there is nothing like it; but much as we relish this jovial, this rapid and delugeous way of conveying one's views and impressions, when we would not converse but meditate, we pray for a man's diamond edition of his thought, without the colored illuminations in the margin, — the fishes and dragons, and unicorns, the red or the blue ink, but its initial letter in distinct skeleton type, and the whole so clipped and condensed down to the very essence of it, that time will have little to do. We know not but we shall im migrate soon, and would fain take with us all the treasures of the East; and all kinds of *dry*, portable soups, in small tin canisters, which contain whole herds of English beeves boiled down, will be acceptable.

The difference between this flashing, fitful writing and pure philosophy is the difference between flame and light.   The flame, indeed, yields light; but when we are so near as to observe the flame, we are apt to be incommoded by the heat and smoke.   But the sun, that old Platonist, is set so far off in the heavens, that only a genial summer-heat and ineffable daylight can reach us. But many a time, we confess, in wintry weather, we have been glad to forsake the sunlight, and warm us by these Promethean flames.   Carlyle must undoubtedly plead guilty to the charge of mannerism.   He not only has his vein, but his peculiar manner of working it.   He has a style which can be imitated, and sometimes is an imitator of himself.

Certainly, no critic has anywhere said what is more to the purpose, than this which Carlyle's own writings furnish, which we quote, as well for its intrinsic merit as for its pertinence here.   " It is true," says he, thinking of Richter, " the beaten paths of literature lead the safeliest to the goal; and the talent pleases us most which submits to shine with new gracefulness through old forms.   Nor is the noblest and most peculiar mind too noble or peculiar for working by prescribed laws ; Sophocles, Shakespeare, Cervantes, and in Richter's own age, Goethe, how little did they innovate on the given forms of composition, how much in the spirit they breathed into them ! All this is true ; and Richter must lose of our esteem in proportion."   And again, in the chapter on Goethe, " We read Goethe for years before we come to see wherein the distinguishing peculiarity of his understanding, of his disposition, even of his way of writing, consists !   It seems quite a simple style, [that of his?] remarkable chiefly for its calmness, its perspicuity, in short, its commonness ; and yet it is the most uncommon of all styles." And this, too, translated for us by the same pen from Schiller, which we will apply not merely to the outward form of his works, but to their inner form and substance. He is speaking of the artist. " Let some beneficent divinity snatch him, when a suckling, from the breast of his mother, and nurse him with the milk of a better time, that he may ripen to his full stature beneath a distant Grecian sky. And having grown to manhood, let him return, a foreign shape, into his century ; not, however, to delight it by his presence, but, dreadful, like the son of Agamemnon, to purify it. The matter of his works he will take from the present, but their form he will derive from a nobler time ; nay, from beyond all time, from the absolute unchanging unity of his own nature."

But enough of this. Our complaint is already out of all proportion to our discontent.

Carlyle's works, it is true, have not the stereotyped success which we call classic. They are a rich but inexpensive entertainment, at which we are not concerned lest the host has strained or impoverished himself to feed his guests. It is not the most lasting word, nor the loftiest wisdom, but rather the word which comes last. For his genius it was reserved to give expression to the thoughts which were throbbing in a million breasts. He has plucked the ripest fruit in the public garden ; but this fruit already least concerned the tree that bore it, which was rather perfecting the bud at the foot of the leaf-stalk. His works are not to be studied, but read with a swift satisfaction. Their flavor and gust is like what poets tell of the froth of wine, which can only be tasted once and hastily.   On a review we can never find the pages we had read.   Yet they are in some degree true natural products in this respect.   All things are but once, and never repeated.   These works were designed for such complete success that they serve but for a single occasion.

But he is wilfully and pertinaciously unjust, even scurrilous, impolite, ungentlemanly ; calls us "Imbeciles," "Dilettants," "Philistines," implying sometimes what would not sound well expressed.   If he would adopt the newspaper style, and take back these hard names — But where is the reader who does not derive some benefit from these epithets, applying them to himself ?

He is, in fact, the best tempered, and not the least impartial of reviewers.   He goes out of his way to do justice to profligates and quacks.   There is somewhat even Christian, in the rarest and most peculiar sense, in his universal brotherliness, his simple, child-like endurance, and earnest, honest endeavor, with sympathy for the like.   Carlyle, to adopt his own classification, is himself the hero as literary man.   There is no more notable workingman in England, in Manchester or Birmingham, or the mines round about.   We know not how many hours a day he toils, nor for what wages, exactly : we only know the results for us.

Notwithstanding the very genuine, admirable, and loyal tributes to Burns, Schiller, Goethe, and others, Carlyle is not a critic of poetry.   In the book of heroes, Shakespeare, the hero as poet, comes off rather slimly. His sympathy, as we said, is with the men of endeavor; not using the life got, but still bravely getting their life. "In fact," as he says of Cromwell, "everywhere we have to notice the decisive practical *eye* of this man; how he drives toward the practical and practicable; has a genuine insight into what *is* fact." You must have very stout legs to get noticed at all by him. He is thoroughly English in his love of practical men, and dislike for cant, and ardent enthusiastic heads that are not supported by any legs. He would kindly knock them down that they may regain some vigor by touching their mother earth. We have often wondered how he ever found out Burns, and must still refer a good share of his delight in him to neighborhood and early association. The Lycidas and Comus, appearing in Blackwood's Magazine, would probably go unread by him, nor lead him to expect a Paradise Lost. The condition-of-England question is a practical one. The condition of England demands a hero, not a poet. Other things demand a poet; the poet answers other demands. Carlyle in London, with this question pressing on him so urgently, sees no occasion for minstrels and rhapsodists there. Kings may have their bards when there are any kings. Homer would *certainly* go a-begging there. He lives in Chelsea, not on the plains of Hindostan, nor on the prairies of the West, where settlers are scarce, and a man must at least go *whistling* to himself.

What he says of poetry is rapidly uttered, and suggestive of a thought, rather than the deliberate development of any. He answers your question, What is poetry? by writing a special poem, as that Norse one, for instance, in the Book of Heroes, altogether wild and original; — answers your question, What is light? by kindling a blaze which dazzles you, and pales sun and moon, and not as a peasant might, by opening a shutter.

Carlyle is not a *seer*, but a brave looker-on and *review-*

er ; not the most free and catholic observer of men and
events, for they are likely to find him preoccupied, but
unexpectedly free and catholic when they fall within the
focus of his lens.   He does not live in the present hour,
and read men and books as they occur for his theme, but
having chosen this, he directs his studies to this end.
If we look again at his page, we are apt to retract
somewhat that we have said.   Often a genuine poetic
feeling dawns through it, like the texture of the earth
seen through the dead grass and leaves in the spring.
The History of the French Revolution is a poem, at
length translated into prose, — an Iliad, indeed, as he himself has it, — "The destructive wrath of Sansculotism :
this is what we speak, having unhappily no voice for
singing."

One improvement we could suggest in this last, as indeed in most epics, — that he should let in the sun oftener
upon his picture.   It does not often enough appear, but
it is all revolution, the old way of human life turned
simply bottom upward, so that when at length we are
inadvertently reminded of the " Brest Shipping," a St.
Domingo colony, and that anybody thinks of owning
plantations, and simply turning up the soil there, and
that now at length, after some years of this revolution,
there is a falling off in the importation of sugar, we feel
a queer surprise.   Had they not sweetened their water
with revolution then ?   It would be well if there were
several chapters headed " Work for the Month," —
Revolution-work inclusive, of course, — " Altitude of the
Sun," " State of the Crops and Markets," "Meteorological
Observations," " Attractive Industry," " Day Labor,"
&c., just to remind the reader that the French peasantry
did something beside go without breeches, burn châteaus,

get ready knotted cords, and embrace and throttle one another by turns. These things are sometimes hinted at, but they deserve a notice more in proportion to their importance. We want not only a background to the picture, but a ground under the feet also. We remark, too, occasionally, an unphilosophical habit, common enough elsewhere, in Alison's History of Modern Europe, for instance, of saying, undoubtedly with effect, that if a straw had not fallen this way or that, why then — but, of course, it is as easy in philosophy to make kingdoms rise and fall as straws.

The poet is blithe and cheery ever, and as well as nature. Carlyle has not the simple Homeric health of Wordsworth, nor the deliberate philosophic turn of Coleridge, nor the scholastic taste of Landor, but, though sick and under restraint, the constitutional vigor of one of his old Norse heroes, struggling in a lurid light, with Jötuns still, striving to throw the old woman, and "she was Time," — striving to lift the big cat, and that was "the Great World-Serpent, which, tail in mouth, girds and keeps up the whole created world." The smith, though so brawny and tough, I should not call the healthiest man. There is too much shop-work, too great extremes of heat and cold, and incessant ten-pound-ten and thrashing of the anvil, in his life. But the haymaker's is a true sunny perspiration, produced by the extreme of summer heat only, and conversant with the blast of the zephyr, not of the forge-bellows. We know very well the nature of this man's sadness, but we do not know the nature of his gladness.

The poet will maintain serenity in spite of all disappointments. He is expected to preserve an unconcerned and healthy outlook over the world, while he lives. *Philo-*

sophia practica est eruditionis meta, — Philosophy prac-
tised is the goal of learning ; and for that other, *Oratoris
est celare artem,* we might read, *Herois est celare pugnam,*
— the hero will conceal his struggles. Poetry is the only
life got, the only work done, the only pure product and
free labor of man, performed only when he has put all
the world under his feet, and conquered the last of his
foes.

Carlyle speaks of Nature with a certain unconscious
pathos for the most part. She is to him a receded but
ever memorable splendor, casting still a reflected light
over all his scenery. As we read his books here in
New England, where there are potatoes enough, and
every man can get his living peacefully and sportively
as the birds and bees, and need think no more of that, it
seems to us as if by the world he often meant London, at
the head of the tide upon the Thames, the sorest place
on the face of the earth, the very citadel of conservatism.

In his writings, we should say that he, as conspicuously
as any, though with little enough expressed or even conscious sympathy, represents the Reformer class, and all
the better for not being the acknowledged leader of any.
In him the universal plaint is most settled, unappeasable,
and serious. Until a thousand named and nameless
grievances are righted, there will be no repose for him
in the lap of nature, or the seclusion of science and literature. By foreseeing it, he hastens the crisis in the affairs
of England, and is as good as many years added to her
history.

To do himself justice, and set some of his readers right,
he should give us some transcendent hero at length, **to**
rule his demigods and Titans ; develop, perhaps, his reserved and dumb reverence for Christ, not speaking to a

London or Church of England audience merely. Let *not* " sacred silence meditate that sacred matter " forever, but let us have sacred speech and sacred scripture thereon.

Every man will include in his list of worthies those whom he himself best represents. Carlyle, and our countryman Emerson, whose place and influence must erelong obtain a more distinct recognition, are, to a certain extent, the complement of each other. The age could not do with one of them, it cannot do with both. To make a broad and rude distinction, to suit our present purpose, the former, as critic, deals with the men of action, — Mahomet, Luther, Cromwell; the latter with the thinkers, — Plato, Shakespeare, Goethe; for, though both have written upon Goethe, they do not meet in him. The one has more sympathy with the heroes, or practical reformers, the other with the observers, or philosophers. Put their worthies together, and you will have a pretty fair representation of mankind; yet with one or more memorable exceptions. To say nothing of Christ, who yet awaits a just appreciation from literature, the peacefully practical hero, whom Columbus may represent, is obviously slighted; but above and after all, the Man of the Age, come to be called workingman, it is obvious that none yet speaks to his condition, for the speaker is not yet in his condition.

Like speaks to like only; labor to labor, philosophy to philosophy, criticism to criticism, poetry to poetry. Literature speaks how much still to the past, how little to the future, how much to the East, how little to the West, —

> In the East fames are won,
> In the West deeds are done.

One merit in Carlyle, let the subject be what it may,
is the freedom of prospect he allows, the entire absence
of cant and dogma.   He removes many cart-loads of
rubbish, and leaves open a broad highway.   His writings
are all unfenced on the side of the future and the possible.   Though he does but inadvertently direct our eyes
to the open heavens, nevertheless he lets us wander broad-
ly underneath, and shows them to us reflected in innumerable pools and lakes.

These volumes contain not the highest, but a very
practicable wisdom, which startles and provokes, rather
than informs us.   Carlyle does not oblige us to think ;
we have thought enough for him already, but he compels
us to act.   We accompany him rapidly through an endless gallery of pictures, and glorious reminiscences of
experiences unimproved.   " Have you not had Moses
and the prophets ?   Neither will ye be persuaded
if one should rise from the dead."   There is no calm
philosophy of life here, such as you might put at the end
of the Almanac, to hang over the farmer's hearth, how
men shall live in these winter, in these summer days.
No philosophy, properly speaking, of love, or friendship,
or religion, or politics, or education, or nature, or spirit ;
perhaps a nearer approach to a philosophy of kingship,
and of the place of the literary man, than of anything
else.   A rare preacher, with prayer, and psalm, and sermon, and benediction, but no contemplation of man's life
from the serene oriental ground, nor yet from the stirring
occidental.   No thanksgiving sermon for the holydays,
or the Easter vacations, when all men submit to float on
the full currents of life.   When we see with what spirits,
though with little heroism enough, wood-choppers, dro-

vers, and apprentices take and spend life, playing all day
long, sunning themselves, shading themselves, eating,
drinking, sleeping, we think that the philosophy of their
life written would be such a level natural history as the
Gardener's Calendar and the works of the early botan-
ists, inconceivably slow to come to practical conclusions.

There is no philosophy here for philosophers, only as
every man is said to have his philosophy. No system
but such as is the man himself; and, indeed, he stands
compactly enough; no progress beyond the first assertion
and challenge, as it were, with trumpet blast. One
thing is certain, — that we had best be doing something in
good earnest henceforth forever; that's an indispensable
philosophy. The before impossible precept, "know thyself," he translates into the partially possible one, "know
what thou canst work at." Sartor Resartus is, perhaps,
the sunniest and most philosophical, as it is the most
autobiographical of his works, in which he drew most
largely on the experience of his youth. But we miss
everywhere a calm depth, like a lake, even stagnant, and
must submit to rapidity and whirl, as on skates, with all
kinds of skilful and antic motions, sculling, sliding, cutting punch-bowls and rings, forward and backward. The
talent is very nearly equal to the genius. Sometimes it
would be preferable to wade slowly through a Serbonian
bog, and feel the juices of the meadow.

Beside some philosophers of larger vision, Carlyle
stands like an honest, half-despairing boy, grasping at
some details only of their world systems. Philosophy,
certainly, is some account of truths, the fragments and
very insignificant parts of which man will practise in this
workshop; truths infinite and in harmony with infinity;
in respect to which the very objects and ends of the so-

called practical philosopher will be mere propositions, like the rest. It would be no reproach to a philosopher, that he knew the future better than the past, or even than the present. It is better worth knowing. He will prophesy, tell what is to be, or in other words, what alone is, under appearances, laying little stress on the boiling of the pot, or the condition-of-England question. He has no more to do with the condition of England than with her national debt, which a vigorous generation would not inherit. The philosopher's conception of things will, above all, be truer than other men's, and his philosophy will subordinate all the circumstances of life. To live like a philosopher is to live, not foolishly, like other men, but wisely and according to universal laws. If Carlyle does not take two steps in philosophy, are there any who take three? Philosophy having crept clinging to the rocks, so far, puts out its feelers many ways in vain. It would be hard to surprise him by the relation of any important human experience, but in some nook or corner of his works you will find that this, too, was sometimes dreamed of in his philosophy.

To sum up our most serious objections in a few words, we should say that Carlyle indicates a depth, — and we mean not impliedly, but distinctly, — which he neglects to fathom. We want to know more about that which he wants to know as well. If any luminous star or undissolvable nebula is visible from his station which is not visible from ours, the interests of science require that the fact be communicated to us. The universe expects every man to do his duty in his parallel of latitude. We want to hear more of his inmost life; his hymn and prayer more; his elegy and eulogy less; that he should speak more from his character, and less from

his talent; communicate centrally with his readers, and
not by a side; that he should say what he believes, without suspecting that men disbelieve it, out of his never-
misunderstood nature.   His genius can cover all the
land with gorgeous palaces, but the reader does not
abide in them, but pitches his tent rather in the desert
and on the mountain-peak.

When we look about for something to quote, as the
fairest specimen of the man, we confess that we labor
under an unusual difficulty; for his philosophy is so
little of the proverbial or sentential kind, and opens so
gradually, rising insensibly from the reviewer's level,
and developing its thought completely and in detail, that
we look in vain for the brilliant passages, for point and
antithesis, and must end by quoting his works entire.
What in a writer of less breadth would have been the
proposition which would have bounded his discourse, his
column of victory, his Pillar of Hercules, and *ne plus ul-
tra*, is in Carlyle frequently the same thought unfolded;
no Pillar of Hercules, but a considerable prospect, north
and south, along the Atlantic coast.   There are other pil-
lars of Hercules, like beacons and light-houses, still further
in the horizon, toward Atlantis, set up by a few ancient
and modern travellers; but, so far as this traveller goes,
he clears and colonizes, and all the surplus population of
London is bound thither at once.   What we would quote
is, in fact, his vivacity, and not any particular wisdom or
sense, which last is ever synonymous with sentence [*sen-
tentia*], as in his contemporaries Coleridge, Landor, and
Wordsworth.   We have not attempted to discriminate
between his works, but have rather regarded them all as
one work, as is the man himself.   We have not examined
so much as remembered them.   To do otherwise would

have required a more indifferent, and perhaps even less just review, than the present.

All his works might well enough be embraced under the title of one of them, a good specimen brick, "On Heroes, Hero-Worship, and the Heroic in History." Of this department he is the Chief Professor in the World's University, and even leaves Plutarch behind. Such intimate and living, such loyal and generous sympathy with the heroes of history, not one in one age only, but forty in forty ages, such an unparalleled reviewing and greeting of all past worth, with exceptions, to be sure, — but exceptions were the rule before, — it was, indeed, to make this the age of review writing, as if now one period of the human story were completing itself, and getting its accounts settled. This soldier has told the stories with new emphasis, and will be a memorable hander-down of fame to posterity. And with what wise discrimination he has selected his men, with reference both to his own genius and to theirs, — Mahomet, Dante, Cromwell, Voltaire, Johnson, Burns, Goethe, Richter, Schiller, Mirabeau, — could any of these have been spared? These we wanted to hear about. We have not as commonly the cold and refined judgment of the scholar and critic merely, but something more human and affecting. These eulogies have the glow and warmth of friendship. There is sympathy, not with mere fames, and formless, incredible things, but with kindred men, — not transiently, but life-long he has walked with them.

No doubt, some of Carlyle's worthies, should they ever return to earth, would find themselves unpleasantly put upon their good behavior, to sustain their characters; but if he can return a man's life more perfect to our hands than it was left at his death, following out the design of its author, we shall have no great cause to complain. We do not want a daguerreotype likeness. All biography is the life of Adam, — a much-experienced man, — and time withdraws something partial from the story of every individual, that the historian may supply something general   If these virtues were not in this man, perhaps they are in his biographer, — no fatal mistake. Really, in any other sense, we never do, nor desire to, come at the historical man, — unless we rob his grave, that is the nearest approach. Why did he die, then? *He* is with his bones, surely.

No doubt Carlyle has a propensity to *exaggerate* the heroic in history, that is, he creates you an ideal hero rather than another thing: he has most of that material. This we allow in all its senses, and in one narrower sense it is not so convenient. Yet what were history if he did not exaggerate it? How comes it that history never has to wait for facts, but for a man to write it? The ages may go on forgetting the facts never so long, he can remember two for every one forgotten. The musty records of history, like the catacombs, contain the perishable remains, but only in the breast of genius are embalmed the souls of heroes. There is very little of what is called criticism here ; it is love and reverence, rather, which deal with qualities not relatively, but absolutely great; for whatever is admirable in a man is something infinite, to which we cannot set bounds. These sentiments allow the mortal to die, the immortal and divine to survive. There is something antique, even, in his style of treating his subject, reminding us that Heroes and Demi-gods, Fates and Furies, still exist ; the common man is nothing to him, but after death the hero is apotheosized and has a place in heaven, as in the religion of the Greeks.

Exaggeration! was ever any virtue attributed to a man without exaggeration? was ever any vice, without infinite exaggeration? Do we not exaggerate ourselves to ourselves, or do we recognize ourselves for the actual men we are? Are we not all great men? Yet what are we actually to speak of? We live by exaggeration. What else is it to anticipate more than we enjoy? The lightning is an exaggeration of the light. Exaggerated history is poetry, and truth referred to a new standard. To a small man every greater is an exaggeration. He who cannot exaggerate is not qualified to utter truth. No truth, we think, was ever expressed but with this sort of emphasis, so that for the time there seemed to be no other. Moreover, you must speak loud to those who are hard of hearing, and so you acquire a habit of shouting to those who are not. By an immense exaggeration we appreciate our Greek poetry and philosophy, and Egyptian ruins; our Shakespeares and Miltons, our Liberty and Christianity. We give importance to this hour over all other hours. We do not live by justice, but by grace. As the sort of justice which concerns us in our daily intercourse is not that administered by the judge, so the historical justice which we prize is not arrived at by nicely balancing the evidence. In order to appreciate any, even the humblest man, you must first, by some good fortune, have acquired a sentiment of admiration, even of reverence, for him, and there never were such exaggerators as these.

To try him by the German rule of referring an author to his own standard, we will quote the following from Carlyle's remarks on history, and leave the reader to consider how far his practice has been consistent with his theory "Truly, if History is Philosophy teaching by Experience, the writer fitted to compose history is hitherto an unknown man. The Experience itself would require All-knowledge to record it, were the All-wisdom, needful for such Philosophy as would interpret it, to be had for asking. Better were it that mere earthly Historians should lower such pretensions, more suitable for Omniscience than for human science ; and aiming only at some picture of the things acted, which picture itself will at best be a poor approximation, leave the inscrutable purport of them an acknowledged secret ; or, at most, in reverent faith, far different from that teaching of Philosophy, pause over the mysterious vestiges of Him whose path is in the great deep of Time, whom History indeed reveals, but only all History, and in Eternity, will clearly reveal."

Carlyle is a critic who lives in London to tell this generation who have been the great men of our race. We have read that on some exposed place in the city of Geneva, they have fixed a brazen indicator for the use of travellers, with the names of the mountain summits in the horizon marked upon it, " so that by taking sight across the index you can distinguish them at once. You will not mistake Mont Blanc, if you see him, but until you get accustomed to the panorama, you may easily mistake one of his court for the king." It stands there a piece of mute brass, that seems nevertheless to know in what vicinity it is : and there perchance it will stand, when the nation that placed it there has passed away, still in sympathy with the mountains, forever discriminating in the desert.

So, we may say, stands this man, pointing as long as he lives, in obedience to some spiritual magnetism, to the summits in the historical horizon, for the guidance of his fellows.

Truly, our greatest blessings are very cheap. To have our sunlight without paying for it, without any duty levied, — to have our poet there in England, to furnish us entertainment, and, what is better, provocation, from year to year, all our lives long, to make the world seem richer for us, the age more respectable, and life better worth the living, — all without expense of acknowledgment even, but silently accepted out of the east like morning light as a matter of course

LIFE WITHOUT PRINCIPLE.*

At a lyceum, not long since, I felt that the lecturer
had chosen a theme too foreign to himself, and so failed
to interest me as much as he might have done. He described things not in or near to his heart, but toward his
extremities and superficies. There was, in this sense,
no truly central or centralizing thought in the lecture.
I would have had him deal with his privatest experience,
as the poet does. The greatest compliment that was
ever paid me was when one asked me what *I thought*,
and attended to my answer. I am surprised, as well as
delighted, when this happens, it is such a rare use he
would make of me, as if he were acquainted with the
tool. Commonly, if men want anything of me, it is only
to know how many acres I make of their land, — since
I am a surveyor, — or, at most, what trivial news I have
burdened myself with. They never will go to law for
my meat; they prefer the shell. A man once came a
considerable distance to ask me to lecture on Slavery;
but on conversing with him, I found that he and his
clique expected seven eighths of the lecture to be theirs,
and only one eighth mine; so I declined. I take it for
granted, when I am invited to lecture anywhere, — for
I have had a little experience in that business, — that
there is a desire to hear what *I think* on some subject,

* Atlantic Monthly, Boston, October, 1863.

though I may be the greatest fool in the country, — and
not that I should say pleasant things merely, or such as
the audience will assent to; and I resolve, accordingly,
that I will give them a strong dose of myself. They
have sent for me, and engaged to pay for me, and I am
determined that they shall have me, though I bore them
beyond all precedent.

So now I would say something similar to you, my
readers. Since *you* are my readers, and I have not
been much of a traveller, I will not talk about people a
thousand miles off, but come as near home as I can.
As the time is short, I will leave out all the flattery,
and retain all the criticism.

Let us consider the way in which we spend our lives.

This world is a place of business. What an infinite
bustle! I am awaked almost every night by the panting
of the locomotive. It interrupts my dreams. There is
no sabbath. It would be glorious to see mankind at
leisure for once. It is nothing but work, work, work.
I cannot easily buy a blank-book to write thoughts in;
they are commonly ruled for dollars and cents. An
Irishman, seeing me making a minute in the fields, took
it for granted that I was calculating my wages. If a
man was tossed out of a window when an infant, and so
made a cripple for life, or scared out of his wits by the
Indians, it is regretted chiefly because he was thus
incapacitated for — business! I think that there is nothing, not even crime, more opposed to poetry, to philosophy, ay, to life itself, than this incessant business.

There is a coarse and boisterous money-making fellow
in the outskirts of our town, who is going to build a
bank-wall under the hill along the edge of his meadow.
The powers have put this into his head to keep him out

of mischief, and he wishes me to spend three weeks
digging there with him.   The result will be that he will
perhaps get some more money to hoard, and leave for
his heirs to spend foolishly.   If I do this, most will
commend me as an industrious and hard-working man ;
but if I choose to devote myself to certain labors which
yield more real profit, though but little money, they
may be inclined to look on me as an idler.   Nevertheless, as I do not need the police of meaningless labor to
regulate me, and do not see anything absolutely praise-
worthy in this fellow's undertaking, any more than in
many an enterprise of our own or foreign governments,
however amusing it may be to him or them, I prefer to
finish my education at a different school.

If a man walk in the woods for love of them half of
each day, he is in danger of being regarded as a loafer ;
but if he spends his whole day as a speculator, shearing
off those woods and making earth bald before her time,
he is esteemed an industrious and enterprising citizen.
As if a town had no interest in its forests but to cut
them down !

Most men would feel insulted, if it were proposed to
employ them in throwing stones over a wall, and then in
throwing them back, merely that they might earn their
wages.   But many are no more worthily employed now.
For instance: just after sunrise, one summer morning,
I noticed one of my neighbors walking beside his team,
which was slowly drawing a heavy hewn stone swung
under the axle, surrounded by an atmosphere of industry, — his day's work begun, — his brow commenced to
sweat, — a reproach to all sluggards and idlers, — pausing abreast the shoulders of his oxen, and half turning
round with a flourish of his merciful whip, while they

gained their length on him. And I thought, Such is
.the labor which the American Congress exists to protect,
— honest, manly toil, — honest as the day is long, —
that makes his bread taste sweet, and keeps society
sweet, — which all men respect and have consecrated
one of the sacred band, doing the needful but irksome
drudgery. Indeed, I felt a slight reproach, because I
observed this from a window, and was not abroad and
stirring about a similar business. The day went by,
and at evening I passed the yard of another neighbor,
who keeps many servants, and spends much money foolishly, while he adds nothing to the common stock, and
there I saw the stone of the morning lying beside a
whimsical structure intended to adorn this Lord Timo-
thy Dexter's premises, and the dignity forthwith departed
from the teamster's labor, in my eyes. In my opinion,
the sun was made to light worthier toil than this. I
may add, that his employer has since run off, in debt to
a good part of the town, and, after passing through
Chancery, has settled somewhere else, there to become
once more a patron of the arts.

The ways by which you may get money almost without exception lead downward. To have done anything
by which you earned money *merely* is to have been truly
idle or worse. If the laborer gets no more than the
wages which his employer pays him, he is cheated, he
cheats himself. If you would get money as a writer or
lecturer, you must be popular, which is to go down perpendicularly. Those services which the community
will most readily pay for, it is most disagreeable to render. You are paid for being something less than a man.
The State does not commonly reward a genius any
more wisely. Even the poet-laureate would rather not

have to celebrate the accidents of royalty. He must be bribed with a pipe of wine; and perhaps another poet is called away from his muse to gauge that very pipe. As for my own business, even that kind of surveying which I could do with most satisfaction, my employers do not want. They would prefer that I should do my work coarsely and not too well, ay, not well enough. When I observe that there are different ways of surveying, my employer commonly asks which will give him the most land, not which is most correct. I once invented a rule for measuring cord-wood, and tried to introduce it in Boston; but the measurer there told me that the sellers did not wish to have their wood measured correctly,— that he was already too accurate for them, and therefore they commonly got their wood measured in Charlestown before crossing the bridge.

The aim of the laborer should be, not to get his living, to get "a good job," but to perform well a certain work; and, even in a pecuniary sense, it would be economy for a town to pay its laborers so well that they would not feel that they were working for low ends, as for a livelihood merely, but for scientific, or even moral ends. Do not hire a man who does your work for money, but him who does it for love of it.

It is remarkable that there are few men so well employed, so much to their minds, but that a little money or fame would commonly buy them off from their present pursuit. I see advertisements for *active* young men, as if activity were the whole of a young man's capital. Yet I have been surprised when one has with confidence proposed to me, a grown man, to embark in some enterprise of his, as if I had absolutely nothing to do, my life having been a complete failure hitherto.

What a doubtful compliment this is to pay me !   As if he had met me half-way across the ocean beating up against the wind, but bound nowhere, and proposed to me to go along with him !   If I did, what do you think the underwriters would say?   No, no!   I am not without employment at this stage of the voyage.   To tell the truth, I saw an advertisement for able-bodied seamen, when I was a boy, sauntering in my native port, and as soon as I came of age I embarked.

The community has no bribe that will tempt a wise man.   You may raise money enough to tunnel a mountain, but you cannot raise money enough to hire a man who is minding *his own* business.   An efficient and valuable man does what he can, whether the community pay him for it or not.   The inefficient offer their inefficiency to the highest bidder, and are forever expecting to be put into office.   One would suppose that they were rarely disappointed.

Perhaps I am more than usually jealous with respect to my freedom.   I feel that my connection with and obligation to society are still very slight and transient. Those slight labors which afford me a livelihood, and by which it is allowed that I am to some extent serviceable to my contemporaries, are as yet commonly a pleasure to me, and I am not often reminded that they are a necessity.   So far I am successful.   But I foresee, that, if my wants should be much increased, the labor required to supply them would become a drudgery.   If I should sell both my forenoons and afternoons to society, as most appear to do, I am sure, that for me there would be nothing left worth living for.   I trust that I shall never thus sell my birthright for a mess of pottage. I wish to suggest that a man may be very industrious, and yet not spend his time well. There is no more fatal blunderer than he who consumes the greater part of his life getting his living. All great enterprises are self-supporting. The poet, for instance, must sustain his body by his poetry, as a steam planing-mill feeds its boilers with the shavings it makes. You must get your living by loving. But as it is said of the merchants that ninety-seven in a hundred fail, so the life of men generally, tried by this standard, is a failure, and bankruptcy may be surely prophesied.

Merely to come into the world the heir of a fortune is not to be born, but to be still-born, rather. To be supported by the charity of friends, or a government-pension, — provided you continue to breathe, — by whatever fine synonymes you describe these relations, is to go into the almshouse. On Sundays the poor debtor goes to church to take an account of stock, and finds, of course, that his outgoes have been greater than his income. In the Catholic Church, especially, they go into Chancery, make a clean confession, give up all, and think to start again. Thus men will lie on their backs, talking about the fall of man, and never make an effort to get up.

As for the comparative demand which men make on life, it is an important difference between two, that the one is satisfied with a level success, that his marks can all be hit by point-blank shots, but the other, however low and unsuccessful his life may be, constantly elevates his aim, though at a very slight angle to the horizon. I should much rather be the last man, — though, as the Orientals say, " Greatness doth not approach him who is forever looking down; and all those who are looking high are growing poor."

It is remarkable that there is little or nothing to be

remembered written on the subject of getting a living :
how to make getting a living not merely honest and
honorable, but altogether inviting and glorious; for if
getting a living is not so, then living is not.   One would
think, from looking at literature, that this question had
never disturbed a solitary individual's musings.   Is it
that men are too much disgusted with their experience to
speak of it ?   The lesson of value which money teaches,
which the Author of the Universe has taken so much
pains to teach us, we are inclined to skip altogether.   As
for the means of living, it is wonderful how indifferent
men of all classes are about it, even reformers, so
called, — whether they inherit, or earn, or steal it.   I
think that Society has done nothing for us in this respect,
or at least has undone what she has done.   Cold and
hunger seem more friendly to my nature than those
methods which men have adopted and advise to ward
them off.

The title *wise* is, for the most part, falsely applied.
How can one be a wise man, if he does not know any
better how to live than other men ? — if he is only more
cunning and intellectually subtle ?   Does Wisdom work
in a tread-mill ? or does she teach how to succeed *by her
example ?*   Is there any such thing as wisdom not applied
to life ?   Is she merely the miller who grinds the finest
logic ?   It is pertinent to ask if Plato got his *living* in a
better way or more successfully than his contemporaries, — or did he succumb to the difficulties of life like
other men ?   Did he seem to prevail over some of them
merely by indifference, or by assuming grand airs ? or
find it easier to live, because his aunt remembered him
in her will ?   The ways in which most men get their
living, that is, live, are mere make-shifts, and a shirking

of the real business of life, — chiefly because they do not know, but partly because they do not mean, any better.

The rush to California, for instance, and the attitude, not merely of merchants, but of philosophers and prophets, so called, in relation to it, reflect the greatest disgrace on mankind. That so many are ready to live by luck, and so get the means of commanding the labor of others less lucky, without contributing any value to society! And that is called enterprise! I know of no more startling development of the immorality of trade, and all the common modes of getting a living. The philosophy and poetry and religion of such a mankind are not worth the dust of a puff-ball. The hog that gets his living by rooting, stirring up the soil so, would be ashamed of such company. If I could command the wealth of all the worlds by lifting my finger, I would not pay *such* a price for it. Even Mahomet knew that God did not make this world in jest. It makes God to be a moneyed gentleman who scatters a handful of pennies in order to see mankind scramble for them. The world's raffle! A subsistence in the domains of Nature a thing to be raffled for! What a comment, what a satire, on our institutions! The conclusion will be, that mankind will hang itself upon a tree. And have all the precepts in all the Bibles taught men only this? and is the last and most admirable invention of the human race only an improved muck-rake? Is this the ground on which Orientals and Occidentals meet? Did God direct us so to get our living, digging where we never planted, — and He would, perchance, reward us with lumps of gold?

God gave the righteous man a certificate entitling him to food and raiment, but the unrighteous man found a *fac-simile* of the same in God's coffers, and appropriated it, and obtained food and raiment like the former. It is one of the most extensive systems of counterfeiting that the world has seen. I did not know that mankind were suffering for want of gold. I have seen a little of it. I know that it is very malleable, but not so malleable as wit. A grain of gold will gild a great surface, but not so much as a grain of wisdom.

The gold-digger in the ravines of the mountains is as much a gambler as his fellow in the saloons of San Francisco. What difference does it make, whether you shake dirt or shake dice? If you win, society is the loser. The gold-digger is the enemy of the honest laborer, whatever checks and compensations there may be. It is not enough to tell me that you worked hard to get your gold. So does the Devil work hard. The way of transgressors may be hard in many respects. The humblest observer who goes to the mines sees and says that gold-digging is of the character of a lottery; the gold thus obtained is not the same thing with the wages of honest toil. But, practically, he forgets what he has seen, for he has seen only the fact, not the principle, and goes into trade there, that is, buys a ticket in what commonly proves another lottery, where the fact is not so obvious.

After reading Howitt's account of the Australian gold-diggings one evening, I had in my mind's eye, all night, the numerous valleys, with their streams, all cut up with foul pits, from ten to one hundred feet deep, and half a dozen feet across, as close as they can be dug, and partly filled with water, — the locality to which men furiously rush to probe for their fortunes, — uncertain where they shall break ground, — not knowing but the gold is under their camp itself, — sometimes digging one hundred and sixty feet before they strike the vein, or then missing it

by a foot, — turned into demons, and regardless of each
other's rights, in their thirst for riches, — whole valleys,
for thirty miles, suddenly honeycombed by the pits of
the miners, so that even hundreds are drowned in them, —
standing in water, and covered with mud and clay, they
work night and day, dying of exposure and disease.
Having read this, and partly forgotten it, I was thinking,
accidentally, of my own unsatisfactory life, doing as others
do; and with that vision of the diggings still before me,
I asked myself, why *I* might not be washing some gold
daily, though it were only the finest particles, — why *1*
might not sink a shaft down to the gold within me, and
work that mine. *There* is a Ballarat, a Bendigo for
you, — what though it were a sulky-gully? At any
rate, I might pursue some path, however solitary and narrow and crooked, in which I could walk with love and
reverence. Wherever a man separates from the multitude, and goes his own way in this mood, there indeed is
a fork in the road, though ordinary travellers may see
only a gap in the paling. His solitary path across-lots
will turn out the *higher way* of the two.

Men rush to California and Australia as if the true
gold were to be found in that direction; but that is to
go to the very opposite extreme to where it lies. They
go prospecting farther and farther away from the true
lead, and are most unfortunate when they think themselves most successful. Is not our *native* soil auriferous?
Does not a stream from the golden mountains flow
through our native valley? and has not this for more than
geologic ages been bringing down the shining particles
and forming the nuggets for us? Yet, strange to tell, if
a digger steal away, prospecting for this true gold, into
the unexplored solitudes around us, there is no danger

that any will dog his steps, and endeavor to supplant him.
He may claim and undermine the whole valley even,
both the cultivated and the uncultivated portions, his
whole life long in peace, for no one will ever dispute his
claim. They will not mind his cradles or his toms. He
is not confined to a claim twelve feet square, as at Ballarat, but may mine anywhere, and wash the whole wide
world in his tom.

Howitt says of the man who found the great nugget
which weighed twenty-eight pounds, at the Bendigo diggings in Australia: " He soon began to drink ; got a
horse, and rode all about, generally at full gallop, and,
when he met people, called out to inquire if they knew
who he was, and then kindly informed them that he was
' the bloody wretch that had found the nugget.' At last
he rode full speed against a tree, and nearly knocked
his brains out." I think, however, there was no danger
of that, for he had already knocked his brains out against
the nugget. Howitt adds, " He is a hopelessly ruined
man." But he is a type of the class. They are all
fast men. Hear some of the names of the places where
they dig: " Jackass Flat," — " Sheep's-Head Gully," —
" Murderer's Bar," etc. Is there no satire in these
names? Let them carry their ill-gotten wealth where
they will, I am thinking it will still be " Jackass Flat,"
if not " Murderer's Bar," where they live.

The last resource of our energy has been the robbing
of graveyards on the Isthmus of Darien, an enterprise
which appears to be but in its infancy ; for, according to
late accounts, an act has passed its second reading in the
legislature of New Granada, regulating this kind of min-
ing ; and a correspondent of the " Tribune " writes :
" In the dry season, when the weather will permit of the

country being properly prospected, no doubt other rich *guacas* [that is, graveyards] will be found." To emigrants he says : " Do not come before December ; take the Isthmus route in preference to the Boca del Toro one ; bring no useless baggage, and do not cumber yourself with a tent ; but a good pair of blankets will be necessary ; a pick, shovel, and axe of good material will be almost all that is required " : advice which might have been taken from the " Burker's Guide." And he concludes with this line in Italics and small capitals : " *If you are doing well at home*, STAY THERE," which may fairly be interpreted to mean, " If you are getting a good living by robbing graveyards at home, stay there."

But why go to California for a text ? She is the child of New England, bred at her own school and church.

It is remarkable that among all the preachers there are so few moral teachers. The prophets are employed in excusing the ways of men. Most reverend seniors, the *illuminati* of the age, tell me, with a gracious, reminiscent smile, betwixt an aspiration and a shudder, not to be too tender about these things, — to lump all that, that is, make a lump of gold of it. The highest advice I have heard on these subjects was grovelling. The burden of it was, — It is not worth your while to undertake to reform the world in this particular. Do not ask how your bread is buttered ; it will make you sick, if you do, — and the like. A man had better starve at once than lose his innocence in the process of getting his bread. If within the sophisticated man there is not an unsophisticated one, then he is but one of the Devil's angels. As we grow old, we live more coarsely, we relax a little in our disciplines, and, to some extent, cease to obey our finest instincts. But we should be fastidious to the extreme of sanity, disregarding the gibes of those who are more unfortunate than ourselves.

In our science and philosophy, even, there is commonly no true and absolute account of things. The spirit of sect and bigotry has planted its hoof amid the stars. You have only to discuss the problem, whether the stars are inhabited or not, in order to discover it. Why must we daub the heavens as well as the earth? It was an unfortunate discovery that Dr. Kane was a Mason, and that Sir John Franklin was another. But it was a more cruel suggestion that possibly that was the reason why the former went in search of the latter. There is not a popular magazine in this country that would dare to print a child's thought on important subjects without comment. It must be submitted to the D. D.s. I would it were the chickadee-dees.

You come from attending the funeral of mankind to attend to a natural phenomenon. A little thought is sexton to all the world.

I hardly know an *intellectual* man, even, who is so broad and truly liberal that you can think aloud in his society. Most with whom you endeavor to talk soon come to a stand against some institution in which they appear to hold stock, — that is, some particular, not universal, way of viewing things. They will continually thrust their own low roof, with its narrow skylight, between you and the sky, when it is the unobstructed heavens you would view. Get out of the way with your cobwebs, wash your windows, I say! In some lyceums they tell me that they have voted to exclude the subject of religion. But how do I know what their religion is, and when I am near to or far from it? I have walked into such an arena and done my best to make a clean breast of what religion I have experienced, and the audience never suspected what I was about. The lecture was as harmless as moonshine to them. Whereas, if I had read to them the biography of the greatest scamps in history, they might have thought that I had written the lives of the deacons of their church. Ordinarily, the inquiry is, Where did you come from? or, Where are you going? That was a more pertinent question which I overheard one of my auditors put to another once, — " What does he lecture for? " It made me quake in my shoes.

To speak impartially, the best men that I know are not serene, a world in themselves. For the most part, they dwell in forms, and flatter and study effect only more finely than the rest. We select granite for the underpinning of our houses and barns; we build fences of stone; but we do not ourselves rest on an underpinning of granitic truth, the lowest primitive rock. Our sills are rotten. What stuff is the man made of who is not coexistent in our thought with the purest and subtilest truth? I often accuse my finest acquaintances of an immense frivolity; for, while there are manners and compliments we do not meet, we do not teach one another the lessons of honesty and sincerity that the brutes do, or of steadiness and solidity that the rocks do. The fault is commonly mutual, however; for we do not habitually demand any more of each other.

That excitement about Kossuth, consider how characteristic, but superficial, it was! — only another kind of politics or dancing. Men were making speeches to him all over the country, but each expressed only the thought, or the want of thought, of the multitude. No man stood on truth. They were merely banded together, as usual, one leaning on another, and all together on nothing; as the Hindoos made the world rest on an elephant, the elephant on a tortoise, and the tortoise on a serpent, and had nothing to put under the serpent. For all fruit of that stir we have the Kossuth hat.

Just so hollow and ineffectual, for the most part, is our ordinary conversation. Surface meets surface. When our life ceases to be inward and private, conversation degenerates into mere gossip. We rarely meet a man who can tell us any news which he has not read in a newspaper, or been told by his neighbor; and, for the most part, the only difference between us and our fellow is that he has seen the newspaper, or been out to tea, and we have not. In proportion as our inward life fails, we go more constantly and desperately to the post-office. You may depend on it, that the poor fellow who walks away with the greatest number of letters, proud of his extensive correspondence, has not heard from himself this long while.

I do not know but it is too much to read one newspaper a week. I have tried it recently, and for so long it seems to me that I have not dwelt in my native region. The sun, the clouds, the snow, the trees say not so much to me. You cannot serve two masters. It requires more than a day's devotion to know and to possess the wealth of a day.

We may well be ashamed to tell what things we have read or heard in our day. I do not know why my news should be so trivial, — considering what one's dreams and expectations are, why the developments should be so paltry. The news we hear, for the most part, is not news to our genius. It is the stalest repetition. You are often tempted to ask, why such stress is laid on a particular experience which you have had, — that, after twenty-five years, you should meet Hobbins, Registrar of Deeds, again on the sidewalk. Have you not budged an inch, then? Such is the daily news. Its facts appear to float in the atmosphere, insignificant as the sporules of fungi, and impinge on some neglected *thallus*, or surface of our minds, which affords a basis for them, and hence a parasitic growth. We should wash ourselves clean of such news. Of what consequence, though our planet explode, if there is no character involved in the explosion? In health we have not the least curiosity about such events. We do not live for idle amusement. I would not run round a corner to see the world blow up.

All summer, and far into the autumn, perchance, you unconsciously went by the newspapers and the news, and now you find it was because the morning and the evening were full of news to you. Your walks were full of incidents. You attended, not to the affairs of Europe, but to your own affairs in Massachusetts fields. If you chance to live and move and have your being in that thin stratum in which the events that make the news transpire, — thinner than the paper on which it is printed, — then these things will fill the world for you; but if you soar above or dive below that plane, you cannot remember nor be reminded of them. Really to see the sun rise or go down every day, so to relate ourselves to a universal fact, would preserve us sane forever. Nations! What are nations? Tartars, and Huns, and Chinamen! Like insects, they swarm. The historian strives in vain to make them memorable. It is for want of a man that there are so many men. It is individuals that populate the world. Any man thinking may say with the Spirit of Lodin, —

" I look down from my height on nations,
  And they become ashes before me; —
  Calm is my dwelling in the clouds;
  Pleasant are the great fields of my rest "

Pray, let us live without being drawn by dogs, Esquimaux-fashion, tearing over hill and dale, and biting each other's ears.

Not without a slight shudder at the danger, I often perceive how near I had come to admitting into my mind the details of some trivial affair, — the news of the street; and I am astonished to observe how willing men are to lumber their minds with such rubbish, — to permit idle rumors and incidents of the most insignificant kind to intrude on ground which should be sacred to thought. Shall the mind be a public arena, where the affairs of the street and the gossip of the tea table chiefly are discussed? Or shall it be a quarter of heaven itself, — an hypæthral temple, consecrated to the service of the gods? I find it so difficult to dispose of the few facts which to me are significant that I hesitate to burden my attention with those which are insignificant, which only a divine mind could illustrate. Such is, for the most part, the news in newspapers and conversation. It is important to preserve the mind's chastity in this respect. Think of admitting the details of a single case of the criminal court into our thoughts, to stalk profanely through their very *sanctum sanctorum* for an hour, ay, for many hours! to make a very barroom of the mind's inmost apartment, as if for so long the dust of the street had occupied us, — the very street itself, with all its travel, its bustle, and filth, had passed through our thoughts' shrine! Would it not be an intellectual and moral suicide? When I have been compelled to sit spectator and auditor in a court-room for some hours, and have seen my neighbors, who were not compelled, stealing in from time to time, and tiptoeing about with washed hands and faces, it has appeared to my mind's eye, that, when they took off their hats, their ears suddenly expanded into vast hoppers for sound, between which even their narrow heads were crowded. Like the vanes of windmills, they caught the broad, but shallow stream of sound, which, after a few titillating gyrations in their coggy brains, passed out the other side. I wondered if, when they got home, they were as careful to wash their ears as before their hands and faces. It has seemed to me, at such a time, that the auditors and the witnesses, the jury and the counsel, the judge and the criminal at the bar, — if I may presume him guilty before he is convicted, — were all equally criminal, and a thunderbolt might be expected to descend and consume them all together.

By all kinds of traps and signboards, threatening the extreme penalty of the divine law, exclude such trespassers from the only ground which can be sacred to you. It is so hard to forget what it is worse than useless to emember! If I am to be a thoroughfare, I prefer that t be of the mountain-brooks, the Parnassian streams, and not the town-sewers. There is inspiration, that gossip which comes to the ear of the attentive mind from the courts of heaven. There is the profane and stale revelation of the bar-room and the police court. The same ear is fitted to receive both communications. Only the character of the hearer determines to which it shall be open, and to which closed. I believe that the mind can be permanently profaned by the habit of attending to trivial things, so that all our thoughts shall be tinged with triviality. Our very intellect shall be macadamized, as it were, — its foundation broken into fragments for the wheels of travel to roll over ; and if you would know what will make the most durable pavement. surpassing rolled stones, spruce blocks, and asphaltum, you have only to look into some of our minds which have been subjected to this treatment so long.

If we have thus desecrated ourselves, — as who has not ? — the remedy will be by wariness and devotion to reconsecrate ourselves, and make once more a fane of the mind. We should treat our minds, that is ourselves, as innocent and ingenuous children, whose guardians we are, and be careful what objects and what subjects we thrust on their attention. Read not the Times. Read the Eternities. Conventionalities are at length as bad as impurities. Even the facts of science may dust the mind by their dryness, unless they are in a sense effaced each morning, or rather rendered fertile by the dews of fresh and living truth. Knowledge does not come to us by details, but in flashes of light from heaven. Yes, every thought that passes through the mind helps to wear and tear it, and to deepen the ruts, which, as in the streets of Pompeii, evince how much it has been used. How many things there are concerning which we might well deliberate whether we had better know them, — had better let their peddling-carts be driven, even at the slowest trot or walk, over that bridge of glorious span by which we trust to pass at last from the farthest brink of time to the nearest shore of eternity ! Have we no culture, no refinement, — but skill only to live coarsely and serve the Devil ? — to acquire a little worldly wealth, or fame, or liberty, and

make a false show with it, as if we were all husk and
shell, with no tender and living kernel to us? Shall our
institutions be like those chestnut-burrs which contain
abortive nuts, perfect only to prick the fingers?

America is said to be the arena on which the battle of
freedom is to be fought; but surely it cannot be freedom
in a merely political sense that is meant. Even if we
grant that the American has freed himself from a political tyrant, he is still the slave of an economical and moral
tyrant. Now that the republic, — the *res-publica*, — has
been settled, it is time to look after the *res-privata*, —
the private state, — to see, as the Roman senate charged
its consuls, "*ne quid res-*PRIVATA *detrimenti caperet*,"
that the *private* state receive no detriment.

Do we call this the land of the free? What is it to
be free from King George and continue the slaves of
King Prejudice? What is it to be born free and not to
live free? What is the value of any political freedom,
but as a means to moral freedom? Is it a freedom to
be slaves, or a freedom to be free, of which we boast?
We are a nation of politicians, concerned about the out-
most defences only of freedom. It is our children's children who may perchance be really free. We tax ourselves unjustly. There is a part of us which is not
represented. It is taxation without representation. We
quarter troops, we quarter fools and cattle of all sorts
upon ourselves. We quarter our gross bodies on our
poor souls, till the former eat up all the latter's substance.

With respect to a true culture and manhood, we are
essentially provincial still, not metropolitan, — mere
Jonathans. We are provincial, because we do not find
at home our standards — because we do not worship

truth, but the reflection of truth, — because we are
warped and narrowed by an exclusive devotion to trade
and commerce and manufactures and agriculture and the
like, which are but means, and not the end.

So is the English Parliament provincial.   Mere coun-
try-bumpkins, they betray themselves, when any more
important question arises for them to settle, the Irish
question, for instance, — the English question why did I
not say?   Their natures are subdued to what they work
in.   Their " good breeding " respects only secondary objects.   The finest manners in the world are awkwardness
and fatuity, when contrasted with a finer intelligence.
They appear but as the fashions of past days, — mere
courtliness, knee-buckles and small-clothes, out of date.
It is the vice, but not the excellence of manners, that
they are continually being deserted by the character ;
they are cast-off clothes or shells, claiming the respect
which belonged to the living creature.   You are presented with the shells instead of the meat, and it is no excuse generally, that, in the case of some fishes, the shells
are of more worth than the meat.   The man who thrusts
his manners upon me does as if he were to insist on in-
troducing me to his cabinet of curiosities, when I wished
to see himself.   It was not in this sense that the poet
Decker called Christ "the first true gentleman that ever
breathed."   I repeat, that in this sense the most splendid
court in Christendom is provincial, having authority to
consult about Transalpine interests only, and not the
affairs of Rome.   A prætor or proconsul would suffice
to settle the questions which absorb the attention of the
English Parliament and the American Congress.

Government and legislation ! these I thought were
respectable professions. We have heard of heaven-born

Numas, Lycurguses, and Solons, in the history of the world, whose *names* at least may stand for ideal legislators ; but think of legislating to *regulate* the breeding of slaves, or the exportation of tobacco !   What have divine legislators to do with the exportation or the importation of tobacco ? what humane ones with the breeding of slaves ? Suppose you were to submit the question to any son of God, — and has He no children in the nineteenth century ? is it a family which is extinct ? — in what condition would you get it again ?   What shall a State like Virginia say for itself at the last day, in which these have been the principal, the staple productions ?   What ground is there for patriotism in such a State ?   I derive my facts from statistical tables which the States themselves have published.

A commerce that whitens every sea in quest of nuts and raisins, and makes slaves of its sailors for this purpose !   I saw, the other day, a vessel which had been wrecked, and many lives lost, and her cargo of rags, juniper-berries, and bitter almonds were strewn along the shore.   It seemed hardly worth the while to tempt the dangers of the sea between Leghorn and New York for the sake of a cargo of juniper-berries and bitter almonds. America sending to the Old World for her bitters !   Is not the sea-brine, is not shipwreck, bitter enough to make the cup of life go down here ?   Yet such, to a great extent, is our boasted commerce ; and there are those who style themselves statesmen and philosophers who are so blind as to think that progress and civilization depend on precisely this kind of interchange and activity, — the activity of flies about a molasses-hogshead.   Very well, observes one, if men were oysters.   And very well, answer I, if men were mosquitoes.

Lieutenant Herndon, whom our Government sent to explore the Amazon, and, it is said, to extend the area of slavery, observed that there was wanting there "an industrious and active population, who know what the comforts of life are, and who have artificial wants to draw out the great resources of the country." But what are the "artificial wants" to be encouraged? Not the love of luxuries, like the tobacco and slaves of, I believe, his native Virginia, nor the ice and granite and other material wealth of our native New England; nor are "the great resources of a country" that fertility or barrenness of soil which produces these. The chief want, in every State that I have been into, was a high and earnest purpose in its inhabitants. This alone draws out "the great resources" of Nature, and at last taxes her beyond her resources; for man naturally dies out of her. When we want culture more than potatoes, and illumination more than sugar-plums, then the great resources of a world are taxed and drawn out, and the result, or staple production, is, not slaves, nor operatives, but men, — those rare fruits called heroes, saints, poets, philosophers, and redeemers.

In short, as a snow-drift is formed where there is a lull in the wind, so, one would say, where there is a lull of truth, an institution springs up. But the truth blows right on over it, nevertheless, and at length blows it down.

What is called politics is comparatively something so superficial and inhuman, that, practically, I have never fairly recognized that it concerns me at all. The newspapers, I perceive, devote some of their columns specially to politics or government without charge; and this, one would say, is all that saves it; but, as I love literature, and, to some extent, the truth also, I never read those columns at any rate. I do not wish to blunt my sense of right so much. I have not got to answer for having read a single President's Message. A strange age of the world this, when empires, kingdoms, and republics come a-begging to a private man's door, and utter their complaints at his elbow! I cannot take up a newspaper but I find that some wretched government or other, hard pushed, and on its last legs, is interceding with me, the reader, to vote for it, — more importunate than an Italian beggar; and if I have a mind to look at its certificate, made, perchance, by some benevolent merchant's clerk, or the skipper that brought it over, for it cannot speak a word of English itself, I shall probably read of the eruption of some Vesuvius, or the overflowing of some Po, true or forged, which brought it into this condition. I do not hesitate, in such a case, to suggest work, or the almshouse; or why not keep its castle in silence, as I do commonly? The poor President, what with preserving his popularity and doing his duty, is completely bewildered. The newspapers are the ruling power. Any other government is reduced to a few marines at Fort Independence. If a man neglects to read the Daily Times, government will go down on its knees to him, for this is the only treason in these days.

Those things which now most engage the attention of men, as politics and the daily routine, are, it is true, vital functions of human society, but should be unconsciously performed, like the corresponding functions of the physical body. They are *infra*-human, a kind of vegetation. I sometimes awake to a half-consciousness of them going on about me, as a man may become conscious of some of the processes of digestion in a morbi'd state, and so have the dyspepsia, as it is called. It is as if a thinker submitted himself to be rasped by the great gizzard of creation. Politics is, as it were, the gizzard of society, full of grit and gravel, and the two political parties are its two opposite halves, — sometimes split into quarters, it may be, which grind on each other. Not only individuals, but states, have thus a confirmed dyspepsia, which expresses itself, you can imagine by what sort of eloquence. Thus our life is not altogether a forgetting, but also, alas! to a great extent, a remembering, of that which we should never have been conscious of, certainly not in our waking hours. Why should we not meet, not always as dyspeptics, to tell our bad dreams, but sometimes as *eu*peptics, to congratulate each other on the ever-glorious morning? I do **not** **make** an exorbitant demand, surely.

WENDELL PHILLIPS BEFORE THE CONCORD LYCEUM.*

CONCORD, MASS., March 12, 1845.

MR. EDITOR : —

We have now, for the third winter, had our spirits refreshed, and our faith in the destiny of the Commonwealth strengthened, by the presence and the eloquence
of Wendell Phillips; and we wish to tender to him our
thanks and our sympathy. The admission of this gentleman into the Lyceum has been strenuously opposed by a
respectable portion of our fellow-citizens, who themselves,
we trust, — whose descendants, at least, we know, — will
be as faithful conservers of the true order, whenever that
shall be the order of the day, — and in each instance
the people have voted that they *would hear him*, by coming themselves and bringing their friends to the lecture-
room, and being very silent that they *might* hear. We
saw some men and women, who had long ago *come out*,
going in once more through the free and hospitable portals of the Lyceum; and many of our neighbors confessed, that they had had a "sound season " this once.

It was the speaker's aim to show what the State, and
above all the Church, had to do, and now, alas ! have
done, with Texas and slavery, and how much, on the
other hand, the individual should have to do with Church
and State. These were fair themes, and not mistimed;

* From " The Liberator," March 28, 1845

and his words were addressed to "fit audience, *and not* few."

We must give Mr. Phillips the credit of being a clean, erect, and what was once called a consistent man. He at least is not responsible for slavery, nor for American Independence; for the hypocrisy and superstition of the Church, nor the timidity and selfishness of the State; nor for the indifference and willing ignorance of any. He stands so distinctly, so firmly, and so effectively alone, and one honest man is so much more than a host, that we cannot but feel that he does himself injustice when he reminds us of "the American Society, which he represents." It is rare that we have the pleasure of listening to so clear and orthodox a speaker, who obviously has so few cracks or flaws in his moral nature, — who, having words at his command in a remarkable degree, has much more than words, if these should fail, in his unquestionable earnestness and integrity, — and, aside from their admiration at his rhetoric, secures the genuine respect of his audience. He unconsciously tells his biography as he proceeds, and we see him early and earnestly deliberating on these subjects, and wisely and bravely, without counsel or consent of any, occupying a ground at first from which the varying tides of public opinion cannot drive him.

No one could mistake the genuine modesty and truth with which he affirmed, when speaking of the framers of the Constitution, "I am wiser than they," who with him has improved these sixty years' experience of its working; or the uncompromising consistency and frankness of the prayer which concluded, not like the Thanksgiving proclamations, with — "God save the Commonwealth of Massachusetts," but — God dash it into a thousand pieces, till there shall not remain a fragment on which a man can stand, and dare not tell his name, — referring to the case of Frederick ——; to our disgrace we know not what to call him, unless Scotland will lend us the spoils of one of her Douglasses, out of history or fiction, for a season, till we be hospitable and brave enough to hear his proper name, — a fugitive slave in one more sense than we; who has proved himself the possessor of a *fair* intellect, and has won a colorless reputation in these parts; and who, we trust, will be as superior to degradation from the sympathies of Freedom, as from the antipathies of Slavery. When, said Mr. Phillips, he communicated to a New Bedford audience, the other day, his purpose of writing his life, and telling his name, and the name of his master, and the place he ran from, the murmur ran round the room, and was anxiously whispered by the sons of the Pilgrims, " He had better not! " and it was echoed under the shadow of Concord monument, " He had better not! "

We would fain express our appreciation of the freedom and steady wisdom, so rare in the reformer, with which he declared that he was not born to abolish slavery, but to do right. We have heard a few, a very few, good political speakers, who afforded us the pleasure of great intellectual power and acuteness, of soldier-like steadiness, and of a graceful and natural oratory; but in this man the audience might detect a sort of moral principle and integrity, which was more stable than their firmness, more discriminating than his own intellect, and more graceful than his rhetoric, which was not working for temporary or trivial ends. It is so rare and encouraging to listen to an orator who is content with another alliance than with the popular party, or even with the sympathizing school of the martyrs, who can afford sometimes to be his own auditor if the mob stay away, and hears himself without reproof, that we feel ourselves in danger of slandering all mankind by affirming, that here is one, who is at the same time an eloquent speaker and a righteous man.

Perhaps, on the whole, the most interesting fact elicited by these addresses, is the readiness of the people at large, of whatever sect or party, to entertain, with good will and hospitality, the most revolutionary and heretical opinions, when frankly and adequately, and in some sort cheerfully, expressed. Such clear and candid declaration of opinion served like an electuary to whet and clarify the intellect of all parties, and furnished each one with an additional argument for that right he asserted.

We consider Mr. Phillips one of the most conspicuous and efficient champions of a true Church and State now in the field, and would say to him, and such as are like him, "God speed you." If you know of any champion in the ranks of his opponents, who has the valor and courtesy even of Paynim chivalry, if not the Christian graces and refinement of this knight, you will do us a service by directing him to these fields forthwith, where the lists are now open, and he shall be hospitably entertained. For as yet the Red-cross knight has shown us only the gallant device upon his shield, and his admirable command of his steed, prancing and curvetting in the empty lists; but we wait to see who, in the actual breaking of lances, will come tumbling upon the plain.

THE LAST DAYS OF JOHN BROWN.*

JOHN BROWN'S career for the last six weeks of his life was meteor-like, flashing through the darkness in which we live. I know of nothing so miraculous in our history.

If any person, in a lecture or conversation at that time, cited any ancient example of heroism, such as Cato or Tell or Winkelried, passing over the recent deeds and words of Brown, it was felt by any intelligent audience of Northern men to be tame and inexcusably far-fetched.

For my own part, I commonly attend more to nature than to man, but any affecting human event may blind our eyes to natural objects. I was so absorbed in him as to be surprised whenever I detected the routine of the natural world surviving still, or met persons going about their affairs indifferent. It appeared strange to me that the "little dipper" should be still diving quietly in the river, as of yore ; and it suggested that this bird might continue to dive here when Concord should be no more.

I felt that he, a prisoner in the midst of his enemies, and under sentence of death, if consulted as to his next step or resource, could answer more wisely than all his countrymen beside. He best understood his position ; he contemplated it most calmly. Comparatively, all other

* Read at North Elba, July 4, 1860.

men, North and South, were beside themselves.   Our thoughts could not revert to any greater or wiser or better man with whom to contrast him, for he, then and there, was above them all.   The man this country was about to hang appeared the greatest and best in it.

Years were not required for a revolution of public opinion; days, nay hours, produced marked changes in this case.   Fifty who were ready to say on going into our meeting in honor of him in Concord, that he ought to be hung, would not say it when they came out.   They heard his words read; they saw the earnest faces of the congregation ; and perhaps they joined at last in singing the hymn in his praise.

The order of instructors was reversed.   I heard that one preacher, who at first was shocked and stood aloof, felt obliged at last, after he was hung, to make him the subject of a sermon, in which, to some extent, he eulogized the man, but said that his act was a failure.   An influential class-teacher thought it necessary, after the services, to tell his grown-up pupils, that at first he thought as the preacher did then, but now he thought that John Brown was right.   But it was understood that his pupils were as much ahead of the teacher as he was ahead of the priest ; and I know for a certainty, that very little boys at home had already asked their parents, in a tone of surprise, why God did not interfere to save him.   In each case, the constituted teachers were only half conscious that they were not *leading*, but being *dragged*, with some loss of time and power.

The more conscientious preachers, the Bible men, they who talk about principle, and doing to others as you would that they should do unto you, — how could they fail to recognize him, by far the greatest preacher of them all, with the Bible in his life and in his acts, the embodiment of principle, who actually carried out the golden rule ? All whose moral sense had been aroused, who had a calling from on high to preach, sided with him. What confessions he extracted from the cold and conservative ! It is remarkable, but on the whole it is well, that it did not prove the occasion for a new sect of *Brownites* being formed in our midst.

They, whether within the Church or out of it, who adhere to the spirit and let go the letter, and are accordingly called infidel, were as usual foremost to recognize him. Men have been hung in the South before for attempting to rescue slaves, and the North was not much stirred by it. Whence, then, this wonderful difference? We were not so sure of *their* devotion to principle. We made a subtle distinction, forgot human laws, and did homage to an idea. The North, I mean the *living* North, was suddenly all transcendental. It went behind the human law, it went behind the apparent failure, and recognized eternal justice and glory. Commonly, men live according to a formula, and are satisfied if the order of law is observed, but in this instance they, to some extent, returned to original perceptions, and there was a slight revival of old religion. They saw that what was called order was confusion, what was called justice, injustice, and that the best was deemed the worst. This attitude suggested a more intelligent and generous spirit than that which actuated our forefathers, and the possibility, in the course of ages, of a revolution in behalf of another and an oppressed people.

Most Northern men, and a few Southern ones, were wonderfully stirred by Brown's behavior and words. They saw and felt that they were heroic and noble, and that there had been nothing quite equal to them in their kind in this country, or in the recent history of the world. But the minority were unmoved by them. They were only surprised and provoked by the attitude of their neighbors. They saw that Brown was brave, and that he believed that he had done right, but they did not detect any further peculiarity in him. Not being accustomed to make fine distinctions, or to appreciate magnanimity, they read his letters and speeches as if they read them not. They were not aware when they approached a heroic statement, — they did not know when they *burned.* They did not feel that he spoke with authority, and hence they only remembered that the *law* must be executed. They remembered the old formula, but did not hear the new revelation. The man who does not recognize in Brown's words a wisdom and nobleness, and therefore an authority, superior to our laws, is a modern Democrat. This is the test by which to discover him. He is not wilfully but constitutionally blind on this side, and he is consistent with himsel.̈́. Such has been his past life; no doubt of it. In like manner he has read history and his Bible, and he accepts, or seems to accept, the last only as an established formula, and not because he has been convicted by it. You will not find kindred sentiments in his commonplace book, if he has one.

When a noble deed is done, who is likely to appreciate it? They who are noble themselves. I was not surprised that certain of my neighbors spoke of John Brown as an ordinary felon, for who are they? They have either much flesh, or much office, or much coarseness of some kind. They are not ethereal natures in any sense. The dark qualities predominate in them.

Several of them are decidedly pachydermatous. I say it in sorrow, not in anger. How can a man behold the light, who has no answering inward light? They are true to their *right*, but when they look this way they *see* nothing, they are blind. For the children of the light to contend with them is as if there should be a contest between eagles and owls. Show me a man who feels bitterly toward John Brown, and let me hear what noble verse he can repeat. He 'll be as dumb as if his lips were stone.

It is not every man who can be a Christian, even in a very moderate sense, whatever education you give him. It is a matter of constitution and temperament, after all. He may have to be born again many times. I have known many a man who pretended to be a Christian, in whom it was ridiculous, for he had no genius for it. It is not every man who can be a freeman, even.

Editors persevered for a good while in saying that Brown was crazy; but at last they said only that it was "a crazy scheme," and the only evidence brought to prove it was that it cost him his life. I have no doubt that if he had gone with five thousand men, liberated a thousand slaves, killed a hundred or two slaveholders, and had as many more killed on his own side, but not lost his own life, these same editors would have called it by a more respectable name. Yet he has been far more successful than that. He has liberated many thousands of slaves, both North and South. They seem to have known nothing about living or dying for a principle. They all called him crazy then; who calls him crazy now?

All through the excitement occasioned by his remarkable attempt and subsequent behavior, the Massachusetts Legislature, not taking any steps for the defence of her citizens who were likely to be carried to Virginia as witnesses and exposed to the violence of a slaveholding mob, was wholly absorbed in a liquor-agency question, and indulging in poor jokes on the word "extension." Bad spirits occupied their thoughts. I am sure that no statesman up to the occasion could have attended to that question at all at that time, — a very vulgar question to attend to at any time!

When I looked into a liturgy of the Church of England, printed near the end of the last century, in order to find a service applicable to the case of Brown, I found that the only martyr recognized and provided for by it was King Charles the First, an eminent scamp. Of all the inhabitants of England and of the world, he was the only one, according to this authority, whom that church had made a martyr and saint of; and for more than a century it had celebrated his martyrdom, so called, by an annual service. What a satire on the Church is that!

Look not to legislatures and churches for your guidance, nor to any soulless *incorporated* bodies, but to *inspirited* or inspired ones.

What avail all your scholarly accomplishments and learning, compared with wisdom and manhood? To omit his other behavior, see what a work this comparatively unread and unlettered man wrote within six weeks. Where is our professor of *belles-lettres* or of logic and rhetoric, who can write so well? He wrote in prison, not a History of the World, like Raleigh, but an American book which I think will live longer than that. I do not know of such words, uttered under such circumstances, and so copiously withal, in Roman or English or any history. What a variety of themes he touched on in that short space! There are words in that letter to his wife, respecting the education of his daughters, which deserve to be framed and hung over every mantel-piece in the land. Compare this earnest wisdom with that of Poor Richard.

The death of Irving, which at any other time would have attracted universal attention, having occurred while these things were transpiring, went almost unobserved. I shall have to read of it in the biography of authors.

Literary gentlemen, editors, and critics, think that they know how to write, because they have studied grammar and rhetoric; but they are egregiously mistaken. The *art* of composition is as simple as the discharge of a bullet from a rifle, and its masterpieces imply an infinitely greater force behind them. This unlettered man's speaking and writing are standard English. Some words and phrases deemed vulgarisms and Americanisms before, he has made standard American; such as " *It will pay.*" It suggests that the one great rule of composition, — and if I were a professor of rhetoric I should insist on this, — is, to *speak the truth.* This first, this second, this third; pebbles in your mouth or not. This demands earnestness and manhood chiefly.

We seem to have forgotten that the expression, a *liberal* education, originally meant among the Romans one worthy of *free* men; while the learning of trades and professions by which to get your livelihood merely was considered worthy of *slaves* only. But taking a hint from the word, I would go a step further, and say, that it is not the man of wealth and leisure simply, though devoted to art, or science, or literature, who, in a true sense, is *liberally* educated, but only the earnest and *free* man. In a slaveholding country like this, there can be no such thing as a *liberal* education tolerated by the State; and those scholars of Austria and France who, however learned they may be, are contented under their tyrannies, have received only a *servile* education.

Nothing could his enemies do, but it redounded to his infinite advantage, — that is, to the advantage of his cause. They did not hang him at once, but reserved him to preach to them. And then there was another great blunder. They did not hang his four followers with him ; that scene was still postponed ; and so his victory was prolonged and completed. No theatrical manager could have arranged things so wisely to give effect to his behavior and words. And who, think you, *was* the manager ? *Who* placed the slave-woman and her child, whom he stooped to kiss for a symbol, between his prison and the gallows ?

We soon saw, as he saw, that he was not to be pardoned or rescued by men. That would have been to disarm him, to restore to him a material weapon, a Sharpe's rifle, when he had taken up the sword of the spirit, — the sword with which he has really won his greatest and most memorable victories. Now he has not laid aside the sword of the spirit, for he is pure spirit himself, and his sword is pure spirit also.

> " He nothing common did or mean
> Upon that memorable scene,
> Nor called the gods with vulgar spite,
> To vindicate his helpless right ;
> But bowed his comely head
> Down as upon a bed."

What a transit was that of his horizontal body alone, but just cut down from the gallows-tree ! We read, that at such a time it passed through Philadelphia, and by Saturday night had reached New York. Thus, like a meteor it shot through the Union from the Southern regions toward the North! No such freight had the cars borne since they carried him Southward alive.

On the day of his translation, I heard, to be sure, that he was *hung*, but I did not know what that meant; I felt no sorrow on that account; but not for a day or two did I even *hear* that he was *dead*, and not after any number of days shall I believe it. Of all the men who were said to be my contemporaries, it seemed to me that John Brown was the only one who *had not died*. I never hear of a man named Brown now, — and I hear of them pretty often, — I never hear of any particularly brave and earnest man, but my first thought is of John Brown, and what relation he may be to him. I meet him at every turn. He is more alive than ever he was. He has earned immortality. He is not confined to North Elba nor to Kansas. He is no longer working in secret. He works in public, and in the clearest light that shines on this land.

THE END.

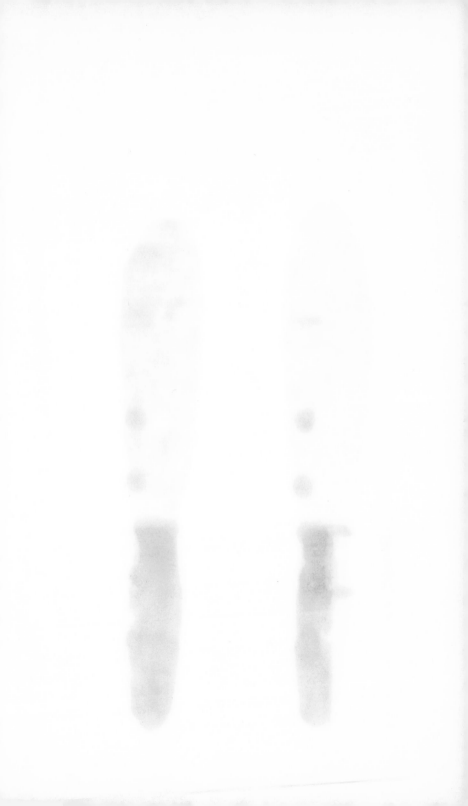

DATE DUE	
OCT 18 2013	
OCT 24 2013	
NOV 03 2013	